THE
RIFLEMEN OF
WELLINGTON'S
LIGHT DIVISION

THE RIFLEMEN OF WELLINGTON'S LIGHT DIVISION

UNPUBLISHED & RARE MEMOIRS OF THE 95TH RIFLES 1808-14

EDITED BY
GARETH GLOVER & ROBERT BURNHAM

FRONTLINE
BOOKS

First published in Great Britain in 2023 by
FRONTLINE BOOKS
an imprint of Pen & Sword Books Ltd,
47 Church Street, Barnsley, S. Yorkshire, S70 2AS

ISBN: 978-1-39908-742-1

CIP data records for this title are available from the British Library

For more information on our books, please visit
www.frontline-books.com, email info@frontline-books.com
or write to us at the above address.

Printed and bound by CPI Group (UK) Ltd, Croydon, CR0 4YY
Typeset by Concept, Huddersfield, West Yorkshire
Pen & Sword Books Ltd incorporates the imprints of Pen & Sword Archaeology,
Atlas, Aviation, Battleground, Discovery,
Family History, History, Maritime, Military, Naval, Politics,
Social History, Transport, True Crime, Claymore Press,
Frontline Books, Praetorian Press,
Seaforth Publishing and White Owl

For a complete list of Pen and Sword titles please contact
PEN & SWORD LTD
47 Church Street, Barnsley, South Yorkshire, S70 2AS, England
E-mail: enquiries@pen-and-sword.co.uk

Or

PEN AND SWORD BOOKS
1950 Lawrence Rd, Havertown, PA 19083, USA
E-mail: Uspen-and-sword@casematepublishers.com

CONTENTS

FOREWORD

Having spent the last two decades scouring the archives for unpublished letters and journals of soldiers who served in the Napoleonic wars, I have not particularly concentrated on the regiments that formed the Light Division in the Peninsular War because I was aware that due to their fame, many memoirs from members of these regiments had already been published and it was therefore highly likely that there was little left to publish.

However, a steady trickle of further memoirs by members of the Light Division have been published in the last twenty years to add to the already impressive total, showing that the mine is far from fully exhausted. These include those of Captain George Miller,[1] Lieutenant James Gairdner[2] and Rifleman George Walton[3] of the 95th Foot, Sergeant Samuel Harrison[4] of the 43rd Foot and Captains George Ulrich Barlow,[5] Charles Kinloch,[6] John Ewart[7] and Lieutenant Charles Holman[8] of the 52nd Foot.

I also received a request from my good friend Robert Burnham, who resides in Hawaii, to help him search the archives for any unpublished

---

1 Published as *The Making of a Rifles Officer: The Life and Letters of Colonel George Miller CB FRS (1786–1843)*. Elizabeth Laidlaw: Edinburgh: Burngrange, 2019.

2 Published as *The American Sharpe: The Adventures of an American Officer of the 95th Rifles in the Peninsula & Waterloo Campaigns*. Gareth Glover. Barnsley: Frontline, 2017.

3 Published as *George Walton 1796–1874: the Journal & Diary of a Rifleman of the 95th who Fought at Waterloo*. Peter Coleman: Studley: Brewin Books, 2016.

4 Published as *The Peninsular War Journal of Sergeant Samuel Harrison of the 43rd Foot 1796–1812*. Gareth Glover: Godmanchester: Ken Trotman: 2017.

5 Published as *A Light Infantryman with Wellington: The Letters of Captain George Ulrich Barlow, 52nd and 69th Foot, 1808–1815*. Gareth Glover. Solihull: Helion, 2018.

6 Published as *A Hellish Business: The Letters of Captain Charles Kinloch 52nd Light Infantry 1806–1816*. Gareth Glover. Godmanchester: Ken Trotman, 2007.

7 Published as *The Peninsular War Diary of Captain John Frederick Ewart, 52nd Light Infantry, 1811–1812*. Gareth Glover. Godmanchester: Ken Trotman, 2010.

8 Published as *52nd (Light Infantry) Eyewitness accounts of the Waterloo campaign*, Gareth Glover: Godmanchester: Ken Trotman 2020.

material by members of the Light Division still existing in the British Library, the National Archives at Kew, the National Library of Scotland, the Royal Green Jackets Museum (now held by the Hampshire Record Office in Winchester) or in the Soldiers of Oxfordshire Museum at Woodstock in Oxfordshire, as part of his thorough preparation for his excellent book on the Light Division in 1810[9] and for his further projected volumes. This search unearthed a virtual treasure trove of material that astounded both of us. There was simply more than we could have possibly imagined there, indeed material was discovered that some of the museums themselves didn't even realise that they had.

From this was spawned the idea of producing a book on each of the three regiments that formed the core of the Light Division, publishing the masses of material unearthed, much for the very first time, or at most has only previously appeared in obscure and very rare publications. This, the third volume, covers the best known of the three regiments and certainly one with a large number of memoirs already published, that is the 95th Regiment of Foot or Rifles. Some seventeen individual memoirs have emanated from this regiment to date.

The three infantry regiments of the Light Division in the Peninsular War maintained quite different characteristics from each other. Captain John Cooke of the 43rd Foot explained not only the brotherhood of regiments, but also their subtle differences at the end of the war in 1814:[10]

Though amongst the regiments which composed it there existed an unanimity which was almost without a parallel in war, yet there was a shade of difference between them, a something peculiar to each corps distinguishing it from the others, which was the more remarkable as amongst them there was a sort of fraternal compact, and it has occurred that three brothers held commissions at the same time in the 43rd, 52nd and Rifle Corps.

The 43rd were a gay set, the dandies of the army; the great encouragers of dramatic performances, dinner parties and balls, of which their headquarters was the pivot.

The 52nd were highly gentlemanly men of a steady aspect; they mixed little with other corps, but attended the theatricals of the 43rd with circumspect good humour and now and then relaxed, but were soon again the 52nd.

9   Published as *Wellington's Light Division in the Peninsular War: The formation, campaigns & battles of Wellington's famous fighting force 1810*. Robert Burnham. Barnsley. Frontline. 2020.

10   *A Narrative of Events in the South of France*, Captain John Cooke, London 1835.

The Rifle Corps were skirmishers in every sense of the word; a sort of wild sportsmen and up to every description of fun and good humour. Nothing came amiss: the very trees responded to their merriment and scraps of their sarcastic rhymes passed current through all the camps and bivouacs.

In this way the brothers of the three regiments met together, each being the very type of the corps to which he belonged.

Some of these attitudes are clearly borne out by the memoirs and letters of the men of each regiment.

With so much new material to be studied, it is inevitable that a great deal of new evidence will be discovered that will change our understanding of many aspects of the life of the troops, the military operations and even their thoughts on their fellow officers and seniors at the very time that incidents occurred.

I hope that you the reader will be as intrigued with what we have unearthed as much as we are.

ACKNOWLEDGEMENTS

A work of this kind cannot come to fruition without the help and advice of a large number of people, but before I make the customary thanks, I must mention one person in particular.

I must thank Robert Burnham, for his help in transcribing the numerous accounts from their original handwriting. He has now been bitten by the bug and has been fully ensnared by the dark arts of transcribing, helping me to prepare these volumes for publication. His help in tracking the movements of the various companies of the 95th is also very much appreciated. I have to also thank John Grehan and Martin Mace of Frontline Books for believing in this project when others were not perhaps so keen.

I also thank the staff of many of the archives around the country, who have cheerfully and patiently dealt with my incessant requests and queries. I have received every help and courtesy from the National Library of Scotland, the National Army Museum, the Hampshire Record Office and the British Library.

I must particularly thank Peggy Ainsworth, Collections Manager/ Deputy Museum Director, for allowing me to literally ransack her archives at the Soldiers of Oxfordshire Museum in the search for material and her unbelievable helpfulness in arranging for copies to be made of literally thousands of documents.

I must also thank Ron McGuigan, with whom I have only ever corresponded by email, but who is the font of all knowledge and finds information on the most obscure subject or person you can ever imagine and rarely fails.

Gareth Glover
Cardiff

1. HISTORY OF THE 95TH RIFLES IN THE PENINSULA AND AT WATERLOO

In January 1800, an Experimental Corps of Riflemen was established from drafts of thirty-four men and three officers each from thirteen Line regiments and further bolstered by twelve men each from thirty-three Fencible regiments then serving in Ireland. In July 1800, three companies of this corps were sent on an unsuccessful expedition to Ferrol, but the Experimental Corps survived and reorganised into a regular battalion of ten companies, many excess or unsuitable men returning to their former regiments. By January 1801, the corps was issued green uniforms and a company served as Marines on ships during the Battle of Copenhagen.

In January 1803 the regiment was officially designated as the 95th (Rifle) Regiment and it proceeded to Shorncliffe camp to begin instruction under Sir John Moore. Here it was joined by a number of other regiments, but eventually none but the 43rd and 52nd Foot remained and these three regiments regularly practised manoeuvring together. Five companies of the battalion then served in Hanover and Bremen in late 1805, but in early 1806 the expedition was removed via the port of Cuxhaven. During 1805 a second battalion of the 95th was also raised.

The 1st Battalion returned to England from Germany in February 1806, but in October five companies sailed for South America, to take part in the Expedition to the River Plate. Three companies of the 2nd Battalion had already sailed on this expedition. All of these troops were involved in the disastrous 1807 campaign of General Whitelock and became prisoners of war, until released under agreement.

Meanwhile, the remainder of both battalions (five companies of the 1st Battalion and five of the seven companies of the 2nd Battalion) accompanied an expedition to Copenhagen led by General Cathcart

1

and Arthur Wellesley, however all of the troops from both expeditions were reunited back in England by November 1807.

1808

In April 1808 three companies of 1st Battalion accompanied General Sir John Moore's force to Sweden, to offer their support to the King of Sweden. However, Moore found it impossible to work with the Swedish king and, having escaped from arrest, the troops returned to England, but did not disembark.

Moore's troops, including the three companies of the 1st Battalion, sailed for Portugal, arriving there in August 1808, where they joined two other companies of the 1st Battalion and four companies of the 2nd Battalion who had accompanied Sir Arthur Wellesley's force to Portugal in July.

In the first campaign in Portugal, the companies of the 2nd Battalion fought at Roliça and they and the companies of 1st Battalion both served at the subsequent Battle of Vimeiro. The fighting then came to an end with the signing of the controversial Convention of Cintra and the French troops were carried in British ships back to France. News of this Convention was heavily criticised by the public and an enquiry was announced, requiring the three most senior generals with the army to be ordered home to testify and leaving Sir John Moore in command.

Moore marched his small army into Spain in an attempt to relieve the pressure on the Spanish forces resisting the French invasion, reaching Salamanca. General Sir David Baird had also been sent out with a reinforcement of some 12,000 men, which landed at Corunna in October 1808 and marched south to meet up with Moore. This force included the other five companies of the 1st Battalion and a further four companies of the 2nd Battalion. After a number of false starts, caused by rumours of advancing French forces, the two forces did not combine until December at Sahagun. Moore, soon discovering that an overwhelming French force was advancing to bring him to battle, a retreat was ordered to Corunna, with the French hot on their heels. Moore split his force at Ponferrada, ordering most of his light troops and the King's German Legion infantry to Ourense and on to the sea at Vigo. This force included 2nd Battalion under the command of Colonel Robert Craufurd. Meanwhile, the main force continued to march on Corunna, including 1st Battalion, which took part in the Battle of Corunna, before the army was able to embark and sail for England.

1809

Having arrived back in England badly depleted, having lost a large number of men to fatigue and sickness, volunteers were sought to replenish the numbers. Far more recruits volunteered for the 95th beyond the number required to replenish the two battalions to their set establishment, so the decision was made on 4 May 1809 to form the 3rd Battalion at Brabourne Lees.

By June 1809 ten companies of the 1st Battalion were already on their way back to Portugal to reinforce the forces remaining there under the command of General Sir Arthur Wellesley, who had been absolved of any blame for the Cintra debacle. The brigade of light infantry under Brigadier General Craufurd hastened to join the army at Talavera before the expected battle occurred; but despite their long, forced march, they arrived the day after the battle. Having arrived with the army they were often used to form a light infantry screen for the army, the advanced guard in forward movements and the rear guard when retreating. The battalion suffered some 300 fever deaths during this unfortunate campaign.

In July 1809 the 2nd Battalion was embarked once again, but it did not go to Portugal, but formed part of the Great Expedition to Walcheren which ended in ignominious disaster in the September, the 2nd Battalion having lost no less than 300 men to the fever that decimated this force and left many too weak for active service for many years.

1810

The 1st Battalion formed a screen along the Coa River for the first half of the year, but the French having successfully besieged Ciudad Rodrigo, the position of Craufurd's troops (expanded in February by the introduction of two battalions of Portuguese Cacadores to become the Light Division) became critical. Due to attrition, the officers and some sergeants from Glass's and Balvaird's Companies of the 1st Battalion were sent home in April, while the riflemen were incorporated into the remaining companies. In July the Light Division was badly mauled at the Coa, Almeida fell in late August following a disastrous explosion in its main arsenal and Wellington ordered a retreat deep into Portugal. The 1st Battalion was heavily engaged at the Battle of Bussaco, but despite a resounding victory Wellington was forced to continue his retreat to take up positions within the Lines of Torres Vedras. Just prior to entering the lines, the Light Division again only narrowly escaped being overwhelmed at Alenquer. The French army suffered great privations in front of the Lines, unable

3

to break through and unwilling to retreat, until a desperate lack of provisions forced them to retreat to a position at Santarem.

The 2nd Battalion remained at Brabourne Lees throughout this year, but the year saw the piecemeal dispatching of companies to Spain, in March two companies (Cadoux and Jenkins) were sent to Cadiz which was besieged by the French and in September one company (Charles Beckwith's) joined the Light Division.

The 3rd Battalion also remained at Brabourne Lees, but in March, three companies (Percival, Knipe and Gray) followed the two companies of the 2nd Battalion to Cadiz. Two additional companies (Fullerton and Pratt) from the 3rd Battalion landed at Cadiz at the end of July. In October Percival's Company was sent from Cadiz to join Wellington. Upon arriving in the Lines of Torres Vedras it was attached to the 1st Division and did not join the Light Division.

1811

Eventually starvation and sickness saw the French retreat, closely pursued by the Light Division, the 1st Battalion taking their part in the actions of Pombal, Redinha, Casal Nova, Foz de Arouce and Sabugal, driving the French completely out of Portugal. The division reverted largely to its role of patrolling the border but fought at the Battle of Fuentes de Oñoro and was part of the covering force during the abortive siege of Badajoz.

In July Hart's company of the 2nd Battalion was sent out to Portugal and joined the Light Division's 1st Brigade in September,

Two companies of 2nd Battalion (Cadoux and Jenkins) and four companies of 3rd Battalion (Gray, Fullerton, Knipe and Pratt) fought at the Battle of Barossa, but the siege of the city continued. All four companies (Gray, Fullerton, Pratt,[11] and Kent[12]) from the 3rd Battalion, left Cadiz and went with Lieutenant Colonel Andrew Barnard to Portugal and joined the Light Division on 1 August. The next day Wellington ordered the 1st Division to release the 3rd Battalion's company[13] which had been with the 1st Division since the previous autumn and sent it to the Light Division.

Meanwhile in December, Jenkins' company of the 2nd Battalion at Cadiz joined the force occupying Tarifa.

---

[11]   Pratt's Company was commanded by Lieutenant James Kirkman. Pratt remained in Cadiz and died there in July.
[12]   John Kent replaced William Knipe, who was killed at Barossa.
[13]   Percival had been seriously wounded at Sobral in October 1810 and was replaced by Captain James Travers sometime after March 1811.

1812

The Rifles were heavily engaged in the successful storming of the fortress of Ciudad Rodrigo (losing Brigadier General Robert Craufurd among many) and the storming of Badajoz. The Light Division was present at the Battle of Salamanca, but was only slightly engaged and they then joined the march on Madrid. They remained protecting the city until Wellington was forced to order his forces to retreat to the Portuguese border again. The Rifles fully participated in this retreat and suffered considerably from the lack of supplies.

In July, a further two companies of 2nd Battalion were sent from England to join the Light Division and in October they were joined by the two companies in Cadiz, making six companies in all.

1813

The Light Division, including the eight companies of the 1st Battalion, six companies of the 2nd Battalion and five companies of the 3rd Battalion, were fully involved in the advance, seeing action at San Millán, Vitoria, Pamplona, the storming of San Sebastian, Vera, the Nivelle and the Nive.

In December, one company from the 1st Battalion, one company from the 2nd Battalion and two companies of 3rd Battalion were sent to Holland with a force under Sir Thomas Graham.

1814

The Light Division continued to be fully involved in the continued advance into France, being involved in the battles of Orthez, Tarbes and Toulouse and also involved in the capitulation of Bordeaux.

All of these troops initially proceeded to England at the termination of the war, but in the September five companies of the 3rd Battalion were dispatched to America, seeing action at Mobile and in the disastrous battle of New Orleans.

1815

With the news that Napoleon was back in Paris, six companies of 1st Battalion joined the company from Graham's force in Belgium; five companies of the 2nd Battalion joined their company in Belgium and the two companies of the 3rd Battalion already in Belgium were not expanded. All of these troops participated fully in the Waterloo campaign and the subsequent Occupation of France.

The 3rd Battalion was disbanded in January 1819.

2. LIEUTENANT COLONEL ANDREW BARNARD LETTERS[14]

Andrew Barnard joined the army as an ensign in 90th Foot in August 1794. Hopping between regiments, he rose through the ranks rapidly and was lieutenant and captain in the 1st Foot Guards in 1799. He became a major in that regiment in January 1805 and gained his lieutenant colonelcy in 1st Foot in January 1809, transferring to the 3rd Battalion 95th Foot in March 1810 and moving to the 1st Battalion in May 1813. He frequently commanded brigades of the Light Division in the absence of senior officers. He saw service in St Lucia in 1795, the Helder in 1799, Cadiz, Barrosa, Ciudad Rodrigo, Badajoz, Salamanca, San Millán, Vitoria, the Pyrenees, Bidassoa, Nivelle, Orthez, Tarbes and Toulouse. He also served at Waterloo commanding 1st Battalion.

Portsmouth, 10 July 1810
To Anne,
I arrived here yesterday, the detachments of the 95th embark tomorrow on board the *Mercury*[15] and we shall sail almost immediately.

24 October 1810
My dearest Anne,
Most sincerely do I feel for you, the melancholy intelligence was not communicated to me till last Saturday.[16] General Graham[17] who had

---

14   These letters are from a number of sources, part from the *Barnard Letters (1778–1824)*, part from The *Journal of the Society for Army Historical Research*, Volume 47, No. 191 (Autumn 1969) and others from The Highland Council Archive.
15   A 28-gun frigate.
16   General James Caitlin Craufurd was married to Barnard's sister, Anne, he died at Abrantes on 24 September 1810.
17   Lieutenant General Sir Thomas Graham.

received a report of it some time, out of kindness to me concealed it still, entertaining a hope that it would prove incorrect but more recent accounts confirmed it beyond a doubt. No circumstance can give me greater pain, independent of the near connection between us and the regard which I bore him on your account, I never knew any friend that I endeared more or any companion that I liked more. I will dwell no longer on a subject, on a future day we may derive a melancholy pleasure from the recapitulation of many circumstances which would now only tend to increase our grief. I know my dear Anne that you are possessed both of fortitude and good sense to a greater amount than most people and that though both must undergo severe trial the welfare of your young family will help you to exert them to the utmost. I will not allow you to trouble yourself by writing to me at present, Sarah[18] will perform that task for you. I shall be very anxious until I hear from her. I must now desire whatever your future plans are, that they may not spring from fear of the expense of them, be checked in anything that may be agreeable to you or advantageous to your children. You have an unlimited power as far as my means extend, I shall request Jack Magnay to write more fully to you on this subject and assure you that the most beautiful satisfaction I can experience will be that of being useful to you. God bless you and yours my dear Anne believe me ever your affectionate brother A F Barnard

To Mrs Isabella Hayes[19]
Isla de Leon, 2 November 1810
My dear Isabella,
I will not dwell upon the loss we have all sustained in poor Craufurd. God knows it has grieved me to the soul, independent of the regard I bore for him as my brother-in-law. He was a man above all others, that I liked in every point. I continue in a state of the greatest anxiety to hear how Anne bears up against so great a misfortune which must be increased by the suddenness of it. Her last letters to me were written in great spirits as she had heard shortly before from him. I hope the packet of which we are in momentary expectation will bring me some letters from Sarah or you.

I must acknowledge my dear Isabella that since my arrival here you have great cause to complain of my negligence as a correspondent, but I assure you that this place is so insipidly dull that except I gave you a dish of Spanish politics I know not how to fill a sheet of paper. Your

---

[18]   Another sister, in 1809 she became the second wife of General Glegg.
[19]   His sister Isabella was married to the Reverend Henry Hayes.

friend Macdonald gives me many admonitions to write constantly to you so that I have no excuse for my silence having as good a flapper as the Deputy Adjutant General.[20] He is a very worthy good fellow and beyond measure attached to every person of the name of Hayes.

I promised you some Spanish politics, they may not entertain you, but Hayes may like to hear a little of them. We have been all surprised at the steady and proper conduct of the Cortes, which proclaim a dawn of liberty in this oppressed and unenlightened country. They have commenced in a quiet way without democratic fury. On the contrary the crown and nobility are supported and the religion of the country is to remain the same but there are strong symptoms of a change in the establishment of the latter so far as political influence is concerned and the abolition of monasterys [sic] is freely talked of. Within these few days they have elected a new regency, at the head of which General Blake,[21] who is thought to be a man possessing some intelligence and energy is placed. He is at Carthagena [Cartagena]. A frigate of ours sailed for him yesterday. Another person the Marchese de Pallacios was chosen as a proxy until his arrival here, when to the great astonishment of everyone he refused to take the oaths and was committed. What is to be done with him is not decided. He is a weak man but cannot absolutely be considered as a traitor, else he would have outwardly confirmed to what was required of him. The Cortes have voted the liberty of the press with certain limitations which are not yet defined but a committee is appointed to regulate them. A priest of the name of Torrera made a most eloquent panegyric on the liberty of the English, declaring at the same time, that we had hitherto been called heretics, that our religion differed only in appearance and that the outward show was greater in Spain that the morality of the English was far superior. This was pretty well for a man bred up in a convent. Adieu my dear Isabella, remember me most kindly to Hayes and believe me ever, your affectionate brother A F Barnard

Isla, 8 March 1811
Dear James,
Hope[22] will give you all the particulars of our short campaign, I shall not therefore enter into a detail of them. I shall only remark that although Graham is his friend and patron it is not in his power to do

---

20   Major John Macdonald, 1st Garrison Battalion, was appointed Assistant Adjutant General and acted as head of department at Cadiz. He became a Deputy Adjutant General in 1811.
21   General Joaquin Blake y Joyes.
22   Brevet Major James Archibald Hope, 26th Foot, served at Cadiz with Graham.

him more than justice, for the military talent energy and temper which he displayed through the whole of it. In the end he alone with the small British force had effected the object of our movements completely, had not the shameful inaction of the Spanish commander made him neglect to profit by our exertions. The French army were routed in the field by the British and a Spanish force of at least 10,000 men remained out of sight. Had half the number moved on Chiclana nothing was left to oppose them, they would have gained possession of the French works without losing a man. The coolness with which Graham extricated his army out of so difficult a situation as it could be placed in and whither he had been led by the solicitation of General la Pena,[23] under fire from a superior force admirably posted and perfectly fresh, and the quickness, but at the same time regularity, with which he made his attack continues still a matter of astonishment to me. Had it not been for the extreme fatigue the British had undergone from a long and harassing night march and being about 20 hours under arms with their packs on, the rout of the French would have been so complete, that I scarcely believe we should have gained possession of the French lines without the assistance of the Spaniards, but the men were unequal to the pursuit. I am highly pleased with the conduct of my little corps, the young officers who had never seen fire before behaved like veterans, not only in point of spirit but intelligence. I received two wounds in the affair but am doing very well.[24]

Isla, 24 March 1811
My dear Anne,
When I reflect that there are two letters of yours laying before me as yet unanswered, I fear you will accuse me of neglect as a correspondent, but I trust the events which have lately taken place in this quarter will plead my excuse.

Should I in the space of a short time meet with the 2nd Battalion 28th, I can then get an account of many circumstances in a more satisfactory manner than you have yet heard them. Abercrombie[25] is a particular friend of mine, he is of the mildest and best disposition capable of feeling in the strongest manner, he is too matter of fact a fellow to colour high, by doing which many persons in order to show their tenderness of disposition are apt really to wound that of the person to

---

23	General Manuel Lapena.
24	Barnard had indeed received two wounds. He was severely wounded in the midst of the battle and while his wound was dressed in the rear, he was wounded a second time.
25	Lieutenant Colonel the Honourable Alexander Abercromby, 28th Foot.

whom they tell their tale, while others by passing them over in a light manner do an equal injury. The love the whole army had for Craufurd must have made all those near him much interested for him, but those not intimately acquainted with his family, however attentive they might be to him as an individual, would not at the moment notice those circumstances which it might have been consolatory or satisfactory for us to have been acquainted with. I was extremely pleased at the tone of your letter of December. When we lose a friend that is really dear to us, so far from suffering our melancholy to recur at the mention of his name, we ought to get the better of that feeling, so that instead of being fearful of his memory occurring to our thoughts, we ought to rejoice in it and never lose sight of him by making him the constant theme of our conversation. I hope my dear Anne that when we meet that your mind will be equal to this. I am sure you must feel the justice of the idea, indeed you have already expressed yourself so to me. My wounds go on as well as possible, but as there are two apertures of some depth to fill up, it may be a little time before I shall be out of bed. Nothing however can be more healthy in appearance than they are and there is a visible improvement daily. I have enjoyed the best of health possible during the whole of my confinement. My room has been always full of visitors, both male and female; the good people of the house where I am billeted, furnish me with beds, pillows, sheets, towels, every comfort that is possible, so were it not that I am fond of an active life, I should be an object of envy, instead of pity.

I did not enter into any detail of the affair in which I suffered, in my last and it will be unnecessary now as I have no doubt that the general will be explicit in his dispatches. But that which can only appear from the events they contain and which probably he will conceal, I may digress upon a little. Nothing but the extraordinary coolness, presence of mind, decision and quickness of arrangement which General Graham showed on that day could have extricated us out of the scrape which our allies had drawn us into. The Spanish force had divided from us in the morning with a view to opening the communication with the Isla, in which they succeeded meeting with little or no opposition. A little before noon, upon the French making some demonstrations, La Pena sent to Graham to desire he would pass through a wood which was in our front and join him with the British. We had advanced accordingly and were entangled about a mile in the mazes of this wood, when word was brought to our general that a strong corps of French had occupied the ground which we had quitted and had taken the baggage. We were instantly faced to the right about and gained the open expeditiously, but the ranks were much confused from the nature of the ground we had moved through. As soon as we gained the plain, we found two strong corps of the enemy very advantageously posted on two different heights. The general ordered an immediate attack with the artillery and light troops, which checked the enemy until he got his battalions disentangled, which was done in an incredibly short time, and so done they commenced a vigorous attack on the two corps of the enemy. A third corps then made its appearance from the wood on our left, but he repulsed it with a single battalion, when the others were put to flight. They were double our numbers in infantry and superior to us in cavalry, but they could not withstand the charge of a single squadron of German hussars who behaved nobly and put the finishing strokes to the business.

Although we occupied the whole force of the enemy and defeated them completely, the Spanish general, not only did not show a single battalion to save us, but he did not profit by the moment and get possession of the French lines which were then deserted. He either wanted curiosity or nerves to come himself to see how the affair was going on with us, he did not send any of his Staff to enquire. I think myself that if the commander in chief did not act in concert with the French, that the chef de etat Major General Lacy who was his principal adviser[26] certainly knew and favoured their plan, which was to cut us off from the Spaniards and then either to capture or annihilate us. General Graham seeing this miserable conduct on the part of our allies, withdrew his army immediately; but to shew you how completely beat the French were, a subaltern picquet of I believe the provost martial's [sic] guard kept possession of the field for two or three days after, brought away not only our own but 500 wounded Frenchmen and all the spoils of the day, not a parley-vous made his appearance. The Spanish general has been superseded and there is talk of bringing him to trial, but everything in Spain is talk, they are sublimity itself in that article, but there is a terrible sinking in poetry when they come to act. Adieu my dear Anne, your ever affectionate brother A Barnard

Isla, 26 March 1811
My dear Isabella,
Captain Lambert of the Guards[27] who is going home in the *Bulwark*[28] will take charge of your guitar. I have desired him to give it in charge to Lady Anne,[29] from whom you can get it by the first good opportunity.

---

26   Brigadier General Luis Roberto de Lacy.
27   Captain & Lieutenant Colonel John Lambert, 1st Foot Guards.
28   HMS *Bulwark* of 74 guns.
29   This must be Lady Anne Lindsay, daughter of the 5th Earl of Balcarres, married to his cousin Andrew Barnard who became Colonial Secretary at the Cape.

I hope it may not be injured by the journey as it is a really superior instrument. I gave a full account of my progress towards convalescence to Anne who will of course communicate it to you. I have really nothing to complain of but confinement to my bed. I have constant society, books and everything to render it as little irksome as possible.

I can never thank you enough for being so regular a correspondent, particularly as I have not written to you very lately. The circumstances which have occurred must plead my excuse, but letters are invaluable to me from their being a constant source of intelligence concerning poor Anne. I perceived by her last letter that the one she had received from Mr Grant had considerably depressed her spirits. It is to be hoped that time will get the better in some degree of the melancholy which must attend her situation which circumstances render peculiarly distressing.

Sarah I suppose is gone to Dublin. I fear that I shall not have time to write to her by the *Bulwark* which conveys this as the bag closes this evening. Nothing will give me greater happiness than promoting with my means any scheme for her future establishment for which I give you a *carte blanche* whenever anything of the sort may take place as you will not have so much delicacy in using it as she might have were I to offer my services to her.

I told Colonel Macdonald[30] of Captain Hamilton's conduct to Mrs Hayes concerning the publication at which he was as much astonished and disgusted as I was, one always hopes that these sort of circumstances may be cleared up for though I do not know Mr Hamilton, yet I dislike to hear of any person being so unfeeling and ungrateful.

But my dear Isabella both Moore Disney[31] and myself have a crow of great magnitude to pluck with you all. William[32] he hears or rather collects from a letter from Mrs M[oore] Disney has got some preferment but what it is we know not, she thinks Sally has written to him and only talks in general terms about a good house, but disagreeable part of the country; sorrow at quitting Finmure being over balanced by the advantage of the exchange &c. Moore is the kindest & best fellow in the world, I have long known this but my present situation makes me feel his cheering good humoured affectionate manner more than ever.

---

30 John Macdonald was now a lieutenant colonel.

31 Major General Moore Disney commanded the Brigade of Guards at Cadiz.

32 His brother the Reverend William Henry, was married to Sarah Disney, sister of General Disney.

Remember me affectionately to Hayes, as also to my good friend Mrs Hayes & the Miss Hayes. Macdonald is returned to England, he is as kind-hearted fellow as lives. Adieu my dear Isabella, your ever affectionate brother A F Barnard

I shall write by every packet to some of you.

El Bodon, 5 November 1811

My dear Anne,

I begin to fear that I shall once more suffer in character as a correspondent with you when I reflect on the length of time which has elapsed since I wrote last. I begin to think that we shall now be quiet for the winter. The French on the 2nd replaced the governor and bullocks which were lately carried off by the corps of Don Julian Sanchez.[33] We marched in the hopes of being able to cut them off, but on our advance Lord Wellington learned that they had got into Ciudad Rodrigo under an escort of cavalry at 2 in the morning having left their infantry about half a league distant. The 3rd and 4th Divisions and cavalry which were coming up to support us were upon this countermanded, but the 95th remained in advance till this day as our general[34] was full of the idea of getting hold of the new supply of cattle. But the enemy drive them into the town every night and watch them so close in the day that were Cacus[35] reanimated he could not steal them. We are therefore returned to our old quarters and in the absence of Mars[36] we cultivate the acquaintance of the Muses Thalia[37] and Melpomene.[38] We have made an excellent theatre out of a ruined chapel at Fuentes de Guinaldo [Fuenteguinaldo] where the 43rd are, and our scenery and drapes are superb considering the small means we have to work on, Lord Wellington comes over to our next. Nor has my old friend Diana[39] deserted me, for his Lordship keeps a pack of hounds and enjoys the fun uncommonly. We also have balls almost every night but the Castilian paysans fare in beauty and grace to my Gaditanians [sic]; but as Mrs Downing used wisely to remark 'for want of company welcome trumpery'. Adieu my dear Anne, though

---

[33] Don Julian Sanchez, a guerrilla known as 'El Charro'.

[34] Major General Robert Craufurd.

[35] Cacus is a character of Roman mythology, he was a three-headed, fire-breathing shepherd who stole some cattle from Hercules and was brutally killed by him.

[36] God of War.

[37] The muse of comedy and poetry.

[38] The muse of tragedy.

[39] The goddess of hunting.

I seem idle, you diligent and let me hear from you constantly. Ever your most affectionate brother A F Barnard

PS Either Harrow or Winchester are good, the former is nearest to you. Would this be a good or bad for Jim[40] your own judgement will direct you, you must put your feelings out.

Villarigo, 25 November 1811
My dear Sarah,
I could not have chose [sic] a worse time to write to you than the present moment, as we are now in movement to endeavour to intercept a convoy which is daily expected at Ciudad Rodrigo. Till this event of our operations is decided both time and news must be scarce, but I am so long in answer to you that I am determined not to allow another post to pass without writing to you.

We have been perfectly quiet the whole of the last & present month with the exception of two or three days and having had the luck to get into one of the best villages I contrived to pass it pleasantly enough but the season is now grown very cold & the houses having neither glass nor fireplaces we shall be rather uncomfortable so long as we are in motion. When quiet there will be little difficulty in building a chimney to the room which I inhabit and which I shall do accordingly.

Since my joining the Light Division I have been in command of a brigade but I expect to be shortly un-brigadiered, as Colonel Beckwith[41] is probably by this time on his way out, my situation is tended with a good deal of extra expense but neither extra pay or allowance. I am nevertheless not displeased at it as it would afford me great opportunitys [sic] of getting into either repute or disrepute should the army continue in the field for any time.

It has given me great pleasure to hear of Harvey Bruce's entire recovery. When you write let me hear all the county politics and how the interests are likely to go on the next election. Best love to Harvey and Letitia[42] and all the younger part of the family. Ever my dear Sarah your affectionate brother A F Barnard

Pastores, 15 January 1812
My dear Anne,

---

[40] Anne and Catlin Craufurd's eldest son James, eventually he became colonel of the 91st Foot.
[41] Brevet Colonel Thomas Sidney Beckwith, he did not return to the peninsula.
[42] His sister Laetitia was married to Sir Harvey Bruce.

I have very little time to write at present but I know you will be better pleased to have a few lines than none.

Thank you for the oil paper[43] and boussole[44] they are just what I wanted. I suppose a Gazette account of the operations will reach you as soon as this, I shall therefore depend upon it for giving you the news the quickness with which Lord Wellington has seized the moment for attacking Ciudad Rodrigo and the energy with which he has carried on the operations must strike everyone. Our 24 pounders are banging away merrily and I trust we shall get into the place tomorrow night. When I am more at leisure I will write you a longer epistle. Adieu, your truly faithful brother A F Barnard

Pastores, 19 January 1812
My dear Isabella,
I am ashamed after so long a silence to write so short an epistle to you, but my time is much occupied at present and as I am determined to write you must excuse brevity.

Lord Wellington will probably send a public dispatch by this mail which will save me the trouble of giving you the news. I can only add my admiration at the quickness with which he has profited of the opportunity of attacking Ciudad Rodrigo with which his mode of carrying on operations have kept pace. Remember me most affectionately to Hayes. Ever your affectionate brother A F Barnard

Undated [mid-January 1812]
I take the opportunity of Colonel Gordon's[45] return to write you a few lines. You will have a full detail from Lord Wellington in the papers of the successful ending of his attack on Ciudad Rodrigo, an operation which has been conceived & executed in a manner truly Wellingtonian. Marmont has been completely caught napping by His Lordship & should he chuse [sic] to visit our quarters now, we are ready to give him a warm reception. The garrison made a gallant defence but our loss is less considerable than we might have expected from the resistance they made.

I have been extremely fortunate. Beckwith will be here in a few days & I was in great fear that I should have resigned the command

---

[43]   Most likely used for waterproofing or to draught-proof windows.
[44]   French for compass.
[45]   Brevet Lieutenant Colonel the Honourable Alexander Gordon, aide-de-camp to the Duke of Wellington, was sent home with the dispatch announcing the capture of Ciudad Rodrigo.

of the brigade without having had the opportunity of doing anything at the head of it; but I shall now return to the humble situation of commandant of a weak battalion with some satisfaction.

La Encina 2 February 1812
My dear Isabella,
I must endeavour to make my peace with you for the two provokingly short letters which I have of late written to you. In the letter which I forwarded through you to George Maquay [sic] I told him that you would send in Thomas's name[46] to Henry Torrens[47] whenever he was old enough to succeed to a commission (16 years old). I shall be glad however to know his exact age as I find it may be necessary for me to make a little interest here. So many volunteers come out to this army who of course must be provided for, it becomes sometimes very difficult to get a lad a commission by applying at home solely, but as I have some good friends at headquarters here, I can help the concern at both sides of the water.

All my military news would be a day too late, nothing has taken place since the capture of Ciudad Rodrigo except that a corps of 4,000 infantry & cavalry came within six leagues of the place to reconnoitre but retired instantly on hearing how matters were.

Our division occupy nearly the same quarters as they did during the siege, the remainder of the army appear to be going to the cantonments which they occupied before the siege. The 5th Division (your friend Leith's[48]) are busy in repairing the works which will soon be stronger than ever.

The other brigade of the Light Division are at Fuenteguinaldo and have got possession of the seat of our theatrical campaign. I know not whether they will undertake the buskin.[49] If they do we have left them a fine stock of scenery &c.

The rains have commenced. It poured torrents last night and as few houses in the country are watertight, we were drenched in our beds. How lucky we were during our operations before Ciudad Rodrigo; the weather was in general intensely cold but always dry and the divisions employed here have not sent a man to hospital since excepting wounded.

I know you will be glad to send me a Christmas box, though the time is past I will suppose it present, so enclose me a nice little Almanack

---

46   Thomas was the son of Henry Hayes and Isabella.
47   Major General Henry Torrens, Military Secretary from 1809.
48   Major General Sir James Leith commanding 5th Division.
49   Indicative of a tragic play in the Greek theatre.

for the year of our Lord 1812.[50] Kindest regards to Hayes, ever your affectionate brother A F Barnard

La Encina, 26 May 1812
My dear Isabella,
Your Almanack is beautiful but when next year arrives you shall send me one such as you describe which I think will answer better for me as it will stand knocking about; that is a very small one bound with real leather.

We are in daily expectation of moving, but none can conjecture in what direction further than it will be in a forward one. The French army are a good deal dispirited by our late success and show their spite by being more oppressive than ever to the poor Spaniards whose dislike of them appears to increase, but the country is so exhausted that the resistance of the latter cannot keep face with their dislike of the yoke. The Spanish government have permitted Lord Wellington to enlist 5,000 men for his army which are to be distributed among the British regiments.[51] I know no way in which the population of the country can be brought to act with so great an effect. They are fine fellows but have been miserably conducted.

I beg when you see Lady Rivers[52] that you will give my kindest regards to her. I can never forget her kindness to me at all times but particularly at an early period. Pray remember me also most kindly to Mrs Storey. I heard of your being at General Steven's[53] in a letter which I received from him by the last post.

I am quite at a loss for any intelligence that can interest or amuse you. We manage to kill time as usual by hunting for which we go out at a very early hour. A grand wolf hunt took place the day before yesterday, 800 persons to beat the woods and three or four hundred posted in different parts of the wood to shoot the wolves, Lord Wellington posted on a hill to look on with a double-barrelled gun. After awaiting the event for two or three hours I returned home to breakfast and found that those who remained two or three more just saw as much of Mr Wolf as I had, that gentleman liking the society of sheep, donkeys and mules better than that of Christians with guns in their paws, so ended the great chase.

---

50   The Gentleman's Almanack or Treble Almanack was published each year, listing all in office in the public and military and also the gentry.
51   A company of Spaniards was to be recruited to each battalion, but the attempt only saw limited success.
52   Lady Rivers was the mother of George Pitt-Rivers, 4th Baron Rivers.
53   General Edmund Stevens.

Lord Wellington reviewed our division yesterday morning. We mustered pretty strong considering our late losses. Kindest regards to Hayes, the same to Mrs & the Miss H[aye]'s when you see them. Your most affectionate brother A F Barnard

Madrid, 25 [August] 1812
My dear Sarah,
Had I time I could furnish you with a volume without recapitulating events, the description of this place and palaces in its neighbourhood would fill a good quarto. I must therefore hope to deliver it to you personally when the war is over as I must be brief at present.

Lord Wellington last night gave a grand ball to the Madrilenas.[54] It was very magnificent the apartments in the Royal Palace where he is now quartered, are in elegance & extent superior to any I have ever seen and are perhaps the finest in Europe. The supper was laid out in the large salon where there was ample room for the whole company, and in stile [sic] the whole entertainment could not be exceeded. The dancing was not over till six this morning.

I have met with nothing in Spain equal to the enthusiasm against the French at this place although there is a considerable party in their favour in the town, yet their voice is overwhelmed by the acclamations of the majority in our favour. The three or four first days after Lord Wellington's entrance the people appeared frantic with joy.

I am lodged in a palace which had been inhabited by the nephew of Madam Joseph Bonaparte soi-distant Queen of Spain. I have the whole house to myself and Staff and inhabit a fine suite of apartments furnished in the most superb stile [sic] with a grand piano forte by Broadwood[55] in the drawing room, lustres,[56] French clocks, pier glasses,[57] marble tables, Turkey carpets in every room & a large bed with damask mattresses & pillows and satin counterpane to repose in &c &c think of the change from sandy ground and muddy water, to which most probably I shall before long return, but the best of all is that we are enjoying these good quarters during the extreme heat and it is probable that every days quiet saves 100 men to the army, the greater part of which are at the Escurial, Anevalli [Arevalo?] & Olmedo. One division and the brigade which I have the honour of commanding are

---

54   The people of Madrid.
55   John Broadwood & Sons of London produced pianos from 1728. It continues in production to this day.
56   Chandeliers.
57   Tall mirrors.

the only British in Madrid. I have collected a little music for the guitar here which I will send by the first opportunity.

I shall not write to Anne or Isabella this post, I must get you to make my excuses to them. Ever my dear Sarah, your truly affectionate brother A F Barnard

9 July 1812
My dear Anne,
We have now been a week in our present situation, the enemy continuing on the opposite bank of the river, whilst we appear to be waiting until he may be so good as to walk off and let us pass without opposition. A general action does not appear to be in the plan of either part for the present. Having seen Salamanca I long to get to the town where Doctor Sangrado[58] practised phlebotomy with such renown. Every step we take being now on classic ground tends not a little to render our movements interesting as far as the non-military part of them is concerned. With respect to the military point of view the best is that this country is covered in all points that we have passed from the Agueda to the Douro with beautiful crops of wheat enough to subsist both our army and the population for the ensuing year, should we be enabled to retain a forward position.

The villagers in this part of the country are very superior to those on the frontier having a number of gentry resident in them and a good number of chateaus and well-furnished houses although put a little out of order by the times. The worst is that hardly a tree is to be seen and our troops are [a] good deal exposed to the sun, which is powerful for some hours during the day. The army notwithstanding continues very healthy and it is always satisfactory when our adversary labours under the same inconvenience which is the case at present. I have received your letter enclosing Lady Liverpool's note.[59] I assure you that the kind interest taken in my behalf both by Lord and Lady Liverpool is more gratifying to me than I can express coming from persons to whom I have long felt a most sincere attachment for their uniform friendship to you, and it must be so gratifying if any exertions of mine in my profession give them cause not to regret their kindness to me. I fear the troubles Lady Liverpool complains of are not at an end, but they are at present of a more satisfactory nature and I most sincerely hope that they will daily decrease and that the new ministry may increase

---

[58]   Doctor Sangrado was a character in *Gil Blas* whose only cure for any illness was bleeding.
[59]   Lady Louisa Jenkinson (nee Hervey), wife of Robert 2nd Earl of Liverpool.

in strength in a proportionate degree. Ever my dear Anne Your most affectionate brother A F Barnard

PS: I understand that there is to be a brevet on the 12th of August, an opportunity will then offer of making me ADC to the Prince Regent or His Majesty; that is to say if there is any intention of giving me a step up, it would be of the utmost importance to me at this moment, as it would probably ensure to me the command of this brigade which I have held in trust for nearly a year but I have never heard a syllable on the subject nor should I had it not been for your letter.

Flores de Avila, 25 July 1812
My dear Anne,
When this reaches you, you will have heard that all the fine manoeuvres of Marmont have ended in his getting a most complete defeat at Salamanca, his army ruined and himself and most of his generals wounded. The details of this glorious affair you will see in the Gazette. During our retreat from the Douro and until the commencement of the action I trembled for Salamanca; the excess of joy shown by the inhabitants at our first entry would have drawn on them the vengeance of the French had we retired further, and they were in a state of despair when the British Army recrossed the Tormes. Their transport at our success you may easily conceive, as it has driven away every apprehension of the return of the enemy. They have flocked out in crowds I understand to assist in administering comfort to the wounded. The day after the action a most brilliant affair took place. During our pursuit the cavalry overtook the rear guard of the enemy at a village called Garcia Hernandez, which was instantly charged by three squadrons of the Heavy Germans.[60] They broke them and took above 1,000 prisoners. We have been obliged to halt here this day to allow the commissariat to come up, I think we shall move tomorrow. They have bundled off at a great rate having got now six leagues start of our infantry. Our cavalry however, still keep close to them and continue to pick up stragglers. Ever my dear Anne, your most affectionate brother, A F Barnard

11 January 1813
My dear Anne,

---

[60]   Squadrons of the 1st Dragoons KGL broke the squares.

You really wrong Jim's drawing talents in comparing them to the miserable efforts of my juvenile pencil. I hope you will make him cultivate his genius for drawing and music as much as possible now that he is young. The former is not only an accomplishment which amuses the possession of it and his friends but is also useful to a degree particularly in the military profession. The second if learnt when very young becomes a *delassement* [relaxation] to a grown up person not a study.

I have been once more in the field, the French made some ridiculous movements one night which put us all in a bustle, but they fled at the first appearance of our attack. The victory cost us but one man and the French who were defeated lost three. Bloodless I grant, but the proportionate loss was what it should be.

The French officers at the advance say that nothing is talked of but war; the senators are detached to their different departments to raise the people.[61] ___[62] they say is near Lyons and Bonaparte on his march to meet him.

I wish we had a few more men and a great deal more money; without the latter we cannot advance at this time of the year, the roads are so bad that our commissariat mules and bullocks for consumption perish in the slough by dozens. We have drawn it is true, considerable and excellent supplies from the country but nothing will secure these regularly to us but immediate payment.

Had we even enough to do this, Lord Wellington might probably endeavour to push on without caring about constant and quick communication with his depots in the rear, but it is great presumption and absurdity in me to speculate as to what his Lordship would do as he generally makes a start contrary to the expectations of everyone. Thank you over and over again for the toothbrush, buttons and ribbon all of which have arrived safe. Pray give my best respects and most kind regards to Mr Craufurd. Love to Joanna, Jim. Ever your most affectionate brother A F B.

Salo [?], 29 January 1813
My dear Isabella,
I return you many thanks for your annual present and letter which found me in rather a better state of health than I ever was before and feeling the consequence of my wound no more than if I had never received it.

---

61   A Senatus-consulte was issued by Napoleon in January 1813 to mobilise 350,000 men to replace his losses in Russia.

62   I have been unable to identify to whom this refers.

I can give you very little public news. That which we receive of the movements of the allies generally reaches England & this part of the world about the same time through the medium of France. You are before-hand with us in authentic intelligence.

Notwithstanding the flattering prospects of this moment I fear some time must elapse before this army can move forward. The roads are nearly impassable and the rains continue with unabating violence.

The French still continue very kind & flattering towards us and are full of assurances that the farther we advance the more hearty will be our reception. Tis deplorable not to be able to give their assertions an immediate trial particularly as large detachments have gone from the army in our part to the interior.

One of the Eeles's has lately got his company[63] and I hope the younger will not be longer without promotion.[64]

James Burns[65] has arrived some time and is really what (without partiality) I think a very fine fellow. I only have to regret that he did not come out sooner, he may yet however have opportunitys [sic] of distinguishing himself acquiring experience as an officer.

Most kind remembrances to Hayes & thank him for his epistle. Ever my dear Isabella, your most affectionate brother A F Barnard

Gallegos [de Argañán], 2 February 1813
My dear Isabella,
The paper in which this is enclosed will let you in to the secret of our present warfare. Our theatre this year is really beautiful. Our scenes are on sliders instead of curtains. We expect the whole of headquarters to patronise the performance.

I hope Anne has received the music safe which I sent her and that you have got a copy of it. I could get nothing well set for the guitar which made me send the required MSS with a piano forte accompaniment.

A thousand thanks for your Almanack and an equal one to Hayes for his which is full of useful information for this part of the world as it contains a calendar of the saints, without a knowledge of which I should give a very unfavourable opinion of my information to the natives. Best regards to H & Mrs & the Miss Hayes's ever your affectionate brother. A F Barnard

---

[63]   William Eeles, 95th Foot, became a captain in December 1813.
[64]   His younger brother Charles Eeles remained a lieutenant, until killed at the Battle of waterloo.
[65]   James Burns joined the 95th in February 1813 as a Volunteer. He did not gain a commission before the war ended.

Lord Wellington has returned to Freineda from Cadiz looking better than I have ever seen him.

Gallegos, 16 March 1813
My dear Anne,
I really think with Lady Liverpool that General Alten[66] is more favourable than those of an official nature generally are, but fear it will be long before HRH may have an opportunity of doing anything for me from the low rank of his present ADCs. But succeed or not I shall ever feel grateful to all those who have so kindly interested themselves for me. I fear I shall soon lose command of the brigade, General Kempt[67] has been long promised to be appointed to the Light Division and is now on his way up from Lisbon. I know no other way that Lord Wellington can fulfil his promise, than by placing him to this brigade, vacant by the appointment of Beckwith to the Staff in Canada. I cannot, however, complain, Lord Wellington has kept me in command of it a long time and I think he will still continue to do so, consistent with his military arrangements. I cannot refrain from enclosing you a letter, which I received from Kempt, about whom I need say nothing further, than to request your perusal of it. Sir Lowry Cole[68] was invested at Ciudad Rodrigo on the 13th. Lord Wellington gave a grand entertainment on the occasion. The rooms of a large house which was Lord Wellington's when the army were at that place last November, were hung with damask hangings of the Palace of San Ildefonso which were brought away by the Intendant of Segovia at the time we retreated. Sixty sat down to a magnificent dinner, after which there was a ball and supper. 250 sat down to the latter, which was equally superb with the dinner. Lord Wellington was dressed out with all his orders amongst others the *Toison d'or*[69] which was presented to him by the Duquesa de Chinchoz [?] since the Battle of Salamanca. I dare not say the value at which it is estimated, but it is something very great. He was in uncommon spirits, danced a country dance, and set off at four in the morning to ride five leagues to Freineda although it was piercing cold weather. The whole company did not break up till six. I have not time to write to Sarah this post; the next I will follow the plan arranged by you. I wrote to you concerning the state of our supplies here. I should be very sorry you inconvenienced yourself on that head as we are admirably off in general, but old pamphlets or rather second-hand new ones and

---

66   Major General Carl von Alten.
67   Major General James Kempt was given command of a brigade in the Light Division.
68   Major General Sir Lowry Cole.
69   The Spanish Order of The Golden Fleece.

political caricatures. What you and your friends are tired of reading or looking at will always be most acceptable, particularly if small enough for the post. I have had a letter from imagined, the banditti tore off your address, but I hope before this you have got the music. Ever your most affectionate brother A F Barnard

I have got the registered addresses, pray destroy Kempt's letter and show it to no one else, as there is a part of it which alludes to another person and not pleasantly.

Espeja, 19 April 1813

Many thanks my dear Sarah for your songs, they have arrived at too late a period for the theatrical campaign of 1812–13, yet they may serve for the ensuing season should we again take the boards. It is now probable that the army will commence moving in the course of a fortnight. Everything portends it. Reports not altogether unauthentic give us reason to believe that the enemy are sending off a considerable portion of their troops to France. If such be really the case I don't think they will be able to stand us on this side of the Ebro, and then they will hardly be able to do more than occupy their strong places. They have certainly evacuated Madrid once more. Joseph Bonaparte has been for some time at Valladolid, but I think we shall shortly turn him out of his palace at that place. The army was never in so fine health and order for the field as it is at this moment and I think it will continue so as there is a prospect of our having crossed the dusty plains of Old Castille before the very hot weather comes on and there is reason to hope that we shall not be obliged to retrograde this year.

This dull part of the world affords little to fill a sheet of paper with, you must excuse my being so very stupid a correspondent you are very good to continue writing to me a kindness which I acknowledge to be more than I deserve. Ever my dear Sarah, your most affectionate brother, A F Barnard

Salamanca, 27 May 1813

My dear Anne,

Your tea arrived safe the day we moved from our cantonments and is most acceptable; although the season of the year does not require muffetees[70] yet the patterns of those you have sent are so elegant and the texture so fine that they do one good to look at them. We moved on the 21st and reached this place yesterday, the French evacuated

---

[70]   A scarf or muffler.

the town without resistance, our cavalry pursued and killed and took about 400 without loss. On our part Fane[71] distinguished himself, they appear quite in the dark as to Lord Wellington's intentions. Does Henry Torrens know of the application Lady Anne has made in my favour. He could forward it as much as any person and I doubt not of his goodwill. I can hardly expect it before a brevet takes place but afterwards think there could be little obstacle, let me know what he says on the subject. You shall hear from me regularly. Ever your affectionate brother A F Barnard

Undated [Late June 1813]
My dear Isabella,
I feel obliged to you beyond measure for your kindness in writing to me so often a moment when it is impossible for me to repay you. I take advantage of a halt this day however to make a little return though my time is so circumscribed that I cannot write a very long epistle. You will have heard so much of Vitoria that the subject will have little merit however I will tell you all the singular circumstances attending that action, it took place on the longest day in the year commenced at daylight and continued till night. Our right was engaged on ground called still the English mountain (Sierra de los Ingleses) from one of our Edwards having defeated the French on it some centuries past.[72] It is also singular that the Prince Regent of Portugal should have created Lord Wellington Duke of Vitoria this year. The quantity of equipage,[73] fine ladies, riches of every sort, guns, ammunition stores, oxen, sheep, poultry, pigs, claret, champaigne [sic], brandy, gauzes, muslins, jewellery &c &c that fell into our hands of our soldiers exceeds anything of the kind that has happened since Darius was defeated.[74] They only carried off one gun and one howitzer out of their immense train[. T]he gunmen of these fell into our hands within a league of Pamplona.

San Estevan, 8 July 1813
My dear Sarah,
I take advantage of a quiet day and a good house to write a few lines to you. I shall not be able to commence a narrative of past events. They are so numerous and my time is so circumscribed that I must refer you to the newspapers. Our army now (with the exception of three

---

71	Major General Henry Fane.
72	The Battle of Inglesmendi (English mount) near Arinez was fought in March 1367.
73	He refers to the results of the Battle of Vitoria fought on 21 June 1813.
74	This refers to the Battle of Marathon in 490 BC.

divisions blockading Pamplona) occupied the passes of the Pyrenees from the sea to the famous pass of Roncesvalles. I hoped to have trod on that chivalric ground.[75] If it is as beautiful as that which we at present occupy it must be sufficient to inspire poetic ideas. The valley in which the town is situated is very fertile and well cultivated and filled with a number of villages and small towns of which I think this is best. The people are lively and good humoured and are very friendly to us, the surrounding mountains romantic with a proper mixture of woods, rocks, heath and pasture.

I cannot form a conjecture whether or not it is Lord Wellington's intention to advance his army beyond the frontier of France, this must depend on a variety of circumstances. Some of our small parties have already been a few leagues beyond the limits of the great nation.

I fear from the late accounts that our allies in the north have not been doing so well.[76] They ought not to have met Bonaparte in the field so soon and with such inferior numbers, the experience of the good effects of retiring to a certain extent before an invading enemy has been lost sight of and he appears to be concluding as usual by overreaching them in negotiating.

I think you mention my old friend McGorty's son[77] in your last letter. He has held a situation in the commissariat for upward of a year and is doing very well for himself and has acquired a good character.

Pray hold the paper upon which this is written, it is out of the French baggage and bears on it the head of Bonaparte. I must conclude my dear Sarah with the hopes you will excuse the shortness of this epistle from your ever affectionate brother, A F Barnard

Lesaca, 4 August 1813
I have but just time to write a few lines to you to go with the dispatch. The army have returned to their old ground after giving the renowned Duke of Dalmatia[78] a lesson which he wanted much to curb his impatience. The events since the 25th of July have raised Lord Wellington's character to a higher pitch than all his former exploits. The whole of Soult's force has been beat by three British divisions, the 2nd, 4th & 6th the Spaniards gave some assistance, the 3rd their countenance, the 7th aided in the demolition of the beaten army and the

---

[75] He refers to the death of Roland in the Pass of Roncesvalles in 778 AD, celebrated in such works in the *Song of Roland*, which heavily influenced the knights chivalric code.

[76] This almost certainly refers to the French victories of Lutzen and Bautzen.

[77] No McGorty appears in the Army List.

[78] Marshal Soult, Duke of Dalmatia.

95th came in for some share of the latter part of the business. From the 25th of July until the 2 August there was a continual roll of musquetry in the mountains during the hours of daylight, a sound which I think must have grown very disagreeable to the nerves of Bonaparte. In this part of the world the Portuguese behaved admirably on every occasion and were very much engaged. The Spaniards are beginning to show symptoms of improvement, and the force of example in a very short time I expect to see them show confidence. The soldiers are naturally as brave a set of fellows as exist, but they have so often fallen a sacrifice to the ignorance and rascality of their generals that it had ruined their morale which the direction of an able chief will improve gradually.

The 4th Division had one of their fights in the Pass of Roncesvalles, the chivalric ground. They were engaged 7 days successively and have suffered very severely, but gave the enemy a most tremendous mauling on the 28th. Lord Wellington was very exposed on that day, the only situation from whence he could command a view of the action was the point of attack where he sat during the whole of it exposed to a most severe fire. Gordon was wounded,[79] the Prince of Orange[80] had his horse killed and many of the rest of his Staff were slightly hit, but luckily for his army and the cause of Europe he escaped.

To Lieutenant Colonel Cameron[81] commanding 1st Battalion 95th, Fort William, North Britain
Camp near Vera, 10 October 1813[82]
My dear Cameron,
T Sarsfield is recommended for a 1st Lieutenancy.[83] I hope he will exchange according to promise, he is not suited to our *species of troop*. The division did a very handsome thing on the 7th, driving the French from a very formidable position, which we now occupy. Our brigade suffered very little, only one officer (Grenville Vickers[84]) wounded. The 2nd Brigade had to attack a redoubt placed in a commanding situation on a narrow tongue of land with a fine glacis. This cost them a good many men, the 2nd Brigade suffered very much, the place was

---

[79]   Captain & Lieutenant Colonel the Honourable Alexander Gordon, 3rd Foot Guards, ADC to Lord Wellington, was severely wounded in the Pyrenees.

[80]   Colonel, His Highness Prince William of Orange, he became a major general the following month.

[81]   Lieutenant Colonel Alexander Cameron, 95th Foot.

[82]   Reference Highland Council Archive/D271/D/I/13/ii

[83]   Thomas Sarsfield was promoted to First Lieutenant, 95th Foot, on 21 October 1813.

[84]   Lieutenant Grenville Vickers (Challis states Gentle Vickers), 3rd Battalion, 95th Foot, was slightly wounded at the Bidassoa.

however carried in fine style by 4 companies of the 52nd under Mein.[85] The sharpshooters suffered from being obliged to keep the ground whilst a body was forming to make a charge. It was all done as well and quick as possible, but from the nature of the ground loss was inevitable. Ever my dear Cameron, most sincerely yours A F Barnard

I am sorry to say poor Algeo[86] of the 1st Cacadores is amongst the killed on the 7th.

General Kempt to Colonel Henry Torrens
Camp near St Pe, 11 November 1813
My dear Torrens,
I grieve to tell you that our excellent friend Barnard received a severe wound on the 10th instant, but he is doing as well as possible & I hope to have ere long the satisfaction of assuring you that he is perfectly out of danger. The ball entered the right breast pretty high up without passing through the lungs & is lodged it is supposed in the shoulder blade. The surgeons have the best hopes of him, for the lungs do not appear to be materially injured ... he breathes freely, suffers but a little pain & is in excellent spirits ... I left him about half an hour ago attended by an excellent surgeon & an officer of his own corps, in a Basque farmhouse and he will be removed to a more comfortable quarter the moment that it is prudent to do so.

I give you all these particulars my dear Torrens because I know the interest which you take in this *prime fellow* & to enable you to relieve the anxiety which his numerous friends of your mutual acquaintance will feel regarding him.

He thought that he might be able himself to write a few lines to his sister, but in all events you will have the goodness to do so upon the receipt of this, for as in the first instance his wound was supposed to be dangerous, unpleasant reports may reach her from other quarters.

Farmhouse near Ascain, 12 November 1813
My dear Anne,
Two lines from me will be more satisfactory than ten from another person. I therefore send an early despatch to tell you that I am going on as well as possible. I shall be moved into Vera this day. I cannot write a great deal as the action of my right arm is a little confined. You must make my excuses to many of my relations and friends to whom I could

---

[85]   Brevet Lieutenant Colonel William Mein, 52nd Foot.
[86]   Brevet Lieutenant Colonel James Algeo, 1st Cacadores, was killed at the Bidassoa.

wish to have transmitted a little early and satisfactory intelligence. It is a great bore to be laid up at so interesting a moment, but I trust my confinement will not be of long duration. Ever my dear Anne your most affectionate brother A F Barnard

From the Marquess of Worcester[87]
St Pe, 12 November 1813
My dear Barnard,
I cannot sufficiently express my delight at hearing from your surgeon today that your wound is not of so serious a nature as we at first had feared it was & it also gave me the greatest pleasure to hear that you did not suffer so much pain as might be expected & that the appearances were in all respects so favourable.

I expect to go home with the dispatches bearing the account of these operations & I shall make a point of seeing Lady Anne Barnard (& your brother if I can) & at all presents should I be prevented from seeing them I will write to them both to tell them how you are.

With regard to the mare, I am very much obliged to you for your anxiety about her, but I always intended her for you in case you liked her & if you will accept of her you will gratify me highly.

We have had no fighting since you left us, but the French have retired quietly & our advance is near 3 leagues in front of this place. Our left is about two miles in front of Bidart on the great road.

We heard a heavy firing on our right today which we suppose came from Sir Rowland Hill's column, but as yet we have not got the accounts from him.

Pray send me your brother's direction by the bearer. I hope & trust that you may not suffer much from your wound & that when I return I may find you quite restored. Let me know if there is anything I can do for you in England & believe me dear Barnard in the hope of your recovering very soon, most sincerely & faithfully yours, Worcester

Vera, 27 November 1813
My dear Anne,
I have continued to mend daily since I wrote last. I am so far recovered that I had proposed moving this day to San [Saint] Jean de Luz where I should have more society, which is always agreeable to a convalescent and this place is uncommonly dull. But unfortunately this changeable climate has marred all my plans, it having rained heavily all this

---

87   Lieutenant Henry Somerset, 10th Light Dragoons, was an ADC of the Duke of Wellington.

morning and when once the rain sets in here it generally lasts a few days. I was on horseback on the fourteenth day after I received my wound, which is pretty well considering that it scratched the right lobe of my lungs. I cannot attempt to give you any news from this quarter, which is now our hospital station, where we know little except the progress we unfortunately are making. I had hoped to have written to you from San [Saint] Jean de Luz in which case I might have at least been able to have described the town and natives who I understand gave John Bull a cordial reception and are not sparing in their abuse of Bony now that they are under our protection. The Spanish army are returned to Spain to be near their supplies which is rather a pleasant circumstance as they were not quite on such good terms with Monsieur,[88] as we his old enemy are.

Expect further intelligence by the next mail, pray give my best respects and most kind regards to Mrs Craufurd and all my other friends in London. Ever my dear Anne your most affectionate brother A F Barnard

San [Saint] Jean de Luz, 9 December 1813
My dear Anne,
I am going to trouble you with commissions without end. Two or three dozen shirt buttons according to the pattern which I send. A box of Spence's toothpowder,[89] and some medal ribbon to enable me to carry the late honours conferred upon me. The cross is really very handsome, I hope to show it to you one of these days. If the toothpowder is folded in papers the whole of these might come under cover through Torrens, if they do not I shall not probably receive them for three, four, five or six months.

My wounds are very nearly closed and I am acquiring strength very fast. I moved over to this place on the 28th and am situated as pleasantly as is possible, being in the midst not only of my headquarters friends but also of my old friends the Guards. The natives are returning fast to this place, the young men have been forbid to quit Bayonne, but they have come through the French posts at night, many of them disguised as women. The inhabitants do not appear uncinical [sic] to us or annoyed at our presence. Those who come over, know little of what

---

88   The Spanish troops perhaps not surprisingly exacted revenge for the crimes enacted by the French previously in Spain. The Duke of Wellington was particularly keen not to encourage resistance from the civilian population of France and he chose to order the majority of the Spanish troops to return to Spain.

89   George Spence of Bond Street, dentist to King George III, had patented a tooth powder and made sufficient money to purchase the estate of Cranford.

is going on in the interior, they report the following placard to have been stuck up at Paris. *'L'Empire a vendre L'Imperatrice a rendre Napoleon a pendre'* [The Empire is for sale. The Empress will hang Napoleon]. This town abounds in comfortable houses and resembles in most respects an English seaport, it may be about the size of Falmouth. There are several comfortable chateaux in the neighbourhood. The country just at the foot of the mountains has been much plundered during the late affairs. I believe the four armies bore nearly an equal share, probably the Spaniards had rather the largest as they were in some degree licenced by their officers and the Spanish peasants descended in flocks to plunder what they could. This town has escaped untouched as well as its environs and everything in front of it; upon the whole the natives do not complain of our conduct as they have seen every exertion made to stop the conduct which necessarily must take place during an affair. Ever my dear Anne your most affectionate brother A F Barnard

San [Saint] Jean de Luz 14 December 1813
My dear Anne,
I am going again to plague you with commissions. Should you be able to pick up for me an old map of France previous to the Revolution, and an old map of Europe of the same date I shall be under an indelible obligation, there is no occasion for either (but the latter particularly) to be upon a large scale. The divisions of kingdoms in the latter and provinces in the former is what I particularly wish to be marked. You know the use of such articles at present are merely as references upon subjects which are now the general topic of conversation and from being almost forgot, occasion little arguments and agreeable blunders. They will therefore make me a man of profound wisdoms should you be able to procure and send them to me. Lord Wellington crossed the river with two divisions (2nd & 6th) and placed his right on the Adour on the 9th, on the 10th Soult made an attack upon the 1st Division (Lord John Hope[90]) on the left with a very overwhelming force. Sir John had only the 5th (a very weak division) and two Portuguese Brigades up. These troops though overpowered and from the nature of the country put in great confusion, managed to check the enemy. Sir John's coolness and personal exertions contributed much to the success of the day.

The Guards came up in the evening and made everything safe. Soult tried the left three days running, but seeing that Lord Wellington had reinforced it much, he passed through Bayonne on the night of the

---

[90]   Lieutenant Colonel Sir John Hope, 4th Earl of Hopetoun, commanded 1st Division.

12th and attacked Sir Rowland Hill yesterday morning, who gave him such a thrashing that I don't think he will trouble right, left or centre any more. He was induced to make great efforts to get our posts off the Adour above Bayonne and across the Nive once more. He is badly off for provisions and means of transport and was principally supplied by boats coming down river, which are now cut off. You will not easily make out my plan [not extant], but if you can, you will be able to understand our situation and that of the enemy. The river separating and their having Bayonne to retire to and pass out on either side of our flanks with all their force gave them a great advantage, which perhaps none but a man of Lord Wellington's genius would have run the risk of contending with. But events justify all his undertakings which no one in this Army can question or criticize. We rather expect that Soult will be obliged to retire from Bayonne for want of supplies. I expect to join the regiment in a day or two, indeed I should have gone out this day or tomorrow were it not that it has commenced rainy weather once more and I don't like running the risk of undoing the state of convalescence that I have acquired. Headquarters returned to this place this day and I think we shall be quiet for a day or two. Pray give my best respects and most kind regards to Mrs Craufurd. Ever my dear Anne your truly affectionate brother A F Barnard

Mr Craufurd of the horse artillery[91] is with the 2nd Division. I have not yet had the good fortune to meet him, but hope it will not be long ere this takes place.

Mont Marsin [Mont de Marsan], 2 March 1814
My dear Anne,
Though I am in a great hurry, I cannot but write you a few lines after our late splendid movements for all which vide dispatch. We have taken large stores of provisions at this place and I understand there is as much more at [blank]. I cannot understand how Soult could think of giving us battle so soon without it was an effort to save these stores. Orders were given that they should be destroyed and the bridges at this place blown up after the defeat of his army. The natives refused to do either and if there were any troops they were not strong enough in numbers or in fight to effect it. The Beaunois [Bayonnaise] and Gascons however showed a little fight at our first appearance but on return of confidence almost immediate, they then overwhelm us with kindness and swear their emperor is a scamp and their army is more abused by them than it was by the Spaniards, all this may be to flatter us but it

---

[91]   First Lieutenant Donald Craufurd was serving with 'F Troop', Royal Horse Artillery.

is evident that they do not consider our entering France as an insult to the country and look forward to the restoration of commerce from it. All the conscripts fly to the rear of the British army as we advance and you never saw such joy as is painted in all their countenances at their escape. William Napier, the 43rd his regiment being absent for its clothing, followed the division in rear, but being unattached he took up his quarters on the night of the 24th at a village at a short distance from the army but unoccupied by any other officer. At night a crowd of plunderers, British and Portuguese, attacked the houses and were committing outrages of every description. Napier went to the robbers, killed two and two prisoners, one a Portuguese escaped through the roof of the prison but the other a British soldier (31st) was hung the next day by order of Lord Wellington. This circumstance had a great effect on the neighbourhood where it took place. It showed the people that we were in earnest in our propositions of kind treatment and that none were guilty of bad conduct but when out of sight of their officers. Kind regards to Mr Craufurd, your affectionate brother A F Barnard

I must delay writing to Tom till next post. We are in the greatest anxiety about Lord March.[92] I most sincerely hope his youth and high spirit will prevent bad consequences from a wound which though as yet no unfavourable symptoms have shown themselves, it is too soon to grow too sanguine. The spirit he has shown in quitting the staff to serve with his regiment during the campaign and the attention to his duty whilst with his corps would be an example to young men whose sole prospects were from their profession and were ambitious of rising in it. With the finest disposition he unites superior sense with a perpetual flow of spirits which I most anxiously hope to see in full force again. George Napier[93] of the 52nd makes many enquiries after you and Mr Craufurd.

St Simon, 1 April 1813 [1814][94]
My dear Cameron,
I thank you for your letter giving an account of the gallant affair at Rueda. I cannot enter into a detail of all the events which have taken place in this part of the world & tell you I will confine myself to the operations of our own corps. You will probably have heard that Lord W[ellington] has been so good as to move the 1st Battalion into the 2nd Brigade which gave me the command of it before the commencement of the campaign, the battalion was on its way up

---

92   Captain George Lennox, Lord Lennox 92nd Foot, but serving with the 52nd Foot, was severely wounded at the Battle of Orthez.

93   Brevet Lieutenant Colonel George Napier 52nd Foot.

94   Highland Council Archive Reference D271/D/I/13/xii.

from San Jean de Luz at the time of the action at Orthez, Snodgrass[95] however with the 1st Cacadores performed the duty which would have fallen to their share with his usual gallantry & activity and was severely wounded, but I am happy to hear favourable accounts of them.

On the 20th when the army advanced before Tarbes we had quite a 95th affair. The 2nd Battalion were sent on a ridge to the left of the division, which was halted on the road from Barbastens [Barbaste] to Tarbes, to observe a corps of French who occupied the further end of it, the enemy having their advance posted in a small wood which was strong from its situation and the form of the ground. I was desired to send some skirmishers to drive them out and three companies of the 1st Battalion under Leach[96] walked them out in a few minutes. Lord Well[ington] had ordered in the meantime the whole division up to the point where the Second Battalion were. The 2nd Battalion advanced to the support of Leach as soon as he gained the wood and protected his right, the enemy formed a considerable body of men & made a very spirited attack on the companies which occupied the wood and had turned their left when Gilmore[97] brought up the other three companies of the 3rd Battalion to that point and put them to an ignominious flight in a moment, the 3rd Battalion in the meantime had attacked up the hill in front of our right and drove the enemy from that point. I assure you the Rifles were laid very short, that the enemy lost as many men as I think it possible to be knocked over in so short a time. The beauty of the business was that we were formed and ready in another attack in a few minutes, Lord W[ellington] saw the whole and was much pleased with [the] rapidity with which the corps made its attacks and equally so with the quickness with which they got together when it was over. Our loss you will see in the Gazette, we all regret Duncan much,[98] Norcott's wound is in the arm,[99] he and all the others are doing well, Simmons had an ugly hit in the knee pad[100] but he writes me word that it is only partially fractured and that he is not apprehensive of the consequences. Miller[101] has been recommended for the brevet in consequence of his having commanded the 2nd Battalion in two

---

95   Lieutenant Colonel Kenneth Snodgrass (from the 52nd Foot) commanded 1st Cacadores.

96   Brevet Major Jonathan Leach, 95th Foot.

97   Brevet Lieutenant Colonel Dugald Gilmour, 95th Foot.

98   Captain John Duncan 95th Foot, killed at Tarbes.

99   Brevet Lieutenant Colonel Amos Norcott, 95th Foot, was severely wounded.

100   First Lieutenant George Simmons, 95th Foot.

101   Captain George Miller, 95th Foot, he did not get the brevet as Major until March 1814.

actions & Charley Beckwith[102] from his having been at the head of a department so long, I have some hopes of getting it for Gray[103] in the next batch.

We have just got the news of the failure at Bergen op Zoom. I see two of my old friends Hog[104] and Muttlebury[105] amongst the list of those who distinguished themselves, I hope to see their names appear soon as Lt Colonels. Remember me particularly to them when you see them, also to Creighton[106] whose name I am glad to see on the Staff & Will if he is in Holland. Also to my friends of the 95th, particularly to Eeles, Fullarton & Kent.[107] I have had caps enough in store to keep the appearance of the 1st Battalion, as it used to be, but the 2nd & 3rd sport 'bang ups', as the soldiers of the 52nd, who were the first in the division that put them on, have christened them. We have a fine town in our front, but the river is so wide & rapid that we have not yet been able to get across. Our leader will manage it for us one of these days however. Believe me my dear Cameron, most sincerely yours A Barnard.

---

[102] Captain Charles Beckwith, 95th Foot, he was serving as a deputy assistant quartermaster general.

[103] He talks of Captain Loftus Gray, 95th Foot, who gained his brevet majority in April 1814.

[104] Major Alexander Hog, 55th Foot.

[105] Major George Muttlebury, 69th Foot.

[106] Probably Captain Abraham Creighton, 55th Foot.

[107] Captains William Eeles, James Fullerton and John Kent, 95th Foot.

3. BREVET LIEUTENANT COLONEL AMOS NORCOTT OBSERVATIONS ON POWDER HORNS AND MAGAZINES

Amos Norcott joined the 33rd Foot in 1793 and served in India under Arthur Wellesley, who helped him pay his gambling debts. He transferred to the 95th Foot in 1802 and rose to brevet lieutenant colonel in 1810. He later commanded the six companies of his battalion at Waterloo.

Observations on powder horns and magazines and suggested Improvements, dated 1816. Description of the large powder horn or magazine
Upon the establishment of the corps, each soldier carried a large cow horn slung from two rings by a green cord; which passing through leather loops on the pouch belt, confined it to the waist about an inch or more above the pouch. The bottom of this horn was made of wood, covered and mounted with brass; the mouthpiece was fitted with a spring such as is usually fixed to a shot belt. The horns varied a little in size, but generally contained from fifty to sixty rounds of powder. The sergeants being equipped with smaller pouches than the men, were furnished with a horn corresponding in size, containing about twenty-five rounds of powder.

Of the small copper powder flask
Each non-commissioned officer and soldier was also supplied with this flask, generally holding thirty rounds of powder. A green cord fastened to the rings, 'which were fixed to the mounting upon the neck of the flask' and was slung round the soldier's collar. The flask was

sometimes carried in a pocket made on the left breast of the jacket band at others, hung by his side. The mouthpiece screwed on the orifice and the measure of powder was thus supplied by pulling back the spring and tilting the flask. The soldier loaded from this flask and it was replenished from the magazine horn as required.

Of the first pouch issued to the corps
The shape was an oblong with the top perfectly flat, side leathers united with the front, thus forming a complete case as a guard against weather. The spare flints were carried in a small leather bag with a running string and this was attached to the body of the pouch under the cover of it. The interior consisted of a tin case divided into two equal parts and a wooden frame with holes for twelve cartridges. The loose balls covered with greased bags were kept in the tin compartments and the ball cartridges in the wooden holes. These latter were intended for use on the outposts at night, in the event of attack in [the] dark, or bad weather, being then more easy to load with, than loose powder and ball.

Of the pouch at present in use
It differs from the former one in no respect as to interior. The form is an oblong curved, in order to sit close to the back of the waist, it has no side guard against bad weather and the place in which the spare flints are placed is unequal to hold them securely, being too small and without any running string to close it.

Of the ball bag
This article is made of leather with a running leather string to close it at the mouth; it has a cover which lays over the mouth about an inch or more all round, fastening with a round leather button to the body of the bag. This bag is fastened to the waist or bayonet belt by two pieces of leather attached to the inside of it through which the belt passes; it is fixed on the right side. The intention of the ball bag is to contain a certain proportion of loose greased balls, which are more at hand for loading than if taken from the patch. These balls when expended are replaced by others from the magazine in the pouch.

Observations on the large horn or magazine and on the small copper flask, with suggestions for their improvement
The first campaign in the peninsula and the service of the corps upon the various expeditions it has been employed on, most clearly proved to the officers and soldiers, that the repair of these articles could not be

kept up; that men who had them in an incomplete state were perfectly useless to the service, and that accidents were continually liable to happen from the quantity of loose powder about the person of the soldier with the mouthpiece of his horn lost or damaged.

The mounting of these horns was worked upon false principles and deficient in strength for the use required. The mouthpieces and springs were continually out of order from a general want of care on the part of the soldier, who was not always particular in handling articles of such nice construction; from accidents and bad weather. It was found extremely difficult and expensive and in many instances impossible to replace and repair them; owing to the local situation of the corps, the want of proper materials at hand and of workmen. Under every circumstance that then existed it was found advisable to discontinue their use and supply the corps with ball cartridge ammunition.

The efficiency of the rifle has been ever since most inferior, even to a musquet. It is not necessary for me to enter into a detail of the comparative merits of a rifle loaded and fired with loose powder and ball and one with ball cartridge, I conceive the use of loose powder and ball to be the only proper ammunition for and true manner of giving to a rifle its destructive qualities, I would suggest that the large cow horn or powder magazine be re-established as a part of the equipment of the corps and prepared in the following manner in place of the principle upon which it was before constructed upon.

I propose to have the cow horn exactly as heretofore, with a wooden bottom, covered and mounted with brass, but extending at least one inch over the edges, with two strong brass rings rivetted upon it. In place of the mouthpiece and spring, I would have nothing more than a cork plug, secured to the neck of the horn by a strong waxed string. The whole of the horn to be covered with black leather sewed tightly round, having a cover (all in one) over the plug and fastening to a leather button. The second ring is on the neck. The price of this horn will be infinitely less than before and it will require neither expense or trouble, to be kept complete in any situation in which the corps may be placed; and in regard to the preservation of the powder and the prevention of accidents, the proposed plan is unquestionably more favourable. I adopted it with the companies of the regiment I had occasionally under my command, in every instance wherein the original horn was rendered incomplete, by the loss of the mouthpiece and spring, or by damage and could not be repaired. I was never apprehensive of an accident, nor did a single one ever occur. The greater part of the horns of the second battalion were fitted up in the proposed manner, during the campaign in Spain under Sir J[ohn] Moore and as it never fired a shot during the retreat to Corunna a good opportunity presented itself of ascertaining the superiority of the new plan over the old one, for upon the arrival of the regiment in its quarters in England, these horns were completely full of powder, perfectly dry and in service order, whereas with the others, the greater part of it was either damp or had been lost through the mouthpiece and spring, which after a little wear always admitted the powder to pass through.

If the magazine horn should be adopted, the small copper flask is absolutely necessary for the soldier to load with.

I would therefore suggest its being again substituted, but upon the following improved principles. The mounting should be considerably deeper and stronger than before, so as to leave no chance of its loosening or being bruised by use. I would further secure the mounting by fixing a brass circle round the exterior of the mounting upon which the rings should be fixed, through which the cord passes, by which it is carried. The rings were fixed upon the old flask in such a manner that after a short use of it, the powder came out continually.

In order the more effectually to prevent the mouthpiece and spring from accident and rust, I would propose in place of carrying this small copper flask in a pocket of the soldier's jacket, or in his breast, by which the article was continually liable to injure and accidents to happen, to have a leather case for it fixed to the waist belt on the left side and made upon the same principles that the present ball bag is constructed upon.

By this plan the flask would be always preserved from injury and bad weather, accidents much less likely to occur and it would be carried in the most safe and easy manner. The two companies of the regiment which I commanded at the siege of Cadiz furnished these leather cases at their own expense, for the copper flask. They were always in service order and the powder complete and in perfect good order. They were highly approved of by all the corps when these companies joined the army near Madrid in 1812.

The expense of what I suggest for the improvement of this flask and for the leather case to contain it, would be very trifling and the colonel would in the end benefit very materially by its adoption.

Observations on the pouch and plan for its improvement
The pouch at present in use with the corps although exactly similar to the old one, as to the interior, is yet very deficient to it in other respects. It has no side guards or case against bad weather, nor is the piece attached to the body of it, equal to hold the required number of spare flints, or to secure them from falling out. The pouch cannot contain,

without the risk of bruising the cartridges in the paper packages as now made up, more than four parcels of ten each; and the wooden holes, twelve, thus making in the whole fifty two rounds, a number infinitely too small for riflemen to have in their possession; it is neither equal to the preservation of ammunition as the edge of the tin box injures it much and the propensity of that metal to rust when damp is also unfavourable to the powder.

Should the magazine horn and copper flask be again introduced into the corps, with loose balls, the very best pouch it can have is the original one, the regiment was furnished with. It is perfect in every respect for the use intended. If however the corps destined to use ball cartridge only, neither of the pouches treated of, are calculated for the preservation of that sort of ammunition, in as much as relates to its being contained in tin compartments. I would therefore suggest under this latter supposition, that the pouches be furnished with two wooden frames containing holes for thirty rounds each and placed one above the other in the pouch; I would give the preference to this latter plan for the whole army; as I know from experience and I have no doubt but most officers will agree in opinion with me, that when cartridges are made up and placed in packages, as now done, much time is lost and ammunition wasted, for when the soldier goes into action, he has to take one of these parcels out of his pouch, unfasten it and then replace the cartridges from whence he took it; it generally occurs afterwards when they are all together in this manner, that he pulls out two or three at a time in place of one when going to load; and this is often done without his knowing it; even if he did, they would not be picked up. I have frequently seen the men after untying the parcels of ammunition, place them on the ground, in order to have them more at hand than when in the pouch and I have as often seen them obliged to quit their station and in so doing the ammunition has been lost.

To obviate this loss of time and waste of powder and ball, the proposed pouch will be found to answer most effectually. It will preserve the cartridges in better form for loading and prevent their being damaged as they generally are from being packed in parcels and squeezed together in the pouch. It is well known that ammunition placed in separate wooden holes in a pouch, is much less liable to injure by damp than a number of cartridges packed together in a paper and kept in a pouch solely of leather in the interior.

Observations on the sword

As the bayonet has been lately substituted to fix on the rifle in place of the sword, I would suggest that it be abolished altogether; the soldier has no use for both. It was always a preventative to his easy marching from the manner in which it was slung; and is very heavy. If it be said that it must be of use upon service in order to cut wood or to hut, I can testify that the Light Division in Spain carried *small* felling axes, purchased by the captains for their men at the particular request of the latter, which they carried on all occasions by squads and used them in preference to either sword or bill hook. They secured more wood with these axes in two hours than the division could have done in two days with the other articles; indeed, I scarcely ever knew the soldier use his sword, but for the purpose of dividing the meat, or for clearing ground to lay on. They were so persuaded of the utility of the felling axe, that it rarely occurred, it was either neglected or lost, and it is a well-known fact that from the use of this article, the Light Division was always hutted and had cooked its provisions, before another one had scarcely began on either. The late General Craufurd praised it most strongly and recommended its being kept up in all situations. The corps composing the Light Division in Spain continued ever afterwards to carry these axes.

The ball bag is so perfect that it is impossible to improve upon it.

The original lock cap furnished is by far the best article of the two kinds that the corps have used. Those latterly issued with sponge above and below, to prevent the water from running down the barrel and on to the lock, have never been found to answer. On the contrary, the sponge collected the water and from the action of the rifle against the shoulder or the hand of the soldier, generally caused more water to pass, than would have done without it.

Amos Norcott, Lieutenant Colonel, Major Rifle Brigade.

4. BREVET LIEUTENANT COLONEL ALEXANDER CAMERON LETTERS

Alexander Cameron volunteered to serve with the 92nd Foot in Holland in 1799, gaining an ensigncy. He joined the 95th Rifles at their conception in 1800 and became a lieutenant but volunteered to serve with the 92nd in Egypt in 1801. He became a captain in the 95th Foot on May 1805 and served in Hanover in 1806, Copenhagen in 1807 and the Peninsular campaign. He was present at the actions of Vimeiro, Corunna, the Coa, Bussaco, Foz de Arouce, Sabugal, Fuentes de Oñoro, Ciudad Rodrigo, Badajoz, Salamanca, San Millán and Vitoria (where he was severely wounded), he also served at Waterloo.

To Captain A[lexander] Cameron, Highland Company,[108] 95th Rifle Regiment, Bremen
Oldenburg, 24 January 1806[109]
My dear Cameron,
It is impossible for me to express the satisfaction your letter gave me and I am very sensible of the assurance of your friendship and all what you said me. Why can I not write better, to express you that what my heart feels for you and to tell you that my dear Cameron the Highlander, shall be holy to my remembrance and that I should by the happiest

---

108   There does not appear to be any official sanction for a 'Highland Company', but Alexander Cameron was Scots and a large number of Scotsmen volunteered to join the regiment including men from Highland regiments. Family history states that Cameron marched at the head of a large number of Scots recruits from Fort William to Horsham. The troops apparently gave up their kilts when they became riflemen, but the company retained a bagpiper. The company was evidently still in operation in 1812.
109   Highland Council Archive/D271/D/I/3/vi.

man of the world, to fix your esteem and friendship for ever. You can think that the news of your soon depart [sic] has much afflicted me, and all your friends in this town. I wish nothing more, I have the pleasure to see you before you leave the country, but I believe it is impossible. Therefore, I write you these lines, to say you my painful adieu. Should it be possible, you see me tomorrow Saturday the 25th in the afternoon to Bremen. I know it shall wound my heart again, when I am obliged to part from my dearest friend Cameron for ever, but I cannot thing [sic – think?] me, I shall not see you once more. I shall do all what I can to bring it about, though I have very few hopes.

When I cannot come tomorrow, I will be most unfortunate. I hope you write me then, in what place you go to be embarqued [sic] and the day when it shall be done. All your friends in the town shall pray for you happy transport and I beg you hearty, to give me assure thereof immediately as you arrive to England. Forget not to send me your address for England and the music of the Scots Reel.

Your friends of both sexes join their wishes for your health and say you the best compliments. Will you remember my best respects to the Colonel, Captain Ross,[110] Lieutenant Fenning[111] and all the other officers from the worthy Rifle Regiment, I have the honour to being acquainted.

Tell to Captain Ross I am most obliged of his letter and his invitation. I hope I shall found occasion to make use of the last lines of his letter. Adieu my dear friend, my wishes accompany you everywhere. I remain with real friendship my dear and worthy Cameron, very sincerely yours for ever, H Anson.[112]

To Captain A[lexander] Cameron, Highland Company, 95th Rifle Regiment, Bremen
Oldenburg 31 January 1806
My dear Cameron,
I send you by this, the little chest. Surely I am very happy, I think by the use of this; you remember you some time, your friend poor H Anson, when you are retired in your far remote country. Being employed to pack up the chest, I find out in the first place two secret drawers. To find these, you must before open the chest and then turn the keys once more as necessary to close the lock. Then can you draw up the right side of the chest, on the iron handles where you meet a little drawer. If you pull it out this, you find a final piece [of]

---

110   Captain John Ross, 95th Foot.
111   No officer of this name or similar served in the 95th Foot at this period.
112   Given the broken English it would seem that H Anson was a local friend in Oldenburg.

wood, with which you draw out another little drawer. I hope you will understand me; if not, I will send you a German description, to let it translate at Bremen.

Since I have left you, my dear friend, I lived very retired. I saw few mans [sic] and find no pleasure, to see anybody. All is still in the town since your departure and we have had this week not once a concert. I beg you to say to Captain Ross my best compliments; and to tell him, that his future shepherd was so happy to meet yesterday with C L [?] on the rampart, but in a such comparing guard, that he never could dare to address her.

Perhaps is it pleasant for you, to know, that Sunday as I was so happy to mess with you at Bremen, my sister had given a supper to Mistress Eichstorff, the two Miss Hatten and their brother, your friend. They drank then your health, and the health of the 95th or Rifle Regiment, with a hip hip, in three times three. You see by this, the interest which all your friends maintain for you.

The new[s] that you stay yet some time at Bremen, is still confirmed. I expect therefore a letter of you, with the greatest impatience. To hear if it is so. I hope then to see you my dear Cameron and any of your friends again here and to assure you personally of the great and particular effusion and friendship, where with I am for ever my dear Cameron, very sincerely yours H Anson.

You will have the favour to remember my best respects; and compliments; to the worthy colonel and all my friends in the Rifle Regiment. My sisters, the family of Hatten, and all your other friends; by her compliments for you. Adieu, my dear friend, God bless you and may preserve your life. H Anson.

To Captain Cameron, 1st Battalion 95th Regiment, Lord Wellington's Army
28 Bryanstone Street [London], 9 November 1809
My dear Cameron,
As I am in great hopes I am on the high road to the preeminent situation. I write best with my military, you suffer I lose also, my more humble means, honesty & friendship and though I have had the most convincing assurances of your confidence, it may not be useless to detail how far I have executed the commission you entrusted with me, as the prize money was not paid till I had left England. I was inculpated to defer the project of the Exchequer bit [bill] on my return in September. I bought one for you for £50; the mare sold for £17 which [Reves] paid me and your mare of Copenhagen was £91 10s. I have no other creditor in

the regiment but Mr Robe[113] should he be with you, will you mention I have received the £25 from Mr Lee's will and that I hold Jenkin's prize money[114] for him. Lieutenant Booth[115] being in the 2nd Battalion did not pass through my hands but have taken care to have it detained, by which I was authorised by Booth and he may receive it off Mackenzie[116] when agent has it. In my solicitude to be absolved from the vexation of accounts and the disagreeable of not separately commanding my time. I yet feel much regret at leaving my friends in the 95th, to many of whom I am attached by a continued service of kindness and I indulge the hope that the casualties of war will hereafter allow me the pleasure & opportunity of soliciting the continuance of their acquaintance. Believe me my dear Cameron yours most truly S Bridge.

If you have any particular appropriation of the money to desire, it shall be most punctually fulfilled. S B

To Captain Cameron 1st Battalion 95th Regiment, Portugal
28 Bryanston Street [London], 17 January 1810
My dear Cameron,
I have the pleasure of your letter of the 22nd instant enclosing Mackenzie's Bit [Bill] for £100. I have assured the statement of your account giving you credit for the interest to the 24th instant at which time your former Bit [Bill] of £109 becomes due by [revenue] to the date of your remittance, that is when they were in cash. I have made for you a set 5 per cent which I hope will meet your expectations. The Bit [Bill] I now receive is not due till the 20 March, from which issue I shall include interest. I have made all the enquiries in my power relative to the 4th Battalion, but I fear it is only the opinion of newspaper writers,[117] as no increase to the establishment of any regiment appears to be ever in contemplation of the modern governments of England till their objective strength outstrips their old quotas and as the 12 battalions we have, little more than seven hundred men, supposing your battalion & those in Cadiz are 1,000 & you are 1,500 men deficient. How far another battalion may assist you some must warrant it, but that measure is not at present pointed out. Indeed the instability of the existing administration leaves more than normal in the dark what will be the principles of the great council of our nation. The Regency appears certain

---

113   Surgeon John Robb, 95th Foot.
114   Captain John Jenkins, 95th Foot.
115   Second Lieutenant William Booth, 95th Foot.
116   Paymaster John Mackenzie, 95th Foot.
117   This refers to rumours that a 4th Battalion of the 95th Foot was in contemplation, it was not true.

of taking place & who can dive into the maxims of a guiding governess. I shall be most alert to give you every information which a poor individual can obtain & although I can't promise more ability, I can pledge zeal & sincerity. I rejoice, you are so well after such an arduous & long campaign. I hear your gallant colonel is better & returned to his command, which has given me great pleasure. Tell our friend J Mackenzie I asked at the War Office to learn the fate of his letter about leave & that I do not write but he should be on his way home last Tuesday, no answer had been determined on. Believe me my dear Cameron, ever yours truly S Bridge.

Last received at Dover	£400
D of Captain Travers[118] for horse	£17
Bit [Bill] on Adair	£77 15s
Copenhagen Prize Money	£91 10s
Of Cox & Greenwood (set)	£50 11s 10d
[Pay] Adair due 24 January	£109 12s 3d
Interest to 19 April	£11 10s
Interest to 24 January	£19 10s
Bit [Bill] on Adair due 20 March	£100
	£877 9s 1d
Deduct paid Macdonald	£36
	£847 9s 1d

***

Elvas 24 May 1811
Sir,
The Commander in Chief having been pleased to direct Lord Wellington to recommend such officers for brevet rank, as may have particularly merited his notice and approbation; I have much pleasure in being the channel of communicating to you that His Lordship has taken this opportunity of recommending you for the brevet rank of Major[119] & I beg you to accept my congratulations on an occasion naturally so gratifyingly to your feelings. I have the honour to be, Sir, your most obedient servant, Fitzroy Somerset,[120] Military Secretary.

---

[118] Captain James Travers, 95th Foot.
[119] He was made a brevet major on 30 May 1811.
[120] Brevet Major Lord Fitzroy Somerset, Military Secretary to Lord Wellington

To Major Cameron 1st Battalion 95th Regiment, Portugal
28 Bryanstone Street [London], 14 February 1812
My dear Cameron,
I was glad to hear from Mackenzie that you were in best health &
spirits, improving in pocket as in rank & bidding fair when the
present arduous campaign is indeed to be enabled to enjoy your
country & friends and take a long farewell of fighting. I say this
much in resolution of many conversations & yet perhaps the king is
deranged; and you are more than ever wedded to war & enterprise,
be it as it may. I shall be most glad to congratulate you on all your
success, or felicitate myself, that you are returned safe & sound to old
England. I write that you may know I am in the land of the living & to
give you a continued account of your account, which I hope will meet
your satisfaction. I request of you to make my kindest remembrances
to Michell[121] & all my friends and believe me my dear Cameron ever
yours most truly S Bridge.

Cash paid Adair for Mackenzie	£17 10s
Balance	£863 19s 1d
	£881 9s 1d
By balance	£847 9s 1d
Interest 20 January	£34
	£881 9s 1d

***

To Major Cameron, 1st Battalion 95th Regiment, Portugal
28 Bryanstone Street, Portman Square, 2 March 1812[122]
My dear Cameron,
I had the pleasure of your letter this day enclosing a Bit [Bill] for one
hundred pounds which I will place to your account. I have yet heard
nothing of the Bit [Bill] you advise of one hundred & sixty pounds,
but it shall be paid. Your account to January I sent about a month ago
which I trust you received, but lest by accident it has miscarried, here
follows a copy.

---

121   Captain Samuel Mitchell ,95th Foot.
122   Highland Council Archive reference D271/D/I/3/iii.

March 26 paid Adair	£17 10s
Balance	£863 19s 1d
	£881 19s 1d
My Book of former account	£847 9s 1d
Interest to 20 January 1812	£34
	£881 9s 1d

The other £100 as well as the Bit [Bill] of 160 to be paid will come into the next account, as you can easily see here [how] the money stands.

I most heartily congratulate you on your brilliant successes and happy escape. It is indeed hard that a man should not keep the laurels his bravery has merited, but I am afraid then that the risks about the winning of name, some risk of favouritism. I was most vexed for poor Brisach.[123] He was I have heard a very excellent & enterprising officer. Pray make my kindest wishes to Mitchell should he be with you. I hope he is by this returned to the regiment. You will have learnt the old use of parties has been confirmed by the prince by his retention of Mr Percival, that the war in the peninsula is to be prosecuted with vigour. Thus, there is no immediate prospect of a termination to the service you are engaged in. I request of you to tell Grey[124] I have received his letter and will immediately commence the mission he entreats to me. My brother Tom and myself spent three months together at Christmas, he was very well. We frequently mentioned his friends in the 95th. God bless you my dear Cameron, believe me ever yours most truly S Bridge.

To Major Cameron commanding 1st Battalion 95th Regiment, Portugal[125]
Colchester, 15 May 1812
My dear Cameron,
I have received your letter with the enclosure also and will attend to your directions about Captain Arnie[126]. I must firstly congratulate you on all the scrapes you have had during your arduous services in Portugal and earnestly pray you may return & enjoy your well

---

123   Lieutenant George William Brisac, 30th Foot, was wounded on the retreat from Burgos.
124   Captain Charles Gray, 95th Foot.
125   Highland Council Archive reference D271/D/I/3/iii.
126   The identity of this officer is not clear.

earnt laurels. Poor Peter,[127] he was a truly good fellow, I felt for his loss as well as his brave companions. I hope Crompton[128] is doing well, pray remember me kindly to him. I should have been happy to have addressed you as lieutenant colonel, but that is still in store for you. I have heard an account of your late gallant affair from Mr Ward, who had a detail of it from his nephew; it appears so incredible & romantic, that I am at a loss to conjecture how you could have proceeded. You are again in the heart of Portugal, I hope you will be ashamed to retire for the remainder of the campaign; but you have a very active & enterprising enemy to contend with. We have been in daily expectation of war in the North of Europe, but it appears as if Russia was afraid & France cherished to the combat. I saw a gent late from Russia, he says the Russian army is 400 thousand strong on the frontiers & that the fortifications towards Petersburg are impregnable, so that should war commence, Nosey will have much to do, to think of the peninsula. You will have heard of the atrocious murder of Mr Percival, he is very sincerely regretted, not only as a man, but as a minister. His death may make Lord Wellesley[129] to the Cabinet, in which case the army in Portugal will continue a first consideration. When you write, address me at Colchester, where I shall be generally the whole summer, command my services in any possible way, they can be useful & assure yourself, none of your friends will be more happy to hear of your health & prosperity than myself. Make my kindest regards to Mitchell & all my old friends & believe me my dear Cameron, ever yours most truly S Bridge.

Tell Mr Burke[130] I sent him the Bit [Bill] from Limerick by an officer of the 4th Regiment which I hope he has received. The receipt I preserve for him.

PRIVATE
[Fuente]guinaldo, 16 May 1812[131]
Sir,
The Earl of Wellington having been informed that it was the intention of His Royal Highness, the Commander in Chief, to promote Major Algeo,[132] in consequence of his having commanded the 1st Cacadores in the attack of Badajoz, I am directed to acquaint you that His Lordship

---

127   Major Peter O'Hare was killed at Badajoz.
128   Richard Wellesley declined to join the new government in 1812.
129   The Duke of Wellington's elder brother, Richard Wellesley.
130   Surgeon Joseph Burke, 95th Foot.
131   Highland Council Archive reference D271/D/I/13/xii
132   Brevet Major J Algeo, 1st Cacadores, was made a lieutenant colonel.

proposes in justice to your services and to your conduct on the night of the 6 April, which was most favourably reported to him by Lieutenant Colonel Barnard, to recommend to the Commander in Chief that he should be pleased to confer upon you the rank of lieutenant colonel in the army.[133] I have the honour to be, Sir, your most obedient servant Fitzroy Somerset Military Secretary.

Rueda, 6 July 1812
To Lieutenant Colonel Cameron, commanding the 1st Battalion 95th Regiment, Light Division
Sir,
I am directed to acquaint you that His Royal Highness the Commander in Chief has been pleased to confer upon you the rank of Lieutenant Colonel in consequence of Lord Wellington's recommendation. I have the honour to be, Sir, your obedient servant Fitzroy Somerset.

Colchester, 20 January 1813[134]
My dear Cameron,
I had truly expected till I had the last letter from Mr Bourke [Burke], that you would long ere this have been in Old England and I had promised myself that whenever it should have taken place you would come & beat up my quarters. I am rejoiced to find you promise me that pleasure when the fate of war allows of your return, believe me I should be most anxious to make your stay pleasant to you & as I am in the midst of many people you must know, can permit you with a page and recommend you to more palatable exercise even. I do not despair of such although I am gratified at your good fortune. I am vexed to see my old friend Mitchell undistinguished he has been on your tails of your military career; till now you have left him many degrees behind. It proves the vast advantage one step may prove & that hence it should be always regarded. Pray say to Mr Mitchell how happy I shall be to congratulate him as a lieutenant colonel. I am sorry to hear so bad an account of poor Mackenzie.[135] I have written to him 4 or 5 times but have not heard from him these 3 months, not since the return of Belliard.[136] The letter you mention he wrote by the last name has not reached me. You will have heard that Sir Sidney [Beckwith] is appointed Quarter Master General to Canada, of course has taken a long farewell of the green jackets. I was much vexed at Lord W[ellington's] late letter to the commanding officers,

---

133 He became a brevet lieutenant colonel on 27 April 1812.
134 Highland Council Archive reference D271/D/I/3/iii
135 Major General John Mackenzie. Whatever his illness, he survived into old age.
136 It has proven impossible to identify this individual.

it created great interest in the country. The glorious news from the north will have ere this reached you, the whole army is annihilated. The late revolt of the Prussians promises great events in the next campaign. I annex a statement of your account, the interest is less than it otherwise would have been from the Bit [Bill] for £140 not being paid for 3 or 4 months. It was made payable to Captain Cameron & you endorsed it as brevet major, but after a long correspondence the Treasury paid it. Accept my best wishes for your health, glory & happiness & believe me my friend ever yours truly S Bridge.

To paid your draft	£160
To paid Captain Allix[137]	£40
Balance	£936 9s 1d
	——————
	£1136 9s 1d
By balance last account	£863 19s 1d
Bit [Bill] due May 2	£100
Bit [Bill] paid out	£140
Interest to 20 January 1813	£1136 9s 1d

Colchester, 24 June 1813[138]

My dear Cameron,

I beg to acknowledge your letter covering a Bit [Bill] for £80 which I will place to your account. I made a trip to Hamburg with my brother to see the cossacks & in my absence your brother received the 20, but I have heard nothing of its repayment. John Mackenzie has not made his appearance nor have I heard of him. There has been some fatality in our letters, mine he complains do not reach him and excepting two I have had none since he left England. I am very, very sorry to hear poor Mitchell is so unwell, he is a truly valuable fellow & I trust in God he will return to receive the recompense of his arduous services. The campaign in the peninsula opens merrily & I think you will give a good account of him. Gilmour has been in Essex,[139] he is still very unwell and in no hurry to leave England. Walter Clark[140] lives very near this, he has married & moves in high style, a very elegant carriage &c,

---

137   Lieutenant & Captain Charles Allix, 1st Foot Guards, brother of Lieutenant William Allix, 95th Foot, who died at the storming of Badajoz.
138   Highland Council Archive reference D271/D/I/13/vii.
139   Brevet Lieutenant Colonel Dugald Gilmour, 95th Foot.
140   First Lieutenant Walter Clerk, 95th Foot, had retired from the Army in January 1810.

but he is still the same good fellow. My brother who is [with me] begs his best regards. Pray my dear Cameron, remember me to our friends and believe me ever yours truly, S Bridge.

I will not forget the fees of commission.

Colchester, 11 February 1814[141]
To Lieutenant Colonel Cameron, commanding 95th Regiment, British Army, Holland
My dear Cameron,
I write a hasty serant[142] to say I have been in anxious expectation of your draft issue the 24th. I wrote to John Mackenzie asking if he knew who had it, that might be in the way, have positively remained with my brother for the last ten days. I thought at first the inclement season had delayed the mails, but as the man has assured the communication generally, I apprehend some mistake. I have the money at the bankers ready & as I have had not even a line or hint the delay seems not with me. Pray give me a line to assure I can remit the account I have for 63 to Mackenzie and paid £12 to my brother. I looked anxiously for your name in the late business but as you were not mentioned conclude you had not joined.

My brother is appointed to the 63rd & has the appointment of Brigade Major in Dublin, he begs his best regards. Forgive haste, it is the publication of my new [prospect?] & have only time to say I am my dear Cameron, ever yours S Bridge.

Layham, 28 March 1814[143]
My dear Cameron,
I was rejoiced to find that you my good friend were not on the unfortunate attack on Bergen op Zoom. What an escape, I shall not venture to you, as a military man, what I think on that ill-fated attempt. There is a little cherub who actively watches over you, may you be spared from such future instruction. Every exertion is making here to reinforce the army. Detachments are arriving at Colchester, from which 3 battalions of 800 each are to be formed and the *great* Lord Buckingham[144] and 2 other Provisional Battalions[145] are destined to put

---

141   Highland Council Archive D271/D/I/3/iii.
142   Latin – composition.
143   Highland Council Archive D271/D/I/3/iii.
144   Richard Temple Grenville, 1st Duke of Buckingham.
145   Three Provisional Regiments of militia were being prepared for overseas service, but did not sail before the war ended in 1814.

you in force again to [face?] the enemy. Affairs do not appear so near as set as when you wrote your old friends in the south, have revived the old principle in France & we here anxiously hope the race of Napoleon will be extirpated. Your mare is arrived safe, she is in great health & beauty, evidently improved since her arrival in these quarters; she is too skittish for any other purpose than exercise, which she has separately every day in the meadow. She was desired to be kept up and fed with 3 feeds, which has been attended to. Whenever you wish it, she can be sent to Harwich and five guineas will take her to you I should think, as there are frequent, nay constant opportunities of sending her across. I have heard not one word of your Bit [Bill] of [£]400. I cannot account for this because if a line had been sent, where the Bit [Bill] was lodged, I could have taken it up. Perhaps your namesake means to give you the receipt of his future kind intentions, but alas he has a family. Write explicitly what you wish should be done, remember the [£]400 remain idle. I shall see you in a month. I am determined to take a trip and though I mean to keep out of step, I shall crack if not a pate,[146] a bottle with you. I was gratified at the orders, it is the greatest pleasure to hear a corps I so respect, so justly appreciated. I have not heard from Mackenzie since the mare arrived. I have written him a feeling letter. God bless my dear Cameron, ever yours most truly S Bridge.

Layham, 14 June 1814
My dear Cameron,
My brother Tom kept me at Harwich till last Saturday. I sent to the post Friday and Monday preceding, expecting a line by return of post and had I received it, I should have broken Tom's hospitable bondage to have seen you in town. On my return, I found your letter, but I knew not what to do, not being able to speculate on your stay. I hope you will not think your mare the worse for my stable; she has never been used; but than for 2 or 3 miles by Henry B but she was too gay and too sassy. She has never been *hazard* by my weight. She has however been regularly exercised. I sent you an account to [inspect?] by a friend to put it into the Newark post. I fear [if] it miscarries, I have not my memorandum back (it is at Brunswick) or I would send a copy. I recollect the only sums charged are £20 to your brother; [£]12 to Tom; [£]63 to Mackenzie and [£]400 to General Cameron[147] & you have a credit of *£80* remitted to me, so that you cannot be in [the] dark by putting these to the last account, but I will when I next hear from you

---

146   A head.
147   Major General Sir Alan Campbell.

a set time & particular statement. I thank you for your kind wishes about John, he has done the thing well, he is the second senior Brigade Major in Ireland and as he is under the wing of Sir George I hope he will not fall into obscenity by this dream of pacification. The army has outlived its splendour such is the state of Europe, that swords may be sheathed without the expectation of ever again drawing them. The prince would like a large establishment but John Burke[148] in the house, will every year hunt it down, so that no one can tell what be the final peace establishment. How sorry I am your native attachments draw you so far north. Pray do you go with any ideas of permanent residence [?] I think you and John Mackenzie might have stretched a point and came this way. You must have had the best motive. God bless you, ever yours truly, S Bridge.

I am anxious to know what you alluded to in your letter, what is it you mean to ask for? I hope some good thing and that you have with your claims great chance of success.

---

[148] John Burke was a Whig politician.

5. BREVET MAJOR JONATHAN LEACH LETTERS ON VIMEIRO, BUSSACO AND THE COA

Jonathan Leach was a captain in the 95th Rifles from May 1806, having served previously in the West Indies. He became a brevet major in June 1813 and a lieutenant colonel immediately after the Battle of Waterloo. He saw service at Roliça, Vimeiro and Vigo, the Coa, Bussaco, Fuentes de Oñoro, Ciudad Rodrigo, Badajoz, Salamanca, San Millán, Vitoria, the Pyrenees, Vera, Bidassoa, Nivelle, Nive, Tarbes & Toulouse.

[Undated letter regarding the Action at Roliça & Vimeiro – written at Lisbon, August 1809?][149]

Rolica
The 60th [Foot] and ourselves attacked the enemy's right and threw in so destructive a fire on their columns, such as we could get within shot of, as to make them retreat in great disorder. You cannot conceive nor can anyone who was not present on that day the situation of ourselves and the 60th. We had to ascend first one mountain so covered with brushwood that our legs were ready to sink under us, the enemy on the top of it lying down in the heath keeping up a hot and constant fire in our face and the men dropping all round us. Before we could gain the summit, the French had retreated to the next hill when they again lay concealed and kept up a running galling fire on us as we ascended. Having beaten them off the second hill and taken possession of it the enemy retreated to a wood, there being a valley between us and it and recommenced a most tremendous fire, having received

---

[149]   Quoted in Verner's *History of the Rifle Brigade.*

a reinforcement. The action now became very severe. About this time I had a most providential escape. I was almost faint with anxiety to get the men properly placed and with the immense heat and fatigue. In short, I was like most of the others, completely fagged and would have given a guinea for one mouthful of water, when one of our officers asked me if I would take a mouthful of wine. He held his canteen to my mouth and it was not there a second when a shot went through his hand and the canteen which was in my mouth and covered my face with wine. The poor fellow dropped immediately. I left a soldier with him and proceeded with my company, pitying the officer who was wounded, but fully convinced that the ball was better through his hand than my head, which has proved the case as he is quite recovered. The action lasted till about five or six in the evening, in which time I am sorry to say we lost many a gallant officer and soldier as Sir A[rthur] Wellesley's dispatches will show. My servant whom I have had ever since I came to the regiment was killed, poor fellow. We had three officers wounded.

Vimiero

On the night of the 20 [August] I was on an out-picket with a field officer and 100 men. Nothing occurred during the night but about seven in the morning the enemy began to appear on some hills in our front and shortly, some of their cavalry advanced towards the left of our army. I recollected that the French in Egypt feigned an attack on the side which they did not really mean should be attacked and concentrated their grand force on the other flank. It struck me that this would be the case now and I mentioned it to the Field officer. We had not much time to consider about it before several immense columns made their appearance towards the right and centre to take our guns which were in the first line. The pickets being only a handful of men, by way of a lookout to prevent surprise, were ordered to check the French columns by a running fire as much as possible and to retreat firing. We remained in the wood until several men were killed and the shots flew like hail, when the Field officer of the pickets ordered us to retreat precipitately as our artillery dared not fire a shot at the French columns (which were pressing hastily on) till we fell back. We retreated down a vineyard and up another hill before we could gain the British lines, the whole time exposed to the fire of a battalion of infantry. In the retreat, the Field officer of the picket received two wounds of which I believe he is since dead. I received a blow, how I cannot conceive, unless a stone was knocked up by the shot against my thigh, which gave me great pain for some days and made me lame.

When we reached the lines, the artillery opened with most wonderful effect. The 97th [Foot] fired a volley and charged the French, on which they retired. I gathered the few of my scattered picket which I could get together and found our companies with the 50th Regiment in the thickest of it and here there was nothing else (I can describe it no better) than a hail-shower of bullets. The French had brought up their guns certainly with the greatest gallantry, under a very heavy fire from us, but the gallant resistance they met with from the British on this (I trust for ever memorable day) will teach them that we can beat them on the 21 August as well as on 21 March.[150] The regiments which we could see engaged were the 97th, 50th, 43rd, 52nd and 60th, the other part of the army being on our left at a good distance. We had something else to do than to look for them. I can only say that no men could behave with greater bravery than all those we saw.

Unpublished & undated letter of Jonathan Leach regarding the Action on the Coa [End of July 1810?].[151]

I think I mentioned in my last letter that Ciudad Rodrigo had fallen after a severe bombardment, on which we retired nearly to Almeida. Since writing you from Val de Mula [Vale da Mula] the French pushed on a considerable force of cavalry and infantry towards that village. On their approach we retired almost under the guns of the garrison of Almeida. The infantry and artillery belonging to our division encamped near the town, the cavalry a short distance to our front and right (it being entirely an open country between Almeida and Val de Mula [Vale da Mula]). Thus we remained tolerably quiet until the morning of the 24th when about daybreak our pickets of cavalry posted on the plain began to retire, skirmishing with the French dragoons and mounted chasseurs. I have always the luck of being on picket when anything is going on, so it happened on this day. I had with me my own company and one company of Portuguese light infantry belonging to old Spry's Regiment. Another company of ours was on picket on my left about two English miles distant. In a very short time, the cavalry skirmishers being obliged to fall back and the country which I occupied being somewhat enclosed, some work immediately fell to my lot. The French cavalry were rather staggered at our opening a fire on them from the enclosures and began to retire, but this was only momentary. In an instant, the hills in front of Almeida exhibited columns of cavalry,

---

150   The date of the Battle of Alexandria in 1801.
151   Hampshire Archives 170A12W/D/0024-33.

infantry and artillery in great force, evidently moving forward for the complete investment of Almeida. They were cannonaded in their advance by our artillery. They moved immediately on our right, left and centre and (as is invariably their system of attack) made a rapid movement to turn both flanks with their light troops and mounted chasseurs acting in conjunction with each other and assisting each other according to the nature of the ground. Excuse egotism when I mention that my picket covered the right of the division and another company of ours the left. By the time we began to retire, the ground becoming most tremendously rough, full of vineyards, rocks etc, the cavalry became no more of use and were ordered to retire through a narrow road with the artillery and get over the bridge of the Coa which was distant several miles from our position.

That you may comprehend me, I ought to describe the country we had to retire through. In the first place our division posted so far in advance of the main body of the army and so far from any support, was merely as a corps of observation and (as it is said) General Craufurd received positive instructions from Lord Wellington not to risqué [sic] an action, but to retire over the Coa on the approach of the French towards Almeida, he well knowing of course that when they did advance, their vast superiority of numbers could render it destructive to us, should we engage them. The division consisted of three British regiments, the 43rd, 52nd and 95th, about 2,600 men at the utmost, besides two Portuguese battalions.[152] The cavalry, as I observed before, was totally useless and incapable of acting in the country through which we had to retreat. The heavy rains which fell the night before, rendered the fords of the Coa impassable for cavalry or infantry, so that a narrow bridge was the only way over the river. But I must return to my account of the retreat, which was of course determined on before the enemy came near us. I have often described to you the nature of the ground on which we engaged the scoundrels on the 17 August (Roleia), this was if possible still more rough and damnable intersected with rocks, stone walls too, which afforded admirable cover for their light infantry. Well, the old 95th and one wing of the 43rd was ordered to cover the retreat of the division, which as I observed, retired in column down the road towards the bridge, at least they began their march on the road, but before they got down the hills, all was confusion.

The troops destined to cover the retreat extended right and left of the road and no sooner was the retreat of the division perceived by the enemy, than down they sent their light infantry in abundance

---

152   1st and 3rd Cacadores.

like swarms of bees and they were regularly relieved by fresh troops so that our poor devils not only laboured under the disadvantage of numbers, but fresh men who hunted us down the mountains like deer. We disputed the ground as well as we could, taking about two hours to retire to the bridge. By the time I got in sight of it I think half the division had crossed and the others were getting over as rapidly as the narrow defile would admit. We withdrew pretty leisurely towards it firing, as we retired and wonderfully regular considering the heart-breaking country we had already got through and still had to surmount before we could reach the bridge. And now the fire began (as you may naturally fancy) to be cursedly hot from the French because the nearer we drew to the bridge the more we concentrated and from behind every wall and rock they directed their fire at the bridge and its vicinity.

I had the lot of being one of the last who crossed and for this I must account to you very easily and without taking any credit to myself. I was [near?] the enemy on the first attack of the picket and consequently among the last who reached the bridge at the critical period, when about fifty of ours and as many of the 43rd were keeping possession of a hill commanding the bridge. About five minutes before the last of us crossed, both the officers of my company were wounded within three minutes of each other. They are brothers, one badly wounded in the thigh, the other in the leg. I had just time to get them carried off, saw them clear over the bridge and then we dashed over helter-skelter, the devil take the hindmost. The French in a second, occupied the hill which we left, blazed at us in crossing and as we ascended the opposite heights [they] made damnable work amongst us. On the bridge stood two artillery cars. An officer of artillery cried out 'don't let me lose my tumbrils, stand by me riflemen.' Our boys lined the battlements of the bridge, keeping up a constant fire whilst he got his horses harnessed and got clear off. Then away we went and ascended the heights on the other side, which were exactly the same as on the Almeida side of the river. Most providentially for us the ground on the Almeida side was such as to prevent the French from getting down their artillery to bear on the bridge or by heaven we must have been annihilated in crossing. Having ascended the heights on this side (as I shall now term it) our men were completely exhausted; many had expended all their ammunition. At this time we lost numbers from the French sharpshooters. The firing across the river at each other was still kept up without intermission. About an hour after we had got up the heights and while the firing was going on from both parties, we perceived large columns coming down from the opposite side, which our artillery astonished with shells, making them fly in all directions.

59

However, a party of grenadiers headed by an officer in the most gallant manner possible, charged over the bridge. They were no sooner on it than such a fire was directed on them from our men as soon covered the bridge and both sides of it. The officer who headed the party crossed unhurt, followed by four others, who attempted to ascend the heights, he was shot on this side and most of his men. I fired at him myself with my little rifle (which still stands my friend) and cursed my stupidity for missing him, but a running person is not easily hit. His right-hand man was killed close to him. They continued charging over the bridge, but finding that we were not to be *licked up the hill,* at last retired leaving both sides of the bridge and the bridge itself strewed with killed and wounded. About four o'clock the firing ceased on both sides and I may safely say that from its commencement at six in the morning, till four there was no cessation even for a second. The loss of the division is altogether 331 including officers. This you will think trifling and say very naturally that in nine hours, more should have been killed, but you must recollect that there was very little artillery against us and that only at the commencement of the business. It was completely a fight of light infantry and the excessive fatigue which is beyond my powers to describe, added much to the severity of the day's work. About twelve o'clock it rained as hard as I ever recollect and continued till five or six in the evening. All the night before, we were drenched with rain, for a more tremendous night I never wish to see and we had no cover, but huts made of boughs of trees which kept out no rain. About five o'clock we broke our fast and never were poor devils more completely knocked up. We retired about six English miles that night and lay down about ten amongst some rocks. We made fires which in some measure dried our clothes. I never slept more soundly, but in the morning the general complaint was rheumatism. We are now refreshed and got into a village distant a few leagues from the enemy.

I have still more remarks to make and I fear you are already tired with this long, tough story. I cannot help thinking how fortunate I have been, never yet to have been touched by musket shot or anything else. The only narrow escape that I am conscious of having had in this last affair was a cannon shot which struck the particles of a rock against me.

By some deserters of the enemy we learn that the French, knowing our division to consist of light infantry, picked some thousand of their best marksmen from the whole army to engage us and they say also that the officers belonging to those corps so embodied from different regiments belong to the Legion of Honour. How far this may be true I know not, so however the deserters say. Certain it is that no troops except British can do anything against them, particularly their light troops. Oh; if we had men enough, they would see us damned before they would dare to come near us. One little charge made at them by our men of the 43rd, sent them off like sheep, although we charged up the hill at them. The loss of our regiment is 130 killed, wounded and missing, including ten officers; two officers killed, seven badly wounded and one taken prisoner while retiring with the picket on the left of the division. I understand he was surrounded by the cavalry before he could get off the plain.

Once more excuse my bringing self into the question, when I say that I certainly killed one French grenadier with my little rifle near the bridge and I sincerely hope hit many others. At all events I did my best and fired until my ammunition was expended and my rifle got so hot that it would fire no longer.

Well now, I have another thing to mention, but as this letter may possibly miscarry, I shall forbear from saying much on the subject. You have heard how universally General Craufurd was hated and detested in the retreat to Corunna. If possible, he is still more abhorred now and has been so ever since we landed in Portugal. He is a damned tyrant and a great blackguard and has proved himself totally unfit to command a company, much less a division. I understand he has just got into a scrape with Lord Wellington for pitching on ground for his position which the most uninstructed boy of one month's standing in the army would have known better than to have taken up. I am fully confident that any sergeant in the army would have brought off the division in better order, God be praised. If we had not all done something like our duty, I know not but the division might have been now on its march to Verdun. If we ever meet I will tell you more about his. Lord Wellington was with us yesterday and our old friend General Spencer[153] whose paternal care cannot be too highly appreciated is riding about our posts. You have often heard me speak of his [Remainder of letter missing].

Undated letter describing the Battle of Bussaco [October 1810?][154]

As for the fighting at Busaco you will make it out from the official despatches better than from my account. If ever we meet (which I trust we soon shall) I will endeavour to explain the whole business. You will naturally wonder to see by the returns that our regiment lost no officers. I will account for it in two ways. In the first place we lost so

---

153   Major General Brent Spencer.
154   Quoted in Verner's *History of the Rifle Brigade*.

many officers at the Coa, which have not yet joined in consequence of their wounds (and three of whom are since dead) that we had a great scarcity, scarcely enough to do the duty. In the second place, the hills occupied by the Light Division were extremely high and the approach to them near the summit full of craggy rocks. Amongst these and some fir trees, our companies lay scattered and had such excellent cover that I am puzzled to conceive how we contrived to lose forty-one men. Not an officer was hit. The 43rd and 52nd were formed on the summit of the heights and by [the] most excellent management of Lord Wellington were kept rather behind the brow of the hill so that the French in their advance to the attack could see nothing but our green jackets peeping out from among the rough and broken ground and making every shot tell amongst them without their being able to do us any material injury. All the prisoners who were taken agreed in the report that even the general who led on the attack did not conceive that the hill was defended by anything more than a few skirmishers and they were therefore not agreeably surprised on their reaching the summit to be saluted with a volley and charge of bayonets from the 43rd and 52nd who were formed in line and ready to receive them. In an instant the irresistible three cheers and the cold steel sent the whole column to the right about and you may then fancy the confusion and destruction amongst them. Our artillery and riflemen and two light battalions firing into a whole division racing down almost a precipice. You could see them tumbling headlong over each other, even those who were not hit. I will not attempt to say how many were destroyed by our division alone, but from a remark which I shall just now make, you can give a rough guess. The division which attacked us was Loison's.[155] General Simon[156] commanded one brigade of it and General Ferrez [Ferey][157] the other. Simon was wounded and made prisoner whilst leading on his men in a most undaunted manner. Ferrez [Ferey] is said to be wounded. We must give the French their due and say that no men could come up in a more resolute manner. When the almost insurmountable nature of the ground is considered, I only wonder that Massena should have thought it possible to force British troops out of such a position. A flag of truce came into us towards evening for the purpose of burying their dead or rather of carrying off their wounded. During this cessation we went down amongst them for the sake of curiosity and as you may imagine it was a sad carnage. By heaven! One little village was full

---

[155]   General Louis Loison.
[156]   General Edouard Simon.
[157]   General Claude Ferey.

of killed and wounded. The attacking division was composed of the following French regiments, as I was enabled to ascertain from their buttons. The 6th, 26th, 66th, 82nd, a battalion of their Hanoverian Legion and the Legion du Midi. Those regiments had nearly reached the summit of the hill when they were attacked. On the day after the battle we got the return of the 26th Regiment, which was 700 killed and wounded. A deserter from the Hanoverian Legion told me in English 'My company come up the hill one hundred and he come back twenty-two men only.' From those remarks you may suppose their loss in this attack was immense. The French 82nd and Legion du Midi are old Vimiera friends. The 26th, 66th and 82nd are *Bridge of Lodi Boys,* but of the heights of Busaco, I daresay they will be less proud. Our regiment lost more men than the 43rd and 52nd together and were in short, engaged with the French light troops constantly, more or less for three days and were much harassed. Our position being very extensive I could not see what was going on when General Picton was attacked, who was some miles on our right. General Pack's Portuguese Brigade formed line and charged in a most regular and spirited manner under a cannonade of round-shot from the enemy's batteries. It shows what improvement they have made since British officers and good discipline have been introduced amongst them. I was quite hoarse with cheering and halloaing. Whenever we saw the Portuguese about to charge, who were nearly a mile distant, we all set up a howl which undoubtedly spirited them on and they behaved uncommonly well, much better than the most sanguine could have expected. The 88th and 45th I am told made a delightful charge, they met our old Vimiera friends, the 32nd and 70th, which are two of their choice regiments. Indeed it is ascertained that Massena's best troops made the attack on that day.

6. CAPTAIN WILLIAM COX
DIARY[158]

William Cox, brother of John Cox, joined the 95th Foot as a second lieutenant on 6 June 1805 and became a first lieutenant in November 1807, before becoming a captain in September 1813. He was on Recruiting Service in Ireland in 1806, before serving at Copenhagen in 1807 and Portugal in 1808 with the 2nd Battalion, seeing action at Óbidos, Roliça and Vimeiro and Vigo. He returned to England in January 1809 but returned to Portugal in June 1809 with the 1st Battalion, returning to serve in England and Ireland in April 1810. He returned to the 1st Battalion in Portugal in April 1813 and saw action at San Millan, Vitoria, the Pyrenees, Vera, Bidassoa, Nivelle and Nive. He then served with the 3rd Battalion in the south of France, seeing further service at Orthez. He served with the regiment in Occupied France from 1815 to 1818, although he was not at Waterloo. In 1820 he transferred to 1st Dragoons England and to the Cape of Good Hope cavalry in 1823.

6 June 1805: In this month I was by the interest of my friend Lieutenant Colonel John Grey[159] gazetted to be 2nd Lieutenant in the 95th of Rifle Regiment commanded by Major General Coote Manningham on the formation of a 2nd Battalion to the corps, and I joined them at Brabourne Lees Barracks in Kent in the beginning of August where both battalions were stationed, the 1st Battalion was commanded by Lieutenant Colonel Sidney Beckwith and the 2nd Battalion by Lieutenant Colonel Hamlet Wade.

October 1805: I marched in this month with 5 companies 2nd Battalion under Major Gardner[160] to Weeley Barracks in Essex, to

---

158   Only his journal up to 1818 has been extracted from his 'Recollections and Military Memoirs of Major General William Cox K H' held at the National Library of Ireland, Dublin.
159   Lieutenant Colonel John Grey, 113th Foot.
160   Major Thomas Gardner, 95th Foot.

whom I acted as Adjutant and did the duty of which in garrison with the 79th, 91st and 92nd Regiments.

1806: We received a route and marched to Faversham in Kent where we joined the remainder of the battalion and from this shortly afterwards, I was with several other officers ordered to Ireland to get volunteers from the Irish Militia. I proceeded to London and from then to Dublin by Parkgate with Lieutenant Loftus Gray[161] of my own corps going on the same duty. On our arrival we were ordered to our different stations. I was ordered to Cashel in the County of Tipperary to get men from the Tyrone Regiment but this regiment being ordered very soon after into Clonmel all the officers of the line were ordered there also. I took lodgings at a Mrs Luther's with Captain Hamilton of the 71st Regiment.[162] I remained the greater part of this summer at Clonmel and got about 35 men from the Tyrone and Kilkenny Regiments of Militia. Having occasionally gone over to Caher where the latter regiment was quartered. The men I got from this regiment were remarkably fine and proved afterwards excellent soldiers. The greater part of them were killed at the storming of Badajoz in Spain in 1812 at the head of the storming party.

In August we were ordered to proceed with our men to our different regiments. I marched with mine and several other parties to Waterford where we were embarked for Bristol. We sailed from Passage[163] but the weather being very bad and being short of stock for the men, we put into Tenby in South Wales where we disembarked and next day I marched both Lieutenant Hunt of the 3rd Regiment,[164] Lieutenants Simpson[165] & Dundas[166] of the 43rd Regiment, Lieutenant Hill 14th Regiment[167] and Lieutenant Cuthbertson 48th Regiment[168] to Carmarthen and from thence on to Bristol, from this we got fresh routes. I proceeded with my own party and that of the 43rd to Kent, where our corps were stationed and after a fatiguing and expensive march of 30 days I joined my regiment at Brabourne Lees Barracks. While I was away from the regiment, 3 companies had gone on the expedition to South America under Major Gardner and were at the storming and taking Montevideo, where we lost a very excellent fine fellow

---

161   First Lieutenant Loftus Gray, 95th Foot.
162   Captain Ralph Hamilton, 71st Foot.
163   Passage near Cork.
164   Lieutenant Robert Hunt, 3rd Foot.
165   Lieutenant Robert Simpson, 43rd Foot.
166   Lieutenant George Dundas, 43rd Foot.
167   Actually Ensign Henry Hill, 14th Foot.
168   Actually Ensign John Cuthbertson, 48th Foot.

Captain Dickenson.[169] About Christmas we changed our quarters to Hythe Barracks, where we remained with the 43rd Regiment till ordered on the expedition to Denmark.

1807: I marched with 5 companies under Lieutenant Colonel Wade to Deal where we embarked in two vessels. I was with the headquarters in Captain Balvaird's company.[170] Captain Creagh's,[171] Honourable H[enry] Pakenham's[172] and Leach's companies[173] were in the other ship. A few days after embarking, the whole fleet sailed from the Downs under the command of Admiral Lord Gardner.[174] The land forces were commanded by Lord Cathcart.[175]

August: The fleet anchored near the Castle of Cronberg [Kronborg] and not far from Elsinore, but removed in two days after further down the Sound and the whole of the troops were disembarked without opposition within ten miles of Copenhagen, the Reserve under Sir Arthur Wellesley were the first that landed. The corps composing it were the 43rd 1st Battalion, 52nd 1st Battalion, 1st Battalion 95th 5 companies and 2nd Battalion 95th 5 companies, and the 92nd Regiment. We immediately moved on and lay in the street of a village that night, and next day invested Copenhagen and had that day some sharp skirmishing with some Danish infantry, this was the first time I saw a shot fired. I was on picket with my men and Captain Pakenham's company this night at a chateau close to the town and having taken a patrole [sic] of the enemy and they having ascertained likewise where we were, they opened a mortar battery on us very early next morning, we lay very quiet in a small ditch and fortunately none of the shells did us any harm, though they repeatedly fell very close to us. We were relieved by some light companies who were very soon dislodged with loss. We remained cantoned in the farmhouses close to the town till the batteries were all completed and had opened on the town when the Reserve marched in two columns into the interior of the country, the enemy having collected a force. Our battalion was in the column commanded by General Linsingen,[176] the other in which was the 1st Battalion was commanded by Sir A[rthur] Wellesley. After some day's marching we came up with the enemy at Kioge, they were

---

169   Captain Richard Dickinson, 95th Foot.
170   Captain William Balvaird, 95th Foot.
171   Captain Jasper Creagh, 95th Foot.
172   Captain Hercules Pakenham, 95th Foot.
173   Captain Jonathan Leach, 95th Foot.
174   Admiral Alan Gardner, 1st Lord Gardner.
175   General William Cathcart, 1st Earl Cathcart.
176   Major General Charles von Linsingen commanded the KGL cavalry brigade.

principally composed of the militia with some guns and a regiment of dragoons, they were instantly attacked by the column under Sir A Wellesley and almost as instantly broken, having scarcely made any stand. The column I was with came at the same time on their flank. We had but a few shots with them when they were completely routed, we took all their guns and generals, but their cavalry escaped to one of the adjacent islands. We then marched to Ringsted, a good town and halted some time.

September: And here we learned a few days afterwards of the surrender of Copenhagen by capitulation, by which we became possessed of all their fleet and naval stores, we moved from Ringsted after a stay there of three weeks, which we enjoyed much, having a good mess at a sort of farm. A battalion of German Legion and the 1st German Hussars were with us.

October: After this, the companies were sent to different parts at the extremity of the Island of Zealand, our company was sent of [sic] [to] a ferry house which we occupied to prevent any communication with any of the islands in the Belt or sea which surrounds Zealand.

November: The weather began to get very cold and bad. From this we were ordered to join the headquarters at Wordemburg [?] where the whole army was put in motion to retire out of the country. We were moved in small waggons down to Copenhagen and put on board the *Princess Caroline* a Danish 74-gun ship. I went with a party of our officers from Ringsted to see the town of Copenhagen, we staid [sic] a week there. It received considerable damage from the bombardment, nearly a third of it was destroyed.

19 November 1807: I was promoted this month to a 1st Lieutenancy by the death of Lieutenant Scanlan[177] who died in South America. Zealand is a remarkable fine island being plentiful and full of game. There is a good deal of sameness in the face of the country. It is flat, several large beech woods and lakes, the woods having no underwood or copse are full of deer and the lakes abound with wild fowl and fish of different kinds.

December 1807. On the whole we found this a most pleasing expedition. We lived on good terms with the natives of the country, had frequent balls to which all the best families came and the women are very fair and very handsome the living being good and cheap and very good Rhenish wine and excellency Hock to be had everywhere we would all willingly have prolonged our stay.[178] We had a boisterous

---

177 First Lieutenant Charles Scanlan, 95th Foot, was killed on 26 March 1807.
178 It is not made clear here, but the British forces left Denmark on 21 October 1807.

passage to England, disembarked at Deal and marched next day to Dover and next morning into Hythe Barracks where the whole of the battalion met; those from South America having returned after the disastrous business of Buenos Ayres and where we lost many fine fellows and some excellent officers, amongst the latter were Captain Jenkinson,[179] Turner[180] & Coane.[181]

1808

January 1808: General Manningham was on the Staff here at the commencement of this year. I was quartered at Hythe Barracks in Kent.

6 January 1808: On this day I went to Faversham to get some men from one of the Norfolk Regiments of Militia and returned to Hythe on the 18th instant.

16 March: On this day I accomplished a wish most nearest to my heart, that of having my brother John gazetted to a 2nd Lieutenant in the corps. I had a few months previous to this made an application to Major General Manningham through Colonel Beckwith to appoint him to the regiment and which was done in the handsomest manner by General Manningham in approbation of my own conduct (as he said himself) while in his regiment.

April: My brother joined [at] the end of the month and a better soldier never joined the British Army as he proved himself to be in all the campaigns in the peninsula and in the terrific Battle of Waterloo where he commanded a company of the 1st Battalion 95th Regiment.

9 May: Two companies of the 2nd Battalion under Major Travers were ordered on service and marched to Dover where they embarked. They were Captain Creagh's and Crampton's.[182]

3 June: On the 3rd of this month two more were ordered. Captain the Honourable H[enry] Pakenham's and Captain Leach's. My brother John was attached to the former and I was placed to the latter and we marched to Dover and embarked.

8 June: There this day. Went into the Downs the next day and sailed the day following in the *Agincourt* transport for Cork harbour where the expedition was to rendezvous.

19 June: We anchored this day in Cork harbour which was full of ships with troops on board. Here we remained while the expedition was in preparation but our commander Sir A Wellesley having arrived ...

---

179   Captain John Jenkinson, 95th Foot, was killed.
180   First Lieutenant Patrick Turner, 95th Foot, died of his wounds.
181   First Lieutenant James Coane, 95th Foot, was severely wounded but survived.
182   Captain Jeremiah Crampton, 95th Foot.

12 July: ... from London we sailed early in the morning of this day. We found our stay in this harbour very agreeable having made several aquatic excursions in this beautiful harbour.

19 July: We crossed the Bay of Biscay with a heavy rolling sea which made us all very ill.

21 July: We made Cape Ortegal this day.

26 July: On the 26th we came to anchor in Mondego Bay, coast of Portugal; as our destination was hitherto uncertain, we were now relieved from all doubts. Knowing as we did that the French army occupied Portugal. We were ordered to prepare immediately for disembarkation and which we set about doing in the highest spirts and which we affected at Figueras [da Foz] ...

1 August: ... without being opposed, the enemy not being aware of our intention. The weather was very hot and we had a fatiguing though short march. We encamped at a place called Lavas [Lavos]. Here we prepared for an active campaign as we learned the French had begun to concentrate their forces.

9 August: We marched this day towards Leiria and got there next morning, a French picquet having just left the town before us. We halted here one day and dined with the monks in the bishop's palace, a fine building afterwards entirely destroyed by the French in their retreat through the country in 1811 under Marshal Massena.

13 August: We moved forward and came up with the enemy at a small town Obidos and ...

15 August: ... had a smart skirmish with their rear guard. They occupied the town and fired on our advanced guard as they approached it. They were instantly driven from the town and being followed too far by Captain Pakenham's company which formed the advanced guard, it brought on a smart skirmish in which we lost Lieutenant Bunbury killed,[183] a gallant young fellow, Captain Pakenham was slightly wounded. We took a position in front of the town and remained next day...

17 August: ... but moved forward the following day to attack the enemy under General Laborde[184] who had taken a position in a strong defile at Rolica but which we carried after a severe loss on our part. The Honourable Colonel Lake[185] of the 29th and Colonel Stewart of the 9th Regiment[186] were killed. We had Captain Creagh and Lieutenants

---

[183]   First Lieutenant Ralph Bunbury, 95th, Foot was killed on 15 August.
[184]   General Henri Delaborde.
[185]   Lieutenant Colonel the Honourable George Lake, 29th Foot, was killed at Roliça.
[186]   Lieutenant Colonel John Stewart, 9th Foot, was killed at Roliça.

T[homas] Cochrane[187] and Pratt[188] & Hill wounded.[189] A singular thing occurred of which I was a witness during the action. Captain Leach asked Lieutenant Cochrane for a drink from his canteen and while the latter was holding it to Leach's head a ball struck Cochrane's hand, went through it and broke the canteen in pieces while Captain Leach was drinking from it. This was the first time I had seen Frenchmen and was struck with their maneuvering [sic] and soldier like appearance. We moved forward this evening and the next day and so on to Vimeiro on the 20th.

20 August: Where we took us a position in which we were attacked by General Junot, Duc of Abrantes ...[190]

21 August: ... with the whole of the French force he could collect and for which purpose he marched from Lisbon. I was on the advance picquet this morning and was early engaged. The attack commenced about 8 o'clock in the morning. The enemy advanced in close columns, first on the part of the position where we were (the right), where General Fane's Brigade was posted, in which they were repulsed, they then endeavoured to deploy, in the act of which they were charged by the 50th and 97th Regiments, our corps and the 52nd 2nd Battalion and part of the 9th Regiment, when they were completely routed at this point. They tried the same mode of attack on the left, where they were repulsed by General Ferguson's Brigade[191] and eventually at all points, we took all their guns, two general officers and killed & wounded a great many and had Lord Sir A[rthur] Wellesley, our gallant commander not been superseded in the moment of victory, the whole French army must have been taken prisoners. Our army was quite fresh, the action not having lasted above four hours, but unfortunately both Sir H[arry] Burrard and Sir H[ew] Dalrymple[192] both arrived as the battle was gained and by not moving on, we lost the golden opportunity. My brother John received a musket ball in the shoulder in this action.

22 August: The next day General Kellerman[193] came in with a flag of truce when a suspension of arms took place which afterwards led

187 Second Lieutenant Thomas Cochrane, 95th Foot, was slightly wounded.

188 First Lieutenant Mathias Pratt, 95th Foot, was wounded at Vimeiro not Roliça.

189 Lieutenant Dudley St Leger Hill, 95th Foot was slightly wounded at both Roliça and Vimeiro.

190 General Jean-Andoche Junot, Duke of Abrantes, commanded the French forces in Portugal.

191 Major General Ronald Ferguson.

192 Lieutenant Generals Sir Harry Burrard and Sir Hew Dalrymple arrived, both being of superior rank to Arthur Wellesley, and took command of the army.

193 General de Division Francois Kellerman.

to the celebrated Convention of Cintra [Sintra] by which the French evacuated Portugal taking with them their arms, baggage &c &c.

23 August: On this day we moved forward towards Lisbon. Here we had halted and had some bad wet weather which we felt much, having no tents.

28 August: We marched again this day to Torres Vedras where we staid [sic] three days ...

31 August: ... and moved on again till we came ...

2 September: ... to Saint Antonio de Tojal [Santo Antão do Tojal] where we halted again. The Archbishop of Lisbon has a handsome palace here with large reservoirs of water in the gardens in which we bathed and found it a great luxury in this warm weather.

9 September: We moved again, passed through the village of Bucellas [Bucelas] and encamped at Campo Grande[194] near Lisbon a handsome kind of small park. We were hailed everywhere with joy by the habitants.

13 September: We moved this day to Campo Pequina [Pequeno] a suburb close to Lisbon and encamped in some handsome grounds here. For the first [time] I entered Lisbon with Captain Leach, the French army were still in the squares. They appeared much annoyed at their recent discomfiture. We enjoyed ourselves much in this town, there was an excellent opera open here and we had constant balls and entertainments, but we were soon to be employed again and we moved to our ground near Belem.

24 September: Preparatory to the army being newly brigaded for moving under Sir John Moore into Spain, the place we encamped at was the high grounds above Belem called Monte Santo [Monsanto]. Here we remained encamped ...

15 October: ... till the 15 of October when our four companies marched to Sacavem on their route to Spain. We were attached to General Beresford's Brigade[195] but the whole army marched by independent regiments to the frontier of Portugal, the whole to unite at Salamanca.

16 October: We got to Villa Franca [Vila Franca de Xira] this day.

17 October: Next to Alquentra [Alcoentre]

18 October: To Rio Mayor [Rio Maior] where we halted one day.

20 October: This day to Carvallos [Carvalhais].

21 October: Next day to Leiria.

22 October: Halted one day here.

---

194   Now the site of the Universidade de Lisboa.
195   Major General William Carr Beresford.

23 October: Marched to Pombal where there is a fine old castle belonging to a count of this realm.

24 October: Next day Condeixa [-a-Velha] and the following day into …

25 October: … Coimbra where we halted till the 30th.

30 October: The detachment marched on the 30th of last month [October] but having got a severe cold and sore throat with a slight feverish attack, which confined me to my bed. I was most unwillingly obliged to remain behind and felt considerably at separating from my brother as we had not [been] apart since he joined. By a little care, I recovered sufficiently to move on my route …

14 November: … on the 14th to Mealhada next day …

15 November: … to Morteagoa [Mortagua] and on …

16 November: … to Tondella [Tondela] …

17 November: … and endeavouring to push on I was benighted, lost [my] way and should have been out all night, but that I fell in with a party of muleteers who brought me into the village of Fagal [Fail], where I got some supper from a peasant …

18 November: … and next morning got on to Fornos de Cilgodes [Fornos de Algodres]…

19 November: … from this I moved to Celorico [da Beira] …

20 November: … and next day into Trancoso. Here I was kindly treated in the family of a very worthy nobleman, a hildalgo as called here, his name was Castano Alexandre de Foncesa Pinto, his house was [the] best in this town which like most of the old towns has a Moorish castellated wall round it.

22 November: I moved on to Pinhel and into …

23 November: … the fortress of Almeida.

24 November: Next I entered Spain near Fort Concepcion and slept at Gallegos [de Argañán].

25 November: On to St Esprit [Sancti Spiritus].

26 November: Next day to Alameda [Aldehuela de la Bóveda?], I passed through Ciudad Rodrigo but I did not halt there …[196]

27 November: … and this day joined the army at Salamanca. Where we were all united under Sir John Moore.

1 December: Our detachment (the 4 companies 2nd Battalion) were moved to a village in front of Salamanca. The French having sent patrols in the neighbourhood, we staid [sic] here a few days …

5 December: … when we marched to Ladezma [Ledesma] with the 2nd Battalion 43rd & 9th Regiment under General Beresford, here we remained till the 11th …

---

196   This should appear before Sancti Spiritus.

11 December: … when we made an amazing long harassing march to Zamora. I don't know that I ever felt so tired, I could scarcely crawl to my billet and when I made out the house, I was kept half an hour knocking at the gate, before I was let in and could then only procure by much entreaty a small cup of chocolate about the size of an egg cup. The house belonged to a priest, however by frightening the old fellow a little, I at last I got something to eat and next morning we learned that the constituted authorities had a superb dinner prepared for all the British officers with which our commanding officer Major Travers was made acquainted but did not tell any of us. He took good care to go himself and partake of it. This was of a piece with all his other conduct to us while under his command. He was an ill-tempered tyrannical selfish fellow.

12 December: We halted one day here, it is a good clean town.

13 December: I remained behind the brigade one day here to give some evidence against a Spaniard who fired at and wounded a man of the 43rd Regiment and whom I assisted in telling …

14 December: …and next day went on to Toro, where we were joined by the Hussar Brigade under Lord Paget[197] from Sir D[avid] Baird's[198] army which had landed at Corunna. The Reserve under Sir Edward Paget[199] was here also.

15 December: All the troops moved on next day. We lay at Bene Fortes [Benafarces] this …

16 & 17 December: … and the following night and next marched to San Pedro [de Latarce]. The weather was very cold but fine for marching and as long as we got into the villages at night, we did not feel much of the severity of it.

18 December: This way we got to ride in a van …

20 December: … and on to Villa Bon [Villalón de Campos]

21 December: Next day to Villa Oca … [Villada]

22 December: … and the next day we joined Sir D[avid] Baird's army at Sahagun and our detachment joined Colonel Wade under Brigadier General R[obert] Craufurd.[200] …

23 December: … in a large convent at this place, from this the whole army marched [on] a desperate cold night to attack Marshal Soult …

24 December: … on the Carrion River but having learned that he had been reinforced we commenced our disastrous …

25 December: … retreat on Christmas Day from Sahagun and marched the first day to the Convent of Monasteria [Monasterio de Vega] and on

---

197   Lieutenant General Lord Henry Paget.
198   Lieutenant General Sir David Baird.
199   Major General Sir Edward Paget.
200   Brigadier General Robert Craufurd.

26 December: to St Michael del Valla [San Miguel del Valle]

27 December: the next day to Castro Pepe [Castropepe] ...

28 December: ...and next day we got to the bridge of Benavente which we remained at and destroyed. That night we spent a most uncomfortable night, the French cavalry frequently came close up to us and ...

29 December: ... next morning we witnessed at a distance a very gallant action between our hussars under Lord Paget and General Lefebre[201] having a body of the French Imperial Guard Light cavalry. He was taken prisoner himself and many of his men killed, wounded and taken. We marched on to La Baneza ...

30 December: and this day to a village near Astorga from which place we separated from Sir J[ohn] Moore's army[202] and marched on the road to Vigo with General Baron Charles Alten's[203] and R[obert] Craufurd's Brigade.

31 December: We got to Foncevedon [Foncebadón] but our men began to feel the want of shoes. I was very ill myself from an attack of dysentery. Our road lay through a bad difficult mountainous country.

1809

5 January 1809: to Orense [Ourense] here we halted two days and got on to Rila Dacia [Ribadavia] which we got to late at night, as we did to all our halting places. We were to have lay in the large old convent here, but the two leading companies had but got on the gallery of the convent when the whole loft gave way and the height being about thirty feet, several of the men were seriously hurt. We moved on to Vigo where ...

12 January: ... we embarked for England to our great joy, having lost our baggage and not taken off our clothes for a considerable time. We had excessive bad weather in the Channel and landed at Portsmouth in a few days from whence we marched to Hythe Barracks [in] Kent.

We learned on arriving at Portsmouth of the action fought at Corunna and the death of our late commander Sir J[ohn] Moore who was much regretted. He was placed in a most critical situation and displayed considerable talent in extricating the army as he did. We had Captain Bennett[204] and Lieutenant Noble[205] in the action, our 1st Battalion having been particularly engaged.

---

201   General Lefebvre-Desnouettes.

202   They actually separated near Ponferrada.

203   Brigadier General Carl Count von Alten.

204   Captain L H Bennett, 95th Foot, died of wounds 14 January 1809.

205   First Lieutenant Charles Noble, 95th Foot, was killed at Corunna.

From Hythe, the battalion was ordered to Riding Street Barracks near Tenterden and the greater ...

February: number of the officers were sent to get men from the approaching volunteering of the Militia.

2 March: I went to Folkstone to the Rutland Regiment. We were remarkably fortunate, in consequence of which we got a third battalion ...

May: ... to the corps in this month, by which my brother John was promoted to 1st Lieutenancy and both him, myself and a few other officers were ordered to join the 1st Battalion at Hythe, preparing for service. This we did and marched to Dover where we embarked with the 1st Battalions of the 43rd & 52nd Regiment. Each of these regiments were above 1,000 strong and three of the finest regiments that ever left England. General R[obert] Craufurd commanded the brigade. We sailed from the Downs and anchored at Cowes, Isle of Wight.

4 June: Where we were detained a few days with a foul wind. After a tolerable good passage we came to anchor in the Tagus at Lisbon. Here we staid [sic] about a week when we were transported by bateau in the transport boats to Sacavem. We marched to Abrantes where the brigade was united under General Craufurd and we proceeded by rapid marches to join Lord Wellington's army which we did at Talavera ...

29 July: ... on the morning of 29 July the day after the battle fought here the day before. Our march was one of the most rapid ever marched by troops and our arrival prevented the enemy making any further attempts on our position.

August 1809: After a halt here of two days the army still in position, the British troops marched to attack Marshal Soult at Plasencia, leaving the Spanish army in position at Talavera, but which place they entered from the day after we marched, in consequence of which we were obliged to change our route and move towards Truxillo [Trujillo]. The Light Brigade under General Craufurd was ordered to defend the ford at Almaraz.

September 1809: Here the brigade suffered a great deal of privation for three weeks, not being supplied with any rations and exposed to the heavy dews at night. The consequence was a great deal of sickness afterwards.

October: The whole army moved towards Badajoz which became headquarters.

November: Our brigade marched by Caceres, Valencia de Alcantra, Castillo de Vide, where I was attacked with the ague. Portalegre and to Campo Major [Maior]. Here General Craufurd's Brigade, the 43rd,

75

52nd, 95th Regiments and Colonel Donkin's Brigade[206] the 45th & 88th Regiments and one squadron 16th Light Dragoons remained for the winter.

May 1810: I continued being with several other officers, so much so that I was obliged to go to Lisbon, from whence I was obliged to go to England in a very weak condition with a bad ague and from there I was a time recovering. After a stay of a couple of months in England I went to Ireland ...

July 1810: ... staid a few weeks in Dublin and went down to Carrick [on Suir] and having spent some time with my good and worthy friend Michael Cox Esq at Castletown,[207] I was ordered to take charge of a recruiting party, sent me to Waterford ...

September: ... where I went very soon and took lodgings. I also began to recover fast but had occasionally this winter very severe rheumatic attacks.

December: I spent the Christmas at Castletown and in the spring of this year I went to Tramore ...

May 1811: ... where by the use of the hot and cold bathing, I got tolerable stout once more and here I formed an acquaintance with a lady who afterwards became my wife 'Miss Catherine Hawtry', sister to Mrs Richard Cox with whom and a party from Castletown, she came to the hotel here.

September: After staying the best part of the summer ...

December: ... I went into Waterford and again spent the Christmas at Castletown.

1812: Early this year I went over [to] England on duty with recruits to Bristol but returned to Waterford after going to Horsham Barracks with the men I brought over. I returned by London and Bristol, spent a couple of days at Clifton where Miss Hawtry was visiting with her sister Charlotte and niece Sally Cox daughter of Richard Cox.

January 1812: My brother John having been very severely wounded at the storming of Ciudad Rodrigo in the month, he returned to England for the recovery of his health ...

May: ...and having come to Ireland he and I took a cottage at Dunmore for ...

July: ... some months and here we spent our [time] very agreeably till his leave having expired and being most anxious to return to the army he left Dunmore for Castletown and I went to my recruiting party at Waterford.

---

206   Brigadier General Rufane Donkin.
207   Mr Michael Cox of Castletown House was the son of the Archbishop of Cashel. He died in 1836.

August: He sailed soon afterwards from Cork for Lisbon.

October: I spent the greater part of this winter at Castletown ...

December: ... going into Waterford on the Return days and having made application to the Horse Guards to be allowed to join my regiment abroad, I got leave and proceeded ...

10 February 1813: ... early this month to Waterford gave up any Recruiting party, returned [the] same day to Castletown ...

23 February: ... came to Carrick on Suir to stay a day or two with my mother before I left home.

25 February: Left Carrick and slept at Clogheen and got into Cork next day.

26 February: Went down to Cove ...

3 March: ... embarked on board the *Jane* transport and ...

5 March: ...sailed for Lisbon.

15 March: We anchored in the Tagus on the 15th and got a good billet at No 9 Rua Nova, St Julian. Here I staid equipping myself for the army and having made a party with Captain Haverfield[208] and Lieutenant Capel of the 43rd Regiment,[209] who I met here and who has just returned from England, we agreed to march up to the army together.

30 March: We left Lisbon having each a horse to carry our baggage and one cart to ride, I had a soldier servant. They had their boys (Portuguese). We got to Villa Franca [Vila Franca de Xira] the first day.

31 March: Next day to Azembuja [Azambuja] and on the day following to Santarem.

1 April: Here we halted one day ...

2 April: ... and here I hired a very good Portuguese boy as servant who was decoyed from me afterwards at Vitoria where I lay ill of my wound, he was taken by a Commissary whose name I could never learn.

3 April: We went on to Golega.

4 April: Punhete[210] the next and then ...

5 April: ... to Abrantes

6 April: where we halted one day.

7 April: On to Gabia [Gaviao] this day.

8 April: next Niza [Nisa] and on to Cartosi [Cebolais de Cima?] the next day.

10 April: Our next place was Castello [Castelo] Branco.

April 11: This day to Escalio de Lesma [Escalos de Cima]

April 12: And next to Penamacor.

---

208   Captain William Haverfield, 43rd Foot.

209   Lieutenant Thomas Capel, 43rd Foot.

210   Now known as Constancia.

April 13: Here we halted one day and dined with the officers of Captain Cairn's[211] troop of horse artillery. Haverfield[212] had a brother with them.

April 14: This day to Quadraces [Quadrazais] and the next day I joined ...

April 15: ... my regiment at Alameda [La Alamedilla] just as they were at dinner. I was received most cordially by my friends but they had lost some excellent men since I had left them in the different sieges and actions. Majors Stuart[213] & Hare[214] and Captains Creagh[215] & Crampton[216] with many others had been killed. Sir Sidney Beckwith was obliged to go home from ill health and the battalion was commanded by Lieutenant Colonel Cameron.[217]

April 16: Two companies were moved to Castillejos [de] dos Casas in one of which was my brother. We were all now preparing for the opening of the campaign ...

May 17: ... and the division was reviewed on the Espeja plain by Lord Wellington this day.

May 20: On this day Lieutenant Colonel Barnard took the command of our battalion and on the next ...

May 21: ... the Light Division commenced its march. It consisted of two brigades, one commanded by Major General Kempt was composed of the 1st and 3rd Battalions 95th Regiment, 6 companies each, 1st Battalion 43rd and the 17th Portuguese Regiment. The Second Brigade was commanded by Major General Vandeleur and composed of the 2nd Battalion 95th Regiment 6 companies, 1st Battalion 52nd Regiment and the 1st and 2nd Portuguese Cacadores. Major General Charles Alten commanded the division. We had also attached to us a troop of horse artillery commanded by Colonel Ross. The first day we encamped near Felices Chico [Saelices el Chico].

May 22: The next day at St Martin del Rio [Martin de Yeltes?].

May 23: The next on the Huebra near

May 24: Samnoz [San Muñoz], where we halted.

May 25: Moved on to Robalisa [Robliza de Cojos]

---

211   Second Captain Robert Cairnes, Royal Artillery. Cox is in error here as Cairnes was in No. 4 Company, 10 Brigade Foot Artillery, not the Horse Artillery.
212   Assistant Surgeon John Haverfield, Royal Artillery.
213   Major John Stewart, 95th Foot, died of wounds, 16 March 1811.
214   Major Peter O'Hare was killed at Badajoz on 6 April 1812.
215   Captain Jasper Creagh, 95th Foot, died of wounds, 25 July 1810.
216   Captain Jeremiah Crampton, 95th Foot, died of wounds, 18 September 1812.
217   Lieutenant Colonel Alexander Cameron.

May 26: next day to Val de Musca [San Julian de Valmuza?]. We struck tents suddenly when we moved on and crossed the Tormes below Salamanca by fording it and encamped at the other …

May 27: … side of the river.

May 28: Encamped at Aldea Nova de Figerueras [Aldeanueva de Figueroa], where we halted with the 2nd Division under General Hill within a short distance of us. Here we staid till the 2nd.

June 2: When we moved on to the Douro near Toro …

June 3: … which we crossed this day. We moved forward next day

June 4 & 5: to St Essema [San Cebrián de Mazote?] next to Villa Moreda [La Mudarra?]

June 6 & 7: on to Ampudia and Placentia [Plasencia] which latter place the enemy had left in the morning. We moved to the Pisuerga River.

June 8–9: by Tamora [Támara de Campos], Pene Campo [Piña de Campos] and Santa Dilla [Astudillo, Palencia?].

June 10: Where we crossed the river.

June 11: We then moved to Villa Ladreno [Villasandino] and Harasmillada [?]

June 12: Near Burgos early this morning. The French blew up the works at the Castle of Burgos and retired.

June 13 & 14: We moved to Torero [Villatoro?] and Quinta de Heras [Quintanilla Sobresierra?] and this day crossed the Ebro by the bridge of Puente de Arinha [Puente Arenas].

June 15: The appearance of the country was beautiful here, hitherto we had marched over an uninteresting flat country without being able to procure refreshments of any kind, but now we got fruits & vegetables in abundance and excellent fresh butter.

June 16: We moved on to Medina [de Pomar] and

June 17: Rio Losa [Rosio?] and next day at

June 18: St Millan [San Millán de San Zadornil] we came up with a column of the enemy with whom we had a smart skirmish. The company I was with (Captain Loftus Gray's) being the advance guard commenced it and in a short time we had 7 men killed and Lieutenant [William] Haggup[218] badly wounded through the stomach. The enemy were quickly dislodged with the loss of their baggage and some killed and wounded.

June 19: We moved on to Villa Herrera [Villanueva de Valdegovía?] and …

June 20: … halted this day preparatory to the general action about to take place, as we knew the enemy had assembled his whole force under

---

[218]   Second Lieutenant William Haggup, 95th Foot.

Joseph Buonaparte in front of Vitoria. I ascended a hill this evening and saw the forces of the enemy distinctly on the plain in front of Vitoria.

June 21: This morning early the whole army was in motion in high health and spirits and this glorious action soon commenced, which terminated so brilliantly by the total defeat of the enemy with the loss of all their artillery, baggage, stores and military chest. At the close of the action in an attack on the one of the last of the positions the enemy attempted to keep, I received a musket shot in my right leg. I was dressed by a surgeon on the ground and was brought into the town of Vitoria in the evening by some men of my own regiment. I was put into a good house and the people treated me very kindly, but I was very faint and much weakened from loss of blood. I passed a restless night and my wound opened and bled afresh. Two days after, I began to have regular medical attendance.

July: The weather was very hot but in a few weeks my wound began gradually to get better and I got out on crutches for the first time …

August 2: … but my wound got worse from making too free and I was not able [to] leave this till the end of September for the army.

September: We had a captain & a lieutenant killed at Vitoria, Captain Jenkins[219] & Lieutenant Campbell,[220] and before I rejoined the regiment Captain Cadoux[221] was killed in one of the attacks by Marshal Soult for the relief of San Sebastian.

16 September: By this officer's death I got my promotion to be captain but I did not know it for some time after.

23 September: I left this with Major Reid[222] and Captain Stavely of the Staff Corps[223] for the army by the route of Salinas [?], Guipacosa [Guipuzcoa].

September 25: Villa Real [Villareal de Urrechu],[224] Tolosa …

September 26, 27, 28, 29: … Hernani, Oyarzun [Oiartzun], Irun, at which place my wound opened afresh and I staid [sic] a few days with an old friend, Major Todd of the Staff Corps[225] at his billet in a cottage near this place (Irun).

October 6: I was not able to move till this day, when I joined the regiment in camp at Vera [Bera] and next day was in action with the

---

219 Captain John Jenkins was recorded as slightly wounded, but died of his wound on 17 July 1813.
220 Lieutenant Leckie Campbell, 95th foot, was killed.
221 Captain Daniel Cadoux, 95th Foot, was killed at Vera on 31 August 1813.
222 Actually Captain William Read, Royal Staff Corps. He became a major in December.
223 Captain William Stavely, Royal Staff Corps.
224 Now known as Urretxu.
225 Brevet Major Alexander Todd, Royal Staff Corps.

division in the attack of the heights here when we forced the puerta and entered France, in which we encamped and ...

October 10: ... here I took command of Captain Gibbons[226] company in the 2nd Battalion, who was killed in the action of the 7th instant and next day ...

October 11: ... I received the notification of my promotion from England.

October 17: The Light Division changed our ground and encamped near St Jean de Luz in France and ...

October 24: ... this day moved to heights of Le Bagnette ...

November 10: ... and on this morning, early, the whole of the enemy's strong fortified position in front of Bayonne and which Marshal Soult had been strengthening for six months, were attacked and forced by our army. The Light Division forced the centre and principal part of the works having the strong Mount Le Rhune and two strong circular forts to attack, in storming the last of which I received a severe contusion in my left side by a musket ball. The fort was taken and in it a French regiment. I rejoined my regiment soon after the action was over and we moved on to and encamped at St Pic [Saint-Pic] and the weather becoming very wet and the roads almost impassable for artillery.

November 21: We went into cantonments at Arbonne. I got into a comfortable farmhouse with my two subalterns, Lieutenant Thomas Cochrane and Budgen[227] but as we invested Bayonne we had frequent sharp ...

December 9: ... skirmishes, until this day the whole of the left of the army was moved forward under Sir John Hope as a reconnaissance. Our brigade had some sharp fighting and we drove the advance of the army into their works in front of Bayonne but retired at night to our former position and I remained on piquet.

December 10: I was attacked next morning and our picquets driven in. Marshal Soult moved the whole of his army out and attacked our centre and left. He continued his attacks the whole of this ...

December 11: ... and the following day.

December 12: There was little done this day, both armies were in sight of each other and remained constantly at their arms, but at night Soult withdrew the whole of his army through Bayonne and next morning...

December 13: ... made a most determined attack on our right under General Hill, which was most gallantly resisted by the 2nd Division

---

226   Captain George Gibbons, 95th Foot.
227   First Lieutenant John Budgeon, 95th Foot.

commanded by Sir William Stewart. After this Marshal Soult withdrew his whole force from Bayonne with the exception of the garrison and retired up the River Adour.

December 14: We returned to our cantonments at Arbonne, the weather being too bad to move.

December 25: On Christmas Day the officers of the 2nd Battalion dined together and being ordered to join the 3rd Battalion I moved to Arcangues did so this day the 26th of December.

1 January 1814: My three subalterns were Sir John Ribton Bt,[228] Lieutenants Jones[229] and Kirkley.[230] The army remained in their cantonments near Bayonne the remainder of this month, the weather being so bad that the roads were impassable. There was occasionally some skirmishing at the outposts.

February: The beginning of this month the army put in motion leaving the 1st and 5th Divisions under Sir John Hope to invest Bayonne. We crossed the Gave de Pau and Oleron with little opposition, Marshal Soult having collected his whole force at Orthez in a formidable position in rear of the town.

February 27: We attacked him on this morning, when after a well contested action he was completely beat at all points and obliged to make a most precipitous retreat in which he lost a great many men.

February 28: The Light Division made a rapid march to Mont [de] Marsan where we took a large store of provisions. It was the principal depot of the enemy.

March: We left this town the day after our arrival and one division of the army under General Beresford marched to Bordeaux. The remainder of the army moved after Marshal Soult. The roads through this country were in a very bad state and the men marched above their knees in puddles. The country is all sandy and very flat.

March 18: We had some skirmishing with the rear guard of the enemy and …

March 19: at Vic [-en-Bigorre] there was a severe one and on the morning of this day the enemy showed his whole force in a position near the town of Tarbes …

March 20: … in which we attacked him. Some companies of the Rifles were first ordered to dislodge them from a commanding hill. Mine was one of them, but on gaining the summit of the hill we found a much

---

228 First Lieutenant Sir John Ribton, 95th Foot.
229 First Lieutenant Loftus Jones, 95th Foot.
230 First Lieutenant Thomas Kirkley, 95th Foot.

larger force than was supposed to be there and we had to sustain a very severe fight against a large force before the remainder of our corps was sent to support. We drove the enemy (who fought remarkably well here) from the hill, but suffered a good deal in retaining it and in which Captain Duncan[231] was killed and twelve of our officers wounded. My brother John received a musket shot in his left leg while commanding a company in the 1st Battalion and I got one also in the right leg having passed through it.

March 20: We were with the other wounded officers brought in here this evening and suffered a great deal of pain the first night besides being in a noisy uncomfortable quarter.

March 21: Next day we were moved into a very good house where we had every comfort we required. We staid [sic] here till the end of this month when all the wounded here with the hospital staff were ordered to Pau.

April: The moving was painful to us. After a few days, my brother and I got into a most excellent quarter, the house of a Monsieur de Bourie, Colonel of the National Guard here. From whom and his family we received the most marked kindness. The scenery of the surrounding country of this neighborhood is most beautiful. The old castle and park in which Henry the Fourth was born in, will always make this an interesting place to a traveller. Being sufficiently recovered, my brother and I left this place in the diligence for Toulouse ...

May 15: ... in which were three French officers, one that had been wounded the day before, he been in a skirmish with our troops. The other two was a father and his son, a major of light cavalry and his son a cornet. They amused us much, particularly the young cornet, who was constantly quizzing his father and getting him into a rage. We slept at Auch and got into Toulouse next evening. It appeared a large fine old town. I went over the position on which the action was fought a short time before. The graves of the brave men who fell here were still fresh and the ground had all that appearance where a battle had been fought. It was the last gallant exertion of the Peninsula army and they maintained their noble reputation until the last.

After a stay of a fortnight here, we left Toulouse by water for Bordeaux with several other wounded officers and men.

May 21: We have been in several boats of a large kind and were three days making the voyage. We landed at night and lay in some of

---

[231]   Captain John Duncan, 95th Foot, was killed at Tarbes.

the villages. The scenery the whole way is delightful and particularly fine on approaching Bordeaux, which is a beautiful town, the finest I have seen on the continent. It was now full of British troops, some on their way to England and some for America. My brother and I staid [sic] here three weeks. I spent a short time most agreeably here ...

6 June: ... when we embarked and sailed for England ...

16 June: ... which we reached on the 16th instant, having landed at Portsmouth and next day left for London, where we took lodgings. It was now remarkably full, the Allied sovereigns having arrived in England. Here we enjoyed the luxuries of a London life for a short time, having three years pay to receive. One of arrears and two given me for wounds received in the Peninsula and France.

27 July: Though I still had leave of absence for the recovery of my wounds, I went down to Hythe where the regiment had arrived to see any old companions and being recommended sea bathing for [my] leg I took lodgings at Sandgate ...

30 August: ... which place I left the end of this month for Town. I staid only a few days and ...

3 September: ... went down to Little Hampton, Sussex, to meet Miss Hawtrey and her sister by agreement and when I did expect to be married. I spent a short time most agreeably here.

September 9: We visited *Worthing* and several places in the neighbourhood. Some circumstance preventing our marriage here.

September 15: We left for Clifton.

September 16: Lay at Southampton and got to the hot wells [of] Bristol the next day.

September 17: I took up my quarters at the Gloucester House and the Miss Hawtrey's at their own in Albermarle Row and having made all necessary arrangements for this event, on the 27th of this month I was married by licence in Clifton Church to Catherine Hawtrey, fourth daughter of the Reverend Ralph Hawtrey of the City of Waterford in Ireland. The ceremony was performed by the Reverend Thomas Connolly Cowan. From the church we proceeded to Bath where we breakfasted and went on immediately to Stourton, Wiltshire where we spent our honeymoon and returned to Clifton.

October 3: The following week, Miss Charlotte Hawtrey and her niece Sally Cox came with us to Stourton.

October 18: We continued in Albermarle Row till the 18th, when my leave having expired we left Clifton for the regiment. Lay at

Marlborough the first and got to London next day and staid [sic] at the Peterburgh Hotel, Dover Street ...

October 22: ... till the 22nd when we went down to Sandgate in Kent. The 3rd Battalion depot being at Shorncliffe which I took the command of. The remainder of the battalion having gone on the expedition to New Orleans, America.

November 4: We took a very comfortable small house here and spent a most agreeable winter here. I remained here all the winter with the depot of the 3rd Battalion and which became the headquarters of it from the promotion of Lieutenant Colonel Gilmore[232] who took the command. Two of our companies were still in Flanders, where we sent a reinforcement and from the return of Napoleon from Elba.

1815

March 25: Our 2 battalions embarked at Dover and sailed for Ostend.

May 15: I left Sandgate with my wife for Bath as I expected daily to be ordered on service.

May 18: We got to Bath where I left her with her sister and returned by London ...

May 24: ... to Shorncliffe Barracks.

June 18: After some days of considerable anxiety we got an account of the great Battle of Waterloo fought by the Duke of Wellington and Napoleon in person commanding the French army. It was of a most sanguinary description and completed the overthrow of Napoleon's dynasty in Europe. My brother John commanded a company of the 1st Battalion Rifle Brigade in this action and myself as well as all others were very anxious for the arrival of the Gazette account of the killed and wounded. To the friends of those fine fellows who fell this day it was a melancholy list, fortunately my brother escaped himself.

July 8: We got a route for three companies to march to Dover ...

July 10: ... where we embarked and sailed immediately for Ostend, at which place ...

July 12: ... we landed. The companies were Captains Kent,[233] Travers[234] and mine. The day after our landing at Ostend we were put into the large boats of this country and proceeded by canal to Bruges ...

July 13: ... and on by the same mode ...

---

232   Brevet Lieutenant Colonel Dugald Gilmour, 95th Foot.
233   Captain John Kent, 95th Foot.
234   Captain James Travers, 95th Foot.

July 14: ... to Ghent, here we halted three days. It is a very large dull town, intersected by canals. We left it on our route to Paris to join the army and marched ...

July 17: ... by Oudenarde the first day ...

July 18: ... to Chievres near Ath the next ...

July 19 & 20: ... and on the following to Mons where we halted one day.

July 21: This day we entered France by Bavay and next day lay at village [near] Cateau Cambresis called Bertry.

July 22: And on this day my little girl Charlotte was born at the Parsonage House Cahircoulish [Caherconlish] County of Limerick where my wife was with her sister, Mrs Richard Cox. This event I did not hear of till some time after when in Paris.

July 23: After a halt of one day ...

July 24: we moved on to Vendhuile near [le] Catelet and next to ...

July 25: Peronne.

July 26: The next day to Roye where we halted.

July 28: We then moved to Gournay [Gournay-sur-Aronde] ...

July 29: ... and on to Pont Saint Maxence and ...

July 30: ... Marly [Marly-la-Ville] and next ...

July 31: day marched into Paris and encamped that night in the Champs Elysee where I had the happiness of seeing my brother and all my old friends of the 1st & 2nd Battalions that survived this memorable campaign.

August 3: I heard from Ireland this day of the *accouchement* of my wife and the birth of my little girl just as I was starting to visit Versailles.

August: I got an excellent billet from Sir A[ndrew] Barnard who was the governor of Paris at No 30 Quai de l'Ecole, the owner was Monsieur Jean Baptiste Renier the King's Jeweller. I was delighted for several days with the amazing number of novelties that this extraordinary city presented at this time. The Louvre which was at this time untouched, was the great attraction as in it was collected everything rare and scientific that Europe could produce as specimens of the arts, both of painting and sculpture. The town was also in military occupancy by almost all the nations of Europe with the Allied sovereigns, the Emperors of Russia and Austria, the King of Prussia and all the distinguished generals of the day and none appeared to be more so than our own, the Duke of Wellington. There were constant reviews of the Allied troops at which the sovereigns were always present and generally commanded in person their own respective troops.

August 12: Our three companies of the 3rd Battalion moved to Franca Nouvelle [?] close to Montmartre. The army being newly brigaded and we being put into Sir Thomas Brisbane's[235] Brigade.

August 21: And this day being the anniversary of the Battle of Vimeira [sic] I had the honour of dining with the Duke of Wellington as was his custom of asking our officers who were in that action. I think not more than six of us remained. It was a splendid entertainment and all the generals and officers of rank who survived and who were at Vimeira were present as were also several foreign officers of distinction.

August 25: This day being the anniversary of the formation of the Rifle Corps the whole of the officers of the three battalions present in Paris, amounting to seventy five having a fine dinner together at the Cordon Bleu on the Boulevards.

September 2: There was a superb review of our heavy cavalry for the Emperor Alexander, their appearance was uncommonly fine.

September 22: And on this day the whole of the British Army, about 65,000 men were reviewed on the plains near Paris at which all the Allied sovereigns and foreign generals were present. It was a representation of the Battle of Salamanca.

September 30: The Austrians took down this day the famous Horses of Corinth brought by Napoleon from St Mark's at Venice.

October: The end of this month, the positions of the army were changed. Our battalion was moved into the village of Monceux [Monceaux] close to the Barriere of the Labehaume, I moved to a billet here myself and we formed a mess here.

November: The weather became cold and wet all the month while we remained at Monceux, but the Articles of Peace being finally settled, our division of the army was ordered to England and with them our battalion.

December 3: We marched from Paris this day to St Denis [Saint-Denis] on our route to the coast.

December 4: The second day to a village near Beaumont [Beaumont-sur-Oise] where the officers got into an old chateau.

December 5: and next day to La Boissière [Laboissière-en-Thelle] near Noailles and …

December 6: then into Beauvais where we halted one day.

December 7: A good town with a very handsome church.

December 8: We moved on to Saint Omer [en-Chaussee] and …

---

[235]   Major General Thomas Brisbane.

December 9: to the Chateau of Mazincourt [Maizicourt], where all of our officers were well entertained by the royalists.

December 10: Next to Wannelle [?] and on

December 11: to Abbeville where we halted one day.

December 12: This is a fine large town and I was well treated by the family I was quartered on here.

December 13: We moved on to Montreuil …

December 14: where we halted again.

December 15: We went on to Courmont [Cormont] …

December 16: and next day to Boulogne.

December 17: … and next into Calais. Here we staid till the 21st waiting for shipping as there were several regiments embarking here at the same time.

December 21: I embarked this day with fifty men and one officer of my own company in a Folkstone fishing smack …

December 22: and landed next morning at Dover and …

December 23: next day marched into our old quarters at Shorncliffe Barracks.

December 24: Took lodging in Sandgate and applied for leave of absence.

December 28: I got my leave this day…

December 29: and started the next for London on my way to Ireland.

1816

2 January: I left London by the mail coach for Milford [Haven] …

4 January: where I embarked and landed after a rough passage …

6 January [landed] at Passage near Waterford. I went on the same day to Castletown, the last of my old and valuable friend Michael Cox Esq, which I left the next morning …

7 January and went on to Clonmel …

8 January and next day got to the Parsonage House Cahircoulish [Caherconlish] the Reverend Richard Cox where I had the felicity of seeing my wife and her little baby, that was born in my absence. Here I remained for nearly three months enjoying the hunting and shooting that the county affords.

3 March The beginning of this month, the regiment hitherto called the 95th was taken out of the line & called the Rifle Brigade …

15 March: & shortly afterwards the 3rd Battalion arrived in Ireland …

23 March: & was ordered to Dublin where they soon arrived …

10 April: and where I joined them shortly after …

8 May: and was followed the next month by Mrs Cox, having taken lodgings at No 46 Henry Street.

1818

8 October – 24 November: An order to that effect having arrived at HQ the 3rd Battalion was *disbanded* at Burr by Major General Kemmis.[236] I was placed to the 2nd Battalion on its way to this quarter from England, having arrived there from France on the breaking up of the Army of Occupation.

[I have chosen to end his account here, which continues throughout his career in South Africa.]

---

[236]   Major General James Kemmis.

7. CAPTAIN CHARLES BECKWITH LETTERS

Charles Beckwith was a first lieutenant in the 95th Foot in June 1805 and became a captain in July 1808. He was a deputy assistant quartermaster general from August 1812 to April 1814. He served at Hanover, the Baltic, Corunna, Walcheren, Cadiz, Foz de Arouce, Sabugal, Fuentes de Oñoro, Ciudad Rodrigo, Badajoz, Salamanca, Burgos, San Millán, Vitoria, the Pyrenees, Vera, Nivelle, Nive, Orthez and Toulouse. He became a brevet major in March 1814.

To Major W Napier at Lady Sarah Napier's, 14 Cadogan Place, Sloane Street.
Alameda, Spain, 1 May 1813
My dear Napier,
… I think we had the pleasure of walking from Salamanca to these parts together and I daresay, you will recollect what sort of a walk it was. Rumour says that we are about to retrace our steps and that we shall not stop until we have driven the French out of Spain. In the meantime, according to custom, the French are represented to be very weak and we very strong; it is said that they will never be able to keep together, though they have lived in that state for the last five months and have even been forming magazines during that period behind the Douro, where the Army of Portugal at present is; the Army of the South is in Salamanca, Avila, Segovia and Madrid, occupying all the country.
   It is generally supposed that we shall find 80,000 men behind the Douro. The first operation, I take it for granted, is to get over the river, next to drive them behind the Ebro and then to take Burgos. I know nothing of the strength of our own army because some people say that it is very strong and others that it is not so strong, and I have no means of informing myself upon this point, but I think, what [the] D[uke of]

W[ellington] said last November was true, I have not overstated the enemy's force … However, I am totally in the dark upon all the points which enable us beings of an inferior description to form any opinion at all.

We have acted some plays since you left us with various success, we have got drunk with constant success and I begin to think that the only thing one can be certain of in this life is that you will certainly get drunk if you will but drink enough.

Our mode of life is exactly the same as when you left us. I ride about all the morning in pursuit of nothing. Barnard[237] smokes segars until the very atmosphere between the Coa and Agueda is impregnated with the 'herbiferous herb' as Dr Morgan says and if you were here again you might draw legs and muscles and Thalia's[238] and Melpomene's[239] until your paint, your paper and your patience were exhausted.

The monotony of the scene is only varied by the reports of Monday which are all found to be lies on Tuesday morning. Sometimes 40,000 Frenchmen march out of the country, sometimes they march in; sometimes the Spaniards have 150,000 men, sometimes 50; sometimes we are to march to France, sometimes to England, sometimes we have plenty to eat and drink and sometimes we have not. Excepting by this last circumstance, I am altogether unconcerned as to what does or does not occur, very few things give me pleasure and very few pain. But in the midst of this chequered scene of joy and sorrow, whether in the Palace of Ildefonso or in the bivouac at San Munoz, in mirth or woe, believe me always, yours very sincerely C Beckwith.

---

237   Lieutenant Colonel Andrew Barnard, 95th Foot.
238   Goddess of Comedy.
239   Melpomene was one of the muses, specifically associated with tragedy.

8. FIRST LIEUTENANT JOHN COX JOURNAL[240]

John Cox joined the 2nd Battalion 95th Foot as a second lieutenant on 16 March 1808 and he served in the actions at Óbidos, Roliça, Vimeiro (wounded) and Vigo. He then transferred to the First Battalion in June 1809 and returned to the peninsula with them, serving at the Coa, Bussaco, Foz de Arouce, Sabugal, Fuentes de Oñoro, Ciudad Rodrigo (severely wounded), San Millán, Vitoria, Pyrenees, Bidassoa, Nivelle, Nive, Orthez and Tarbes (severely wounded). He also served at Waterloo.

17 August 1808: On approaching the place [Roliça], the enemy opened a fire of musketry from a windmill on a rising ground adjoining the place and a few shots came from the town; however a rapid advance of the riflemen drew the French from all points of their posts, but being rather too elevated with this, our first collision with the foe, we dashed along the plain after them like young soldiers, but we were soon brought up by a body of French cavalry advancing from the main force. A retrograde movement was now imperative in which we lost an officer and a few men.

20 August: Vimiero [Vimeiro]. ... by this time the riflemen on the left were considerably forward, having been sharply engaged throughout with large bodies of voltigeurs who were strongly posted in the steep hills, vineyards and enclosures from which they were successively driven.

---

240   These are extracts from his journal, unfortunately the whereabouts of the original are not known. These extracts are taken from copies held at Winchester Archives and the National Library of Ireland, Dublin. The short 1808 section up to Corunna only appears in Verner's *History and Campaigns of the Rifle Brigade*.

13 September: I entered Lisbon for the first time. The French army was still in the square … they appeared much annoyed at their recent discomfiture. We enjoyed ourselves much in this town, there was an excellent opera and we had constant balls and entertainments.

[Nothing further is recorded until late in the march of Sir John Moore's army into Spain.]

11 December: Marched 30 miles to Zamora.

13 December: Marched up the Douro, 20 miles to Toro.

14 December: Halted, joined by the Hussar Brigade. Last night the 18th Hussars and 3rd Hussars KGL had the honour of opening the campaign. Brigadier General Stewart[241] at the head of 100 of the 18th Hussars having surprised a cavalry detachment at Rueda, making 27 prisoners and a French patrol of 15 cavalry were made prisoners by the 18th close to our post last night, the officer only having escaped.

15 December: Affair of cavalry near Valladolid, French light horse and 50 dragoons taken.

19 December: 20 miles to Villa Mayor [Villamayor de Campos].

20 December: 15 miles to Villalon [Villalón de Campos].

21 December: 18 miles to Villada. These marches were very harassing owing to the severe cold with heavy snow on these extensive plains. A very brilliant cavalry action took place in front of Sahagun early this morning between the 10th and 15th Hussars under Lord Paget; the enemy had scarcely time to form outside the town when they were charged and overthrown with a loss of 2 colonels, 10 officers and 150 prisoners, besides those sabred.

22 December: Marched to Sahagun where we hoped to halt for the night, but not so, being ordered on 4 or 5 miles in front to the monastery of Trianis [Monasterio de Santa Maria de Trianos] where we were joined by the rest of the battalion that came out with Sir David Baird. Our march today was 17 miles through snow. Our brigade now consisted of the 1st Battalion 43rd Light Infantry, 2nd Battalion 52nd Light Infantry and 2nd Battalion 95th Rifle Regiment commanded by Brigadier R[obert] Craufurd.

24 December: Advanced on [Marshal] Soult, news of Napoleon's advance. Retreat of the British army, not a very cheering prospect, a winter's retreat through mountains covered with snow lies before us, but we will do our duty come what will.

---

[241]   Brigadier General the Honourable Charles Stewart, he later became the 3rd Marquess of Londonderry.

25 December: Our brigade now on rear guard retired 24 miles on Mayorga and 28 miles more next day to the village of S Miguel [San Miguel del Valle]. During the night Lord Paget fell back with the cavalry from Sahagun and fell in with a body of French cavalry near Mayorga which he attacked with the 10th Hussars, taking 100 prisoners, and the 7th Hussars also retook some baggage which had fallen into their hands.

28 December: On the morning of the 28th, the 18th Hussars had an affair with the French cavalry which they routed and took an officer and some men. Three companies 95th Rifles and two companies 43rd took post on the heights in front of the bridge of Benavente this afternoon so as to protect the engineers mining it. We burnt a posthouse and some buildings here to prevent the enemy obtaining wood for a temporary bridge. After dark a French patrol approached our post but rode off again upon being fired upon, discharging their carbines in return. At midnight we crossed the half destroyed bridge and an arch having been blown up soon after, we joined the Reserve of the army at Benavente. We lay in the streets until daybreak.

29 December: As day dawned, the Reserve filed out of the town followed by our brigade. As we cleared it, a body of the French Imperial cavalry of the Guard crossed a ford of the Esla near the bridge. Our cavalry piquets in observance on the river immediately united under Colonel Otway[242] and disputed the ground while slowly retiring. Brigadier General Stuart [Stewart] arrived placing himself at the head of the piquets while Lord Paget brought up the 10th Hussars in support; a dash was now made on the enemy who could not escape from the fleetness of English horses and were soon overtaken when 60 of them were cut down and considerably more taken prisoners, among them was General Le Febre [Lefebvre]. We lost about 40 in the business. The French on reaching the opposite bank of the river formed up but some guns of our horse artillery arriving soon made them scamper off again. Bunoparte [sic] witnessed the whole affair.

We had a most fatiguing march of about 30 miles to La Baneza, the worst I have hitherto experienced, no provisions having been issued to us at the bridge for two days, some biscuit only was obtained from carts that were too late to pass over it. No change [of clothing] to be had from the baggage which was far away, my last pair of shoes torn in pieces and for the first time in my life compelled to walk

---

[242]   Brevet Lieutenant Colonel Loftus Otway.

barefooted for the last 10 miles over a flinty road, up on duty all the previous night, all combined to stamp misery on the recollection of them. On arriving at La Baneza we were put into a cold convent, the town being crowded with the Reserve and fatigue parties busily employed in throwing ammunition into the water which could not be forwarded. At daybreak the bugles sounded to march. How was I to do this with sore feet? A pair of monk's shoes was obtained without leave from a dusty corner which enabled me to get along. 'Necessity has no law'.

30 December: Retired 15 miles to Astorga ... full of Spanish troops, immense destruction of stores here.

31 December 1808: We commenced the ascent of the Galician mountains and after a severe march reached Fuencebadon [Foncebadón].

1 January 1809: Marched 20 m[iles] to Ponferrada ... here it was decided that the main body of the army should retire by Lugo on Corunna and that our brigade with the 2 light battalions KGL should fall back by the Vigo road to secure that port and form a flanking column.

On 4 January a detachment of 300 of the freshest men were sent on by forced marches to secure passage of the River Minho by the bridge at Orense [Ourense].

8 January: Six days of incessant marching through snowy mountains brought the two brigades of the town of Orense, having traversed from Ponferrada upwards of 100 miles, through almost impassable roads (without baggage, which no doubt took the road of the main column), and frequently benighted far short of our destination, which was sure to be wretched villages half buried in snow and frequently having to feel with poles for doors of the houses and fortunate were they who found any provisions in them, for too often the inmates absconded, after concealing all eatables when they found the men coming. They also drove away their oxen, which caused great difficulty in getting bullocks for the sick carts.

12 January: Arrived at Vigo. On topping the hills that opened to us the view of this fine bay, nothing could exceed the joy that ran through our ranks. The fleet of transports was clearing the bay as we gained the summit of the last ridge of hills going round to Corunna under convoy of the *Victory* 110 [104] guns, *Barfleur* 98 [90] and a frigate, the *Endymion* I believe [of 40 guns], the *Alfred* 74 remaining to convoy us. Headquarters embarked on HMS *Alfred*, the remaining companies being in the *Aid* Transport and *George and Mary* brig. From the 12th to the 20th remained at anchor awaiting orders.

On 21 January sailed, but a gale springing up, had to take shelter under the Bayona Islands and next day returned to the old anchorage.

24 January: Weighed anchor.

26 January: Lay to off Corunna.

28 January: Made the Scillies.

29 January: Furious storm, lost main yard.

30 January: Renewed hurricane, ship disabled.

1 February: Anchored Portsmouth, got news of the Battle of Coruna; had not heard anything since we parted from the 1st Battalion on 3 January.

[He now falls silent again until embarking again for Portugal in June]

4 June 1809: Saw the Isle of Wight at daybreak which we bore up for and dropt [sic] anchor at St Helen's as the wind chopped round against us.

5 June. Heavy squalls coming on, quitted this exposed situation and stood round to anchorage at Cowes. Passed the Russian fleet that they took in the Tagus.[243]

18 June. Weighed at 11 am, passed through the Needles at 2 and at 10 pm abreast of the Bill at Portland standing down Channel wind fair.

24 June. Made coast of Spain at daybreak.

28 June. Saw the craggy mountain called the Rock of Lisbon at daybreak, at noon off the mouth of the Tagus, when the tide setting in, the fleet was soon carried up this noble river (anchoring opposite Lisbon).

3 July. The Rifles and a wing of the 43rd entered the boats that came alongside last night and shoved off at midnight and proceeded up the Tagus; at daybreak opposite Alhandra, the constant grounding of the boats on the sand shoals caused our voyage to be very tedious heightened by exposure to a scorching sun all day; at dusk we arrived at the village of Villada [Valada] got ashore and bivouacked.

4 July. Marched a short distance to the town of Santarem where we halted two days for the rest of the brigade and baggage.

20 July. Entered Spain by crossing the river Elgas [Erges] below Salvaterra [do Extremo] and marched on to Zarza [La] Maior [Mayor]

---

[243] A Russian fleet commanded by Admiral Seniavin sailed from the Adriatic in 1807, arriving in Lisbon, where they remained when the British arrived at Lisbon in 1808. The fleet was forced to surrender and sailed to England.

25 July. Moved over a plain (with the Sierra da Gato topped with snow in view) to the village of Malpartida [de Plasencia] on the River Calzones. Next day crossed the River Tietar by a flying bridge and had a most fatiguing march to Vente de Sarragona [La Bazagona?] and the 27th to Navalmoral [de la Mata], heat oppressive.

28 July. Marched at daylight to the town of Calzada [de Oropesa] where an express met us from the commander in chief, Sir Arthur Wellesley, ordering the brigade to proceed without delay to his position on the River Alberche at Talavera de la Reyna [Reina]. After a short rest we pushed on 2 leagues to Oropesa halting there for 4 hours having already marched 26 miles under a burning sun; the bugles sounded the 'fall in' and onward we marched completing thirty miles more during the night through heavy sandy roads arriving at Talavera [de la Reina] next morning, after the most celebrated march of troops on record viz, 56 miles in 25 hours for the last ten miles was covered with Spanish wounded and fugitive soldiers.

29 July. On arriving at Talavera [de la Reina] the brigade was ordered [to] take the outposts on the Alberche which flows into the Tagus above the town, as we passed through the position found the battle-ground strewed with dead.

30 July. Employed in burning the dead bodies, the intense heat of the sun rendering them very offensive; a slight firing across the Alberche between the French and our outposts.

1 August. At daybreak observed that the enemy's picquets were withdrawn leaving rows of fires; patroles [sic] were sent across the river and some of the French wounded in the villages found.

4 August. The only thing to be done was to cross the Tagus and place that river between us and Soult's army, the passage was affected today by the bridge of Arzobisbo [Arzobispo], leaving some Spaniards there to watch it; we went into bivouac on the banks of the Tagus, where we were joined by Colonel Donkin's Brigade[244] consisting of the 45th, 87th, 88th, and 5 companies 60th, forming with ours the 3rd Division under our brigadier.

5 August. Marched in the night and made but short halts for 14 hours, the soldiers were greatly fatigued not being able to attain a drop of water the small streams being dried up. Lay down for the night on a barren hill.

6 August. A weary march over a wild country brought us to the village of Puerte de las Cazas [?] and Romongordo [Romangordo]. Donkin's Brigade formed a bivouac at the former and ours at the latter

---

[244]   Colonel Rufane Donkin.

in their front, placing out picquets on the fords of the Tagus and at the broken bridge of Almaraz. Soult's videttes being on the opposite bank, a Spanish battalion of militia lay here observing the passes; here we remained a miserable fortnight moving at sunset to a damp valley near the river (where the seeds of ague were sown in hundreds) and returning at daybreak to repose under the shelter of some cork trees which indifferently sheltered us from a scorching sun. No regular issue of rations, which never amounted to more than a handful of coarse flour, a little goat's flesh and neither wine or spirits. Soon after our arrival here the French passed a body of cavalry over the Tagus by fording and compelled the Spaniards to quit their post at the bridge of Arzobisbo [Arzobispo] leaving their cannon behind. The headquarters was first at Truxillo and latterly at Deleitosa.

20 August. Having received the welcome orders to march we quitted the valley of starvation during the last night and at daylight passed through Deleitosa and arrived on the banks of the Rio del Monte halting in an extensive forest of cork oak.

29 August. Entered Portugal by crossing the river below Marvao and proceeded to Castello [Castelo] de Vide where we halted three days in a chestnut wood.

11 September. Marched into Campo Maior a large fortified frontier town of Portugal, here the division lay *3 months in winter quarters*. It lies a short league from the Caya [Caia] which marks the boundary of Spain.

12 December. The Light Brigade commenced the march by regiments for the north of Portugal and assembled at Portalegre on the 17th, proceeded on the 18th to Crato next day to Ponte de Sor and to Abrantes the 20th.

22 December. Left Abrantes and proceeded to Coimbra by Punhete,[245] Tomar, Ourem and Leiria, Pombal and Condeixa, most of these places were passed through with Sir John Moore's army last year.

30 December. Coimbra halt day.

1810

1 January. The Light Brigade marched yesterday to the poor village of Ponte de Murcella [da Mucela] on the Alva which joins the Mondego below this place this day to Louvoza [Lourosa] and Gallizes [Galizes] and the 2nd, continued our route for the frontier by Santa Marinha at the foot of the Sierra de Estrella the highest chain of mountains in Portugal. Celorico the 3rd and to Pinhel next day.

---

245   Now Constancia.

98

6 January. As the advanced posts of the enemy were on the banks of the Agueda the 1st Battalion 95th Rifles were sent to the front this day we crossed the River Coa and occupied the villages of Cinco Villas [Vilas], Villar Torpin [Vilar Torpim] and Reygade [Reigada], distant from Pinhel 2 leagues and held them until the 18th.

18 January. The Rifles moved towards the River Douro into the villages of Figuera [Figueira de Castelo Rodrigo], Matta de Lobo [Mata de Lobos] and Escallao [Escalhão], the 43rd and 52nd marching from Pinhel into villages on our right and as a heavy fall of snow has come down, the enemy is not likely to disturb us. Held this line in quietness until the 27th [February].

27 February. A rifle company was sent on to the Spanish village of Boisa [La Bouza] from which a patrol was sent across the stream Duas Casas to reconnoitre the post of Barba del Puerco,[246] held by the enemy.

11 March. Four rifle companies under Colonel Beckwith occupied Barba del Puerco and a few Spanish soldiers joined us here. On the 14th three more companies took post at Villar de Ciervo watching the fords on the river in front of Villar de Egua [Yegua], 2 leagues higher up, the 1st German hussars were with them, the fords of the Douro were also watched (into which river the Agueda falls). The gorge of the latter at Barba del Puerco is a very bold one, the river here tumbles with a roar over a very rocky bed and is shut in at one point by high cliffs of gray [sic] blocks that project and approach each other within less than point blank musket range. That post was assigned to the Spaniards as a narrow footpath led through the rocks to it from the bridge; to the left of this a bridle road ascends zig-zag through the face of the highest part of the cliff and leads to the village of Barba del Puerco near the summit; the river in the bottom is spanned by a stone bridge 100 yards long by 5 broad. 3,000 French troops under Baron du Feres [Ferey][247] occupied the town of St Felices [Saelices el Chico], half a league from the off (or right bank) with their picquets watching the bridge; we had one company observing it and the other 3 were kept accoutred in the village; thus matters remained until the 19th when the enemy showed a hostile disposition by firing on our advance sentries and picquet, while withdrawing at daybreak.

20 March. Barba del Puerco. The enemy made a most determined attack on this post at half past 11 o'clock last night in the following manner. Baron du Feres [Ferey] moved 1,000 men without knapsacks

---

246   Now Puerto Seguro.
247   General de Division Claude Ferey, Baron de Rosengarth.

down to the pass in perfect silence leaving 400 on the off approach, he pushed 600 across the bridge; the night being dark at the time, their advance could not be perceived and the roaring of the river preventing our double sentry at the bridge from hearing footsteps, these 2 soldiers fell into their hands; the small advance picquet of course, instantly retired before this attacking column who pushed smartly up the zig zag way until it came in contact with the main body of the company under Captain O'Hare[248] who gave them a warm reception but their numbers enabled them to extend to their right and clear the gorge of the rocks. Just at that moment the other 3 companies arrived, one of which was sent to support the Spanish post, which they found abandoned by the Castilians though not attacked. The other 2 companies forthwith attacked the enemy who had gained the summit, the flashing of their musquets [sic] showing up their white cross belts, for a while the firing was within pistol range but *our swords* were soon fixed and giving the war-cheer we closed on the foe sending them helter-skelter into the gorge and down the pass as fast as their legs could carry them; they had previously removed several of their wounded but 2 officers and 18 men lay stretched on the summit. We had Lieutenant Mercer[249] killed and 17 men killed and wounded. We buried our brave fellows at daylight and had the satisfaction of defending our post against double our numbers in a formidable night attack, but the French general was highly censured for this act as the post could not be of any advantage to him, had he gained it, being on this side of the river and not tenable.

21 March. The post was reinforced by 2 more rifle companies, 1 of the 43rd and 2 of the 52nd.

25 March. A very flattering order was issued today to the brigade by order of Lord Wellington.

8 April. Yesterday a strong body of the enemy from St Felices [Saelices el Chico] foraged the right back of the river in front of Villar de Egua [Yegua], we were relieved in all the outpost duties this morning by the 52nd after which the rifles marched into the Portuguese villages of Val de la Mula [Vale da Mula] and Valde la Quelho [Vale de Coelha] on the Touron [Turones] near Fort Concepcion, also Malpartida, the 43rd were cantoned near us.

11 April. Two companies 95th Rifles were broken up and drafted into the others. Captain Ross's[250] troop of Horse Artillery was attached to the brigade.

---

248   Captain Peter O'Hare, 95th Foot.
249   First Lieutenant James Mercer, 95th Foot, was killed at Barba del Puerco.
250   Captain Hew Ross commanding 'A Troop', Royal Horse Artillery.

21 April. A change of cantonments took place today on the 43rd taking the outposts; the enemy has made his appearance before Ciudad Rodrigo. It is a fortified Spanish city on the Agueda and 5 leagues from Fort Concepcion.

29 April. Since last date the enemy has invested this fortress, in consequence of which the Rifles moved to the front into the Spanish villages of Espeja and Gallegos [de Argañán], 3 leagues from the fortress, posting picquets 2 miles in front on the river Azava [Azaba] where the bridge of Marialva [Marialba] spans it. Also placed parties to watch the fords, while the German videttes overlooked the whole country from the heights of Carpio [de Azaba] beyond the river.

30 April. The 1st and 3rd Portuguese Cacadores having now joined we now are called the Light Division. Colonel Donkin's Brigade[251] is moved to another division. A smart firing took place this forenoon with the Spanish and French outposts.

[There is a large gap here, but the diary seems complete. Presumably little happened of note to warrant an entry in his diary.]

11 July. Our brigade ordered out during the night, seven companies [of] riflemen, two companies 52nd, a squadron 14th Light Dragoons and 2 guns, the object of which was to cut off a post which the enemy began to establish at daybreak at the Spanish village of Barquillo [Barquilla] and this force took post at the back of a rising ground which overlooked that place. The 1st German Hussars & 16th Dragoons were at other points. As day dawned a troop of French cavalry followed by a company of infantry, approached the village and threw forward videttes towards the high ground behind which we lay. The Honourable Major Butler[252] instantly led his squadron 14th Light Dragoons at a gallop round the skirts of the village and succeeded in taking prisoners most of the cavalry who broke and fled, but the infantry threw themselves into square and received the successive charges of the German Hussars, 16th and 14th Dragoons that came on without making any impression, in one of which Colonel Talbot[253] 14th Dragoons was killed; 30 men of the cavalry were also killed or wounded and 20 horses, and after all this, [the] handful of French infantry effected their retreat from the

---

251   Colonel Rufane Donkin.
252   Major the Honourable Charles Butler, 14th Light Dragoons.
253   Lieutenant Colonel Neil Talbot, 14th Light Dragoons, was killed on 11 July 1810.

ground, whereas if our brigade had [been] ordered up, even one company of infantry, their fire would soon have compelled them to lay down their arms, or one or two rounds from the artillery would soon dispose of their square while the cavalry should have been merely posted on the plain to cut off their retreat, however the Germans watched their retreat and made several of them prisoners thus ended this ill-conducted affair.

22 July. Early yesterday morning Marshal Massena advanced in great force, driving in our advance posts from the Duas Casas beyond the Turon [Turones] upon which the mines of Fort Concepcion were exploded, our division instantly took up a position. The left covered by Almeida and the right in rocky ground, the Coa in our rear. Cavalry on the plain in front.

24 July. A night of thunder, lightning and heavy rain drenched all through, just as we began to light our fires at dawn of day, the enemy drove in our outposts and as the morning fog cleared away we observed the extensive plains in our front covered with the French army as far as the eye could reach, yet our brigadier [Colonel Robert Craufurd] was determined to fight with the flooded Coa in his rear, over which the only pass was by the bridge. The cavalry and horse artillery being useless in broken ground we occupied, they withdrew across the river followed by the 52nd Regiment and as they had to retire through a long defile, the 43rd and Riflemen had to sustain the repeated attacks of a large body of voltigeurs (which the enemy rapidly pushed forward) until by superior numbers they began to outflank our position. These two regiments now began to fall back towards the bridge, disputing the enclosures and rugged ground, in the execution of this movement the enemy occupied an eminence of importance which commanded the road to the bridge, but were instantly driven from it in gallant style by the 43rd and Rifles who held it until it became necessary to retire across the river. The division then occupied the rocky banks and defended the bridge throughout the day against attacks made on it by the enemy who charged repeatedly, but the few who passed over never returned. Towards sunset few of the muskets or rifles would go off as it rained incessantly, the fire of the enemy ceased and a French officer advanced waving a white handkerchief as a signal for a cessation of hostilities, asking for permission to remove their wounded as the approaches to the bridge lay strewed with them, it was granted to them. Night was now coming on, so the division retired to Carvalhal [de Atalaia], leaving picquets to watch the bridge. Our loss this day in killed and wounded was

27 officers and 336 men. One officer and 55 Riflemen were cut off in a windmill on the mill plain and taken prisoners; the brigadier put them there and could not withdraw them. The whole loss fell upon the 43rd and riflemen, Colonel Hull[254] commanding the former was killed, yet all this blood was shed for no purpose whatsoever. A rear guard should have occupied the ground and the whole division withdrawn over the river when such a superior force was seen advancing.

4 August. In the General Orders of this day the Light Division is formed into two brigades viz the 1st Brigade to be composed of the 43rd Regiment, the right wing of the 95th Riflemen and 3rd Cacadores under Lieutenant Colonel Barclay.[255]

28 August. The enemy attacked our cavalry posts in front of [Baraçal] this morning and were repulsed with the loss of several dragoons taken prisoners, but the attack having been renewed our cavalry posts were withdrawn to Alverca and the Light Division fell back to Celorico [da Beira] and villages in front. A smart affair took place at the cavalry outposts yesterday in which 25 French dragoons and 11 infantry were made prisoners.

2 September. The enemy drove in our cavalry picquets from Alverca, so the Light Division retired on Sampayon [Sampaio] three leagues in rear of Celorico, passed the ruins of the ancient castle of Linhares on the march.

[Strangely no mention is made of the Battle of Bussaco fought on 27 September 1810, perhaps Cox had no time to record his thoughts.]

15 October. At midday the enemy made a trifling reconnaissance at Sobral [de Monte Agraço] and our posts at Arruda [dos Vinhos] but retired on being fired upon. But yesterday a smart affair took place at Sobral close to which were posted a company of the 1st Battalion 95th Rifles and a detachment of the 71st Light Infantry, which were attacked by infantry and artillery to cover a reconnaissance, but the whole were driven back into the town.

---

254   Lieutenant Colonel Edward Hull, 43rd Foot, was killed, having arrived with the regiment from England that very morning.

255   This is an error. Lieutenant Colonel Thomas Beckwith commanded the First Brigade; Lieutenant Colonel Robert Barclay, 52nd Foot, commanded the Second Brigade.

Route of the Light Division from Gallegos [de Argañán] to Arruda [dos Vinhos]		
From	To	Leagues
Gallegos [de Argañán] (in Spain)	Almeida	5
Almeida	Freixedos [Freixedas]	4
Freixedos [Freixedas]	Celerico [Celorico da Beira]	3½
Celerico [Celorico da Beira]	San Pao [Sao Paio]	3
San Pao [Sao Paio]	Cea [Seia] St Romao [São Romão]	2½
Cea [Seia] St Romao [São Romão]	Saragossa [Lajeosa?]	3
Saragossa [Lajeosa?]	Venda de [do] Porco	4
Venda de [do] Porco	Sylverina [Vimeiro?]	4½
Sylverina [Vimeiro?]	Mortagao [Mortagua]	3
Mortagao [Mortagua]	Busacco [Bussaco]	2
Busacco [Bussaco]	Butao [Botao]	2
Butao [Botao]	Coimbra	2½
Coimbra	Condeixa [-a-Velha]	2
Condeixa [-a-Velha]	Pombal	5
Pombal	Boa Vista	3½
Boa Vista	Batalha	3
Batalha	Rio Maior	6
Rio Maior	Alcoentre	4
Alcoentre	Carregoda [Carregado]	4
Carregoda [Carregado]	Alemquer [Alenquer]	2
Alemquer [Alenquer]	Arruda [dos Vinhos]	2
Total		**68 Leagues**

[Cox again fails to note the French retreat to Santarem.]

20 November. Drenched through with torrents of rain all night having bivouacked, the Light Division with a few dragoons advanced at daybreak across the low ground and approached the left of the French position with a view of making them show their force, but they

promptly filled the wooded slopes with hordes of light troops with whom the 95th skirmished, having found the approach very swampy we retired again and the division as also the Brunswick Corps went into cantonments at Valle [Vale de Santarem] and detached houses, the right wing 95th Rifles being in advance.

1811

23 January. The Light Brigade paraded to witness the shooting of three of the Brunswick Corps that attempted deserting a week ago,[256] the remainder of them were sentenced to be transported, but in consequence of so much desertion this corps was sent to the rear after the execution.

9 March. The right wing 95th Rifles and cavalry pushed on at daybreak and after a rapid march of five hours came up with the enemy's rear guard at the junction of the great road from Leiria; the 1st German Hussars made a charge here and took 12 prisoners of the 11th Horse Grenadiers, 40 stragglers also fell into our hands during our march besides horses, gun carriages tacking etc and went into bivouac after dusk.

10 March. Sir William Erskine[257] assumed the command of the Light Division vice Craufurd gone to England on leave of absence. Next morning the enemy's rear guard retired but having occupied the walled enclosure in front of Pombal with voltigeurs, some companies of the 95th and the 3rd Cacadores were ordered to dislodge them which was promptly done, driving them into the town where they disputed the old castle for a time, but [it was] carried by the 3rd Cacadores in a spirited manner.

12 March. The enemy broke up from the ground he held during the night and this morning in position on the extremity of the plain of Redinha, that town being in his rear, his right on the River Soure protected in front by a wooded height filled with voltigeurs and his left on the heights of the Redinha River covered also by woods, this force was the 6th Corps and Montbrun's cavalry. The woods covering the flanks of their position were briskly attacked by both wings of the 95th Rifles and soon carried, the Light and 3rd Divisions were then placed in two lines supported by Pack's Brigade[258] and the cavalry

---

256 General Orders show that Privates Francis Leibental, John Lange and William Morentye of the Brunswick Light Infantry were shot on 23 January 1811. Frederick Getterman was also sentenced to death and presumably met his death at the same time, making four in total.

257 Major General Sir William Erskine took command; he was not popular.

258 Brigadier General Denis Pack, commanding a Portuguese brigade.

with the other divisions in reserve. The lines of attack having been beautifully formed under a sharp command from the enemy and strong bodies of light troops thrown out, a general advance was made on the French position, from which he broke by retreating in battalions from his right, but was soon thrown into disorder by the pressing forward of the light troops, who drove their rear through the town of Redinha in great confusion, where numerous prisoners were taken and many drowned in trying to ford the river, the bridge having been blocked up by others here, the 50th French Regiment suffered much being the last to retreat, the enemy placed several pieces of cannon to command the bridge, which enabled him to collect his scattered battalions & cover them with a new position. The 3rd Division crossed the river and moved on his left while the Light Division and light troops from the 1st Division and Pack's Brigade followed by cavalry advanced on his front forcing him back on his main body at Condexia [Condeixa-a-Velha], we then bivouacked for the night.

13 March. Again in motion at daybreak & found the enemy strongly posted in great force at Condeixa [Condeixa-a-Velha] the only approach to which being by a causeway enfiladed by several guns, the 3rd Division were sent around by a mountain road to turn their left which movement made them evacuate the town. They retired to Casa Nova [Casal Novo] in the mountains, followed by the division, but his main body still held a strong position on the heights, which was necessary to turn by flank movements, so the Light Division with Pack's Brigade got round his right by a mountain road, while the 3rd Division turned his left, forcing him from his position after giving us a few volleys (this forced the retreat to Ponte du Murcella [da Mucela] and Coimbra).

14 March. As soon as the morning fog cleared away we perceived the enemy in the same strong position as yesterday, having two corps there with a large body of voltigeurs on a small hill in advance which was promptly attacked and carried by the left wing 95th Rifles under [Brigade] Major Stewart[259] who received his death wound there; an excellent officer lost to the service, the cross walls lined by the enemy were also carried by the right wing Rifles and the whole advanced post were successfully driven back.

19 March. Our cavalry made 800 of the enemy's rear prisoners, in crossing the plain in our front, among them is an aide [de] camp of Loison's[260] a Portuguese.

---

259   First Lieutenant James Stewart, 95th Foot, acting brigade major, died at Freixedas on 28 March 1811.
260   General Louis Loison commanded VI Corps.

20 March. The division moved through Gallices [Galizes] and bivouacked, the enemy retired with greater celerity today but were closely followed by our cavalry and horse artillery who took all their stragglers, horses, tumbrils, carts & marked their retreat.

21 March. The cavalry cut off 200 more of the rear guard, the division halted in the fir groves above Marceira [Maceira] and the enemy at Celorico [da Beira] which being a strong position they were enabled to hold it five days.

28 March: [Brigade] Major Stewart's body brought in. He was killed in the streets of Freixedas.

3 April. Operations commenced on the enemy's left by Colonel Beckwith's Brigade of the Light Division, crossing the Coa at a ford half a league above Sabugal, the 95th driving in their picquets and descended the height overlooking the ford, the rest of the brigade following. In front was a wood of large horse chestnut trees which was warmly disputed by the 14th French Light Infantry [Legere], but the galling fire of the 95th Rifles at point blank range soon compelled them to retire, but rallying with strong supports, the wood again became the scene of sharp work and close-firing. The enemy shortly advanced on us in three columns in solid masses with their charge beating and covered by rounds of grape shot from a howitzer close up. The 43rd formed line giving their fire, we skirmishers rapidly forming up on their left opening our fire on the advancing columns, the 52nd pushed up on the right followed by their brigade and the enemy having almost reached our line, reeled under the close fire and fell back and as we followed them up with a general charge, they warmly disputed the possession of the howitzer with the 43rd who had taken it but they were again driven back. The 3rd Division who in the meantime had crossed at a ford lower down, now opened a fire with their light troops on the right of the retiring enemy supported by the 5th Regiment while the 5th Division crossing at the bridge of Sabugal threatened his right and rear and our cavalry held the plain on his left, these dispositions had the desired effect, for Regnier [Reynier][261] broke into a retreat to cover which he made two serious attacks on the Light Division which were repulsed at once, he then abandoned the field (favoured by a heavy descent of rain) with the loss of more than 1,000 men. The Light Division got Sabugal for quarters as the chief fighting fell on it, the other troops had a wet bivouac.

3 May. Massena advanced this morning with the Army of Portugal, which consists of the 2nd, 6th, & 8th Corps, a division of the 9th

---

[261]   General Jean Louis Reynier.

Corps and a very large cavalry force, the latter being very superior to ours in numbers, gave them an advantage on the plains. The French marshal moved in 3 columns on the Duas Casas, the Light Division retired before them, covered by our dragoons and took post behind the village of Fuentes d'Onoro [Fuentes de Oñoro]. Here Lord Wellington formed in battle order behind the above river, his right resting on the Portuguese village of Naves de Aver [Haver] which was occupied by the celebrated guerrilla chief Don Julian Sanchez with his corps, the centre at Fuentes d'Onoro and left at Fort Concepcion. As the main road to Almeida lay through Fuentes it was evident it would become a point of contention, therefore that village was promptly occupied by the light companies of the 3rd Division, those of General Howard[262] and General Nightingale's Brigades[263] also by those of the King's German Legion supported by the 2nd Battalion 83rd Regiment. Shortly after these troops posted themselves behind the cross walls of the village, the enemy attacked it fiercely with a very strong column which suffered much from fire poured in on them, but from superiority of numbers succeeded at length in making a lodgement in that part of the village near the Duas Casas river and having increased their efforts to force their way on, the 24th 71st & 79th were thrown into the village The 71st charging through it routed the French from the ground they had gained, the contest at this point continued until night put an end to it, the village remaining in our possession held by the 24th, 71st & 79th the other troops were withdrawn after dark. The Light Division was kept in reserve behind Fuentes [de Oñoro] the greater part of the day, and towards evening were sent to support the left, as the enemy were moving troops towards that point. The marshal kept up a general cannonade throughout the day without gaining an inch of ground and his attacks on Fuentes cost him many men.

4 May. The enemy confined himself to a close reconnaissance of our position. General Craufurd assumed the command of the Light Division again. Towards sunset it was moved in rear of the centre.

5 May. This morning the enemy's force opposite Fuentes was considerably increased and he commenced the battle by moving a strong column of cavalry round the right of our position which obliged the Spaniards to retire from Naves de Aver [Haver]. This column continued on towards Poca Velha [Poco Velha] occupied by the 7th Division to which point the Light Division and cavalry were detached, but as a strong body of French infantry also marched on

---

262   Major General Kenneth Howard commanded a brigade of the 1st Division.
263   Major General Miles Nightingall commanded a brigade of the 1st Division.

that village and drove the posts of the 7th Division from it, and by gaining the passage of the Duas Casas there, he was enabled to turn the right of that division with his cavalry on the plain. A change of position now became necessary by throwing back the right of the army, this beautiful manoeuvre was effected in a masterly manner, crossing a plain in the presence of a great superiority in number of French cavalry. The 7th Division retired (covered by the Light Division) the enemy's dragoons now pressed on but were checked by the fire they received from that division and I never saw a charge of cavalry repulsed in a steadier manner than by the Chasseurs Britanniques. About the same time a brilliant dash was made by some squadrons of our dragoons (headed by General Stewart[264]) on the advance brigade of French cavalry who were pressing on the Light Division squares, they were ridden through, several cut down and a colonel with some of his regiment brought in prisoners. The 7th Division having effected its retrograde [movement] to the new position, the Light Division fell back (covered by the cavalry and filed through the Guards in the 1st Division, drawing up in their rear as a reserve and threw 5 companies [of the] 95th Rifles into a broken valley through which flows the river Teuron [Turones], and assisted by the light companies of the Guards repulsed the French voltigeurs in an attempt to push through it. By the change of position the 7th Division was thrown across the Teuron covering the roads leading to Almeida.

12 May. This morning the enemy drove in our cavalry picquets from Carpio [de Azaba] with a brigade of dragoons, who had the temerity to ride up within fire of Colonel Beckwith's Brigade formed outside Espeja, but our riflemen having got through a wood on their flank soon made them gallop off again and the posts were established as before.

[There is another significant gap here, when nothing of real consequence occurred.]

21 August. We received a rifle reinforcement this day viz 4 companies of the 3rd Battalion 95th under Lieutenant Colonel Barnard[265] which had been serving with the army at Cadiz, they were placed in the 3rd [sic] Brigade under Colonel Beckwith.[266]

7 September. The mountain posts of Robladillo [Robledillo de Gata] Las Herias [Erias] and Aldeajúilla [Ovejuela] were occupied by two

---

264   Major General the Honourable Charles Stewart.
265   Lieutenant Colonel Andrew Barnard, 95th Foot.
266   This is an error, they were added to the 1st Brigade, no 3rd Brigade was formed.

companies Rifles, which they held until the 22nd when they joined the division. In consequence of the advance of Marmont's army from their cantonments, a company of the 2nd Battalion Rifles has joined from England and are attached to the right wing 95th which consists of 4 companies 1st Battalion and 2 [companies] of the 2nd Battalion.

[27] September. On arriving at Forcaylos [Forcalhos] a squadron of the enemy approached the village but were driven back by the right wing 95th Rifles and 3rd Cacadores. In the afternoon a strong body of the enemy drove in our outposts through Aldea de Ponte [Aldeia da Ponte].

1 October. Two more companies [of the] 2nd Battalion 95th Rifles joined the division a few days back.[267]

1812

8 January. The most commanding ground in the immediate vicinity of the town being the hill of St [San] Francisco on which the enemy had constructed a redoubt, the possession of which was indispensably necessary towards future operations, accordingly a detachment from the Light Division of 120 men of the 43rd, 52nd & 95th Rifles making 360 volunteers under Lieutenant Colonel Colborne[268] stormed it after dark and carried it in a very short time, 2 captains and 49 soldiers were taken in the work, the rest fell by the bayonet.

19 January. General Mackinnon's Brigade[269] of the 3rd Division moved on the right breach, storming it with great gallantry and protected by the 2nd Battalion 5th and 94th Regiment. The 2nd Cacadores covered the advance also. The 43rd, 52nd and 95th Rifles formed the left column and advanced under a heavy fire to the assault of the left breach, headed by a storming [party] of 300 men from these regiments and Major George Napier 52nd Regiment[270] proceeded by the right wing 95th Rifles who were destined to clear the breach by its fire and protect the advance of the storming party, a service of much danger, being exposed to the fire from the walls. The 3rd Battalion 95th covered the right of this attack and kept up the communication with the 3rd Division by moving along the ditch to its right. All the troops mounted the breaches with great gallantry and their valour was crowned with complete success, the fortress being in their possession. The enemy threw out several fire balls on the advance of the right

---

267	Captain Samuel Mitchell's company joined in October 1810, while Captain John Hart's company arrived on 7 September. Both were in the 1st Brigade.
268	Lieutenant Colonel John Colborne, 52nd Foot.
269	Major General Henry Mackinnon.
270	Major George Napier, 52nd Foot, was severely wounded at Ciudad Rodrigo.

wing 95th Rifles destined to cover the approach of the storming party, these balls quite illuminated the ground so as to enable the fire from the ramparts to be directed immediately on the assailants, most of the senior officers suffered. Our General Craufurd was mortally wounded, General Vandeleur,[271] Colonel Colbourne [sic] badly wounded, Major George Napier lost an arm, many other officers came into the list of sufferers. Among them was the writer of this journal, who had his left arm completely fractured, a musket ball having parted the bone of the upper arm and being thus put *hors de combat* he must fill up the movements of the Light Division during his absence from the reports of friends in the field.

[On the evidence of his brother William, John returned to Ireland to recover from his wound and only returned to Lisbon in August 1812. He does, however, comment on the Storming of Badajoz which he was not present at.]

[6] April. Fortunately, General Picton succeeded in escalading the castle and having lodged the 3rd Division in it, the breaches were soon abandoned and the place fell, the 95th Rifle Corps had 24 officers killed and wounded among the former was the gallant Major O'Hare who commanded the storming party and fell riddled with bullets on the breach.

[No more of 1812 is discussed]

1813

February. The French army was considerably reduced this month by drafts of ten men per company from the Army of Portugal and larger numbers from the [other] armies having been ordered to France for the purpose of sending them as non-commissioned officers to the Grand Army forming under Bonaparte for the invasion of Russia, several general officers were also ordered to join that army.

21 May. The 2 brigades of the Light Division commanded by Major General Kempt[272] and Vandeleur, broke up from their cantonments yesterday, the former consisting of the 1st Battalion 43rd Light Infantry, 6 companies 95th Rifles, 5 companies 3rd Battalion 95th and the 17th Portuguese [Line] Regiment. The brigade of General Vandeleur was

---

271   Major General John Ormsby Vandeleur, commanded a brigade of the Light Division. He was slightly wounded.
272   Major General James Kempt.

composed of the 1st Battalion 52nd Light Infantry, six companies 2nd Battalion 95th Rifles and the 1st and 3rd Cacadores, Major Ross's troop of Horse Artillery still attached to the division. Baron Alten commanding the whole. This morning the division assembled at Molinos [Casillas] de Flores.

3 June. In the retreat of the enemy yesterday the 19th [sic] hussars charged a body of their cavalry near Morales [de Toro] which were overthrown and 206 prisoners taken, soon after daybreak commenced the passage of the Douro in the best manner we could, by passing the broken arch of the bridge one by one down and up ladders and by one small boat. The horses and baggage animals crossed by a deep ford above the bridge, by midday the whole were over river and the division moved a short distance to the village of Texara Buena [Tagarabuena].

15 June. Crossed the Ebro by the bridge of Puente de Arenas [Puente Arenas]. The appearance of the country was beautiful here.

18 June. Yesterday morning early we moved off (preceded by a squadron of the 1st German Hussars 1st Battalion 95th Rifles following them close up) having passed the villages of Tovillas [?] and Valpuesta we arrived at the small town of Milan [San Millán de San Zadornil] and there surprised the 1st Brigade of the French division under General Maucune[273] which had halted there for the night and were preparing to march, when our German squadron suddenly came on their look-out party of dragoons, which they instantly charged, and all made prisoners. Now the riflemen lost no time in attacking the French infantry filing out of the town and caused much loss to them by hanging on the flank of their column, they attempted to stop us by forming a line but it soon gave way under the punishing fire of the Rifles who actually pulled a chef de battalion and several men out of the melee they got into. The second brigade of this French division had halted at a village a mile in the rear, and being cut off by our attack had no other mode of extricating itself from the defile but by throwing itself into the overhanging mountains on its right with the loss of all its baggage, General Vandeleur's Brigade had turned out of our line of march and made a rapid movement on them, throwing them into great disorder, a Spanish detachment now hunted them down and very few escaped. Now to return to our 1st Brigade which followed the enemy skirmishing through the villages of Villa Nueva and Villa Mana beyond which they were joined by other French troops and having taken up a very strong position that completely commanded the road no attempt was made to dislodge them, however towards nightfall

---

[273]   General Antoine de Maucune.

they retreated and we encamped on the River Onicillo [Omecillo] below Villa Nueva [Villanueva de Valdegovia], St Milan [San Millán de San Zadornil] stands on this stream.

20 May. Halt day. Yesterday [19th] the Light Division moved off at daybreak and crossed the Onicillo [Omecillo] at Villa Maderna [Villamaderne] in its march to Salinas [de Anana] (where are salt springs) from thence to Pobes where we crossed the small River Bayas by a wooden bridge where we encamped. This movement turned the flank of the enemy who disputed a pass on our left with the 4th Division and to keep up the communication with it the 1st Cacadores were detached in the hills and became engaged in a skirmish with the enemy. These defiles lead through a bold range of heights into the plain of Vitoria where the French army had concentrated, when we passed the Ebro consequently our columns closed up today to accept the offer of battle.

21 May. At daylight this morning the Light Division moved to the front leaving the baggage behind, passing through Subijana de Morillo [Subijana-Morillas], Montaviete [Montevite] and Olavere [Ollávarre], having been joined during the march by the 4th Division, on arriving at the heights overlooking the plain of Vitoria we drew up. From this point, the position for the French army could be distinctly traced, the centre resting along the left bank of the River Zadora covering the city of Vitoria. Their right was on heights in front of the river and above Abechuco [Abetxuko] and their left thrown back to the village of Subijana de Alva [Alava], having a strong force posted in the rugged mountains of La Puebla. The battle commenced by an attack on this latter point made by General Hill's Corps, the advance being composed of the 71st Light Infantry and the light companies of regiments aided by a Spanish brigade under General Morillo.[274] At the onset the enemy gave way, but being strongly reinforced, the fight was renewed with obstinacy which ended in their being driven across the Zadora and being followed up closely, they were also compelled to retire from Subijana de Alva. While this contest was going on, the 95th Riflemen drove their voltigeurs from the banks of the Zadora beneath the heights, seizing on one of the bridges.[275] Strange to say, that the French neglected to destroy this, as also two other bridges that lay in front of their position, over which our centre now crossed to the attack, taking advantage of the enemy's having sent troops from our front to support their left where Lord Hill was forcing it. The Light, 3rd

---

[274]   General Pablo Morillo y Morillo, Count of Cartagena.
[275]   This refers to the Bridge of Trespuentes.

and 4th Divisions having passed the river made a rapid attack on the enemy's centre under a sharp cannonade and carried a commanding hill above the village of Arinez. This village being a key-stone to ulterior movements, [they] showed a strong disposition to hold it, but were driven from it by the 88th Regiment and a part of which was taken by the riflemen (25) while endeavouring to escape through the village. The 7th Division now crossed the river and by a general advance the whole line of the enemy's centre was driven back on the city of Vitoria. Sir Thomas Graham's Corps now pressed the enemy's right and drove it from the heights where it was posted; beaten at all points and out-manoeuvred the French army was forced from position to position and compelled to abandon the city, when it may be said that a complete de-route commenced. King Joseph Bonaparte[276] (who commanded in person) seconded by Marshal Jourdan had intended to keep open the Bayonne and Pamplona roads for his retreat, but seeing Sir Thomas Graham's first attack threatened the communications with the former, he sent a strong force to the two villages of Gamarra[277] on the Zadora where the high road passes. One of these villages was instantly carried by General Robinson's Brigade[278] of the 5th Division and General Longa's Spaniards[279] took the other. The enemy collected a strong force to retake these villages, but the possession of Vitoria compelled him to retrograde. Sir Thomas Graham then crossed the Zadora and by forcing the enemy's right and right centre back on the other retiring bodies, the greatest disorder prevailed in the whole of the French army by being thrown upon the Pamplona road, the only one open to their retreat; confusion reigned among their corps and as the allied army still pressed on, the enemy had not time to take advantage of any ground and were compelled to fly in a mob covered by their cavalry, leaving behind them every piece of cannon they had on the field except one, amounting to 151 guns & 415 caissons, all their baggage, money chests and every description of material. The ground being low and much intersected with dykes was most unfavourable for a flying army. Such a disaster by the loss of the battle was never anticipated, as nearly 2,000 carriages and waggons of various descriptions were abandoned near the gates of Vitoria, among them King Joseph's carriage which he quitted and escaped on horseback, the road being still quite blocked up with these impediments, many ladies endeavoured to escape on foot, every politeness was shown

---

276 Napoleon's elder brother Joseph had been installed as King of Spain.
277 Gamarra Menor and Gamarra Mayor.
278 Major General Frederick Robinson.
279 General Francisco de Longa.

to those who fell into our hands, among them was General Gazan's wife.[280] The loss of the enemy in killed, wounded and prisoner was 10,000.[281] The contending armies were nearly equal in number as the 6th Division had not arrived from the rear, when night put an end to the pursuit, our army bivouacked on the plain, having fought over a long line of country.

22 May. The Light Division commenced the pursuit of the enemy this morning, followed by the 3rd and 4th Divisions, the 1st German Hussars & 14th Light Dragoons with the Horse Artillery being in front of the column, passing through some abandoned villages and the old walled town of Salvatierra[282] situated on two streams) we encamped at the village of Alvisera [Alivesa], throughout the day the cavalry harassed the enemy's rear guard and took 50 prisoners. Sir Thomas Graham's Corps marched towards Bilboa on a French column of 12,000 men under General Foy[283] which were in that neighbourhood and supposed to be in march to join King Joseph's army at Vitoria.

23 May. With the light cavalry in front, the Light Division continued to pursue the enemy at daybreak, the 1st Battalion 95th Riflemen being pushed forward at the village of Cordia [Ziordia] we passed the River Burunda[284] into the province of Navarre and following the course of the stream downwards came up with the enemy's rear guard posted at a village, having set the wooden bridge on fire. They were soon dislodged by our horse artillery and we forded the river above and pushed the enemy so hard that they failed in destroying several small bridges. Came up with them again at the village of Echarrianos [Etxarri-Aranatz] which was on fire, a skirmish took place between the riflemen and voltigeurs which compelled the French rear guard to move off rapidly, cannonaded by our light artillery setting all the villages on fire that lay in their retreat. On reaching La Cuenca [Lakuntza] they drew up in columns but the horse artillery soon opened a fire on them which compelled them to retire through Huerta [Uharte-Arakil], the operations ended for the day. The Light Division occupied the Cunca [Lakuntza] and its neighbourhood with cavalry in front at Huerta.

24 May. At daybreak we were in motion again, our advance guard being composed of the 1st & 3rd Battalions 95th Rifle with the cavalry and guns leading, we soon came up with the enemy, when a running

---

280 General Honore Gazan.
281 This is an overestimate, the French lost just under 8,000 all told.
282 Now more often known as Agurain.
283 General Maximilien Foy.
284 Also known as the Arakil.

fight commenced. Whenever the enemy halted, they were instantly attacked by our riflemen and horse artillery. The latter displayed the greatest activity in bringing their guns to bear, at length the French rear guard halted within half a league of Pamplona on the high road and opened a fire from the solitary gun they got off the battlefield of Vitoria. As the approach was by a causeway, the riflemen made a flank movement and the 14th Light Dragoons charging along the road, the enemy gave way, seeking shelter under the walls of Pamplona (having left the one gun and caisson in our hands (a large body of troops were also halted there). The Light Division then occupied the villages of Aldava [Aldaba], Burasso [Berriosuso], Berripluno [Berrioplano-Berriobeiti] & Lauste [Zausti] for the night, having followed up the enemy five leagues.

15 July. Soon after daybreak the Light Division assembled and moving down the Bidassoa passed some look out parties of Longa's guerrillas and on reaching the bridge of Lesaca [Lesaka] we discovered the advanced post of the enemy on the summit of the hill overlooking us. The 1st & 3rd Battalions 95th Rifles immediately ascended the steep eminence, driving the French from the top with little loss. This chain of heights is called Santa Barbara from the ruins of a convent so called and from this point we got a view of the Pyrenees with their advanced post holding the town and valley of Vera [Bera] on the River Bidassoa, with some detached houses, from which after a sharp tirallade [sic] they were driven by the 43rd Light Infantry favoured by the fire of some Spanish guerrillas who held the opposite side of the river. A heavy fire was kept up all day as the enemy held the church and further portion of Vera [Bera]. This ceased at night and both parties established picquets in the portions of the town each held, the 1st Brigade bivouacked on the heights of Santa Barbara in communication with the 7th Division in the mountains on their right and the 2nd Brigade at Vera.

26 July. The 7th Division retired on St. Estevan [Santesteban[285]] and the Light Division crossed the Bidassoa and retired unmolested through Lesaca [Lesaka] and encamping on a ridge between the latter and Sumbillo [Sunbilla].

27 July. The Light Division fell back at night through the valley of Hurin [Ituren] to Zubieta two leagues and a half, which short distance was not accomplished before daybreak owing to the extreme darkness and roughness of the road.

28 July. Encamped at Zubieta and halted throughout the day, a heavy peel of cannon echoed all day through the mountains on

---

[285]   Also known as Doneztebe.

Alexander Cameron, 95th.

Sir Andrew Barnard, 95th.

Nicholas Travers, 95th.

Amos Norcott, 95th.

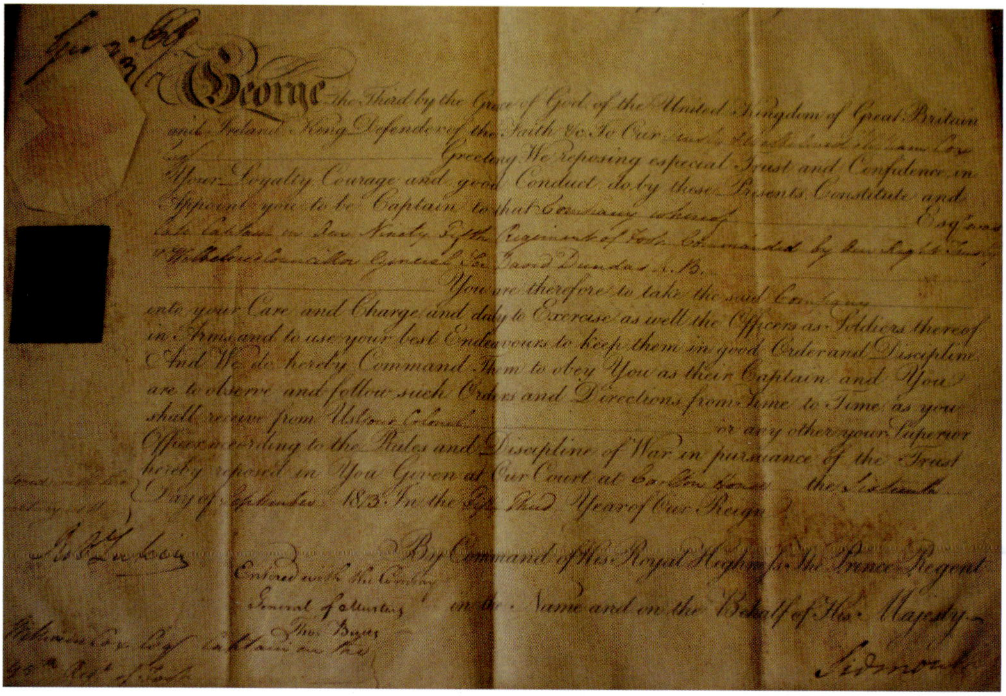

George the Third by the Grace of God of the United Kingdom of Great Britain and Ireland King Defender of the Faith &c To Our
Greeting We reposing especial Trust and Confidence in Your Loyalty Courage and good Conduct do by these Presents Constitute and Appoint you to be Captain to that Company whereof
late Captain in the Ninety Fifth Regiment of Foot
You are therefore to take the said Company into your Care and Charge and duly to Exercise as well the Officers as Soldiers thereof in Arms and to use your best Endeavours to keep them in good Order and Discipline And We do hereby Command Them to obey You as their Captain and You are to observe and follow such Orders and Directions from Time to Time as you shall receive from
or any other your Superior Officer according to the Rules and Discipline of War in pursuance of the Trust hereby reposed in You Given at Our Court at Carlton House the Sixteenth Day of September 1813 In the Fifty Third Year of Our Reign

By Command of His Royal Highness The Prince Regent in the Name and on the Behalf of His Majesty
Sidmouth

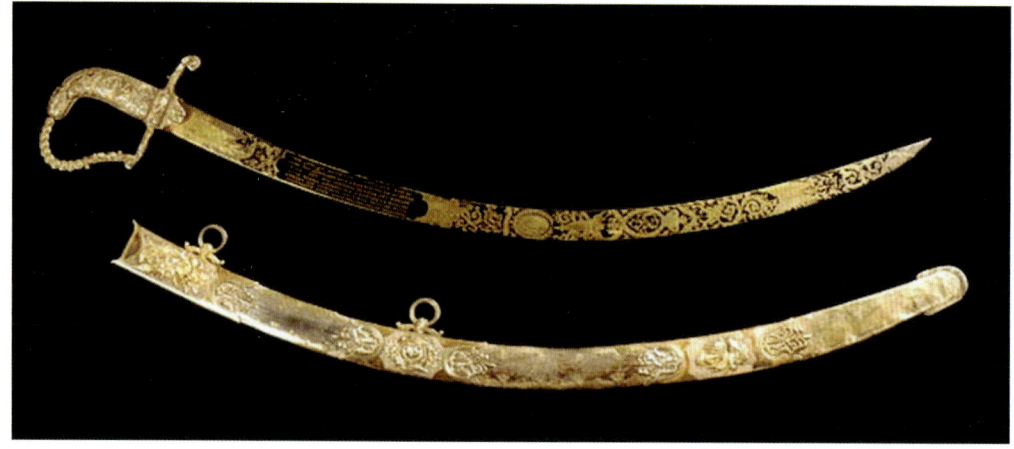

The commission promoting William Cox, 95th, to captain in 1813.

Ceremonial sword presented by the officers of the 95th to Sir Andrew Barnard in 1818.

Early depiction of the 95th Rifles.

George III telescope owned by Horatio Stewart, 95th.

John Molloy, 95th, in Western Australia in later life.

Hospital mate Dr William Sankey in later life.

Craufurd and his troops on the retreat to Vigo.

A 95th officer.

The 95th Rifles at Cacabelos in 1809 by Richard Simkin.

Original Baker rifle and sword bayonet.

James Shaw, 43rd Foot.

Major General Robert Craufurd.

95th Rifles at Tarbes 1814 by Richard Simkin.

the right accompanied with incessant musketry, strongly indicating hard fighting in that direction and that the advance of Soult was well contested. The division moved after sunset on the 29th and encamped at Saldias. The Light Division was instantly marched through the mountains and took up a position on the main road from Pamplona to Tolosa covering the left of General Hill's Corps.

1 August. The Light Division now were pushed forward making a forced march of eight leagues by Escura [Ezkurra], Zubieta and Hurin along the heights on the left bank of the Bidassoa through bad roads and under a scorching sun. In passing the chain of mountains overlooking the village and bridge of Villas [?] we found the enemy strongly posted there in order to cover the retreat of a column from Sumbillo [Sunbilla] along the opposite of the river. The 1st and 3rd Battalion 95th Rifles now pushed on and gained possession of some houses near the bridge after a sharp tiralade [sic], but the enemy [were] too strong to be forced and night coming on the firing ceased on both sides. The rear of the retiring column from Sumbillo [Sunbilla] was thrown into great confusion and was so hurried that the dragoons actually flogged the infantry with their sabres to drive them on before the rear guard, but their baggage was cut off and fell into the hands of the 4th Division who followed up their retreat from Sumbillo [Sunbilla].

2 August. The enemy abandoned Villas [?] during the night and were followed up this morning by the Light Division the 1st Brigade advancing by the main road leading to Vera [Bera], and the 2nd Brigade marched by Yanci [Igantzi] and Lasaca [Lesaka] we soon found ourselves on our former ground at Vera which we occupied without firing a shot, the enemy holding the same posts in the hills as formerly with the exception for the craggy hill on our right on which they retained a force, and as this formed one of the shoulders of the Pass of Echallar [Etxalar] it was necessary to dislodge them from it. Accordingly, towards evening the 1st Brigade was drawn up on the heights of Santa Barbara, from thence the 1st and 3rd Battalions 95th Rifles advanced up the face of the craggy mountain to make a feint first attack with a view of favouring the attack of the 7th Division on the Pass of Echallar [Etxalar] close on our right. On approaching the summit the riflemen sustained and kept up a sharp tiralade [sic], the enemy having 3 battalions on the crown of the craggy peak, a heavy fog now came on, which the riflemen took advantage of and pushed up smartly but were charged back a short distance by the enemy, however as the fog became dense they could not discover the real force opposed to them so they abandoned the hill on being pressed hard again, thus our feint attack turning out so successful that it prevented a real one

taking place in the morning. The 43rd were in support on the base, the brigade returned to camp leaving the 17th Portuguese [Line Battalion] in charge of the post.

1 September. The firing continued with unabated spirit on the wall of San Sebastian for several days past, on the 20th ultimo 250 volunteers were sent from the Light Division under Major Hunt[286] of the 52nd Light Infantry.

[The enemy seeking] the passage of the river moved on and took post at the bridge after having been once repulsed by two companies [of the] 2nd Battalion 95th Rifles who held detached houses opposite, the enemy left a strong force there to secure the bridge and ascended the roads that led to San Sebastian. Those French divisions which crossed to the left bank in the morning were compelled to seek a passage at the bridge of Vera [Bera] in which they suffered considerable losses by the fire of some companies of the 95th Rifles who gallantly maintained their ground although attacked from Vera [Bera].

Crossing of the Bidassoa

7 October. But the most serious task was reserved for the Light Division which had to assault the entrenched Pass of Vera [Bera], this commenced by the 3rd Battalion of the 95th Rifles taking the small hill that overhangs the town which was done in very beautiful style. On this was the advanced post of the enemy, the two brigades then advanced to the assault of the works, the 2nd Brigade under Colonel Colborne 52nd Light Infantry met with considerable opposition in carrying a redoubt on a tongue of land that descends from the summit of the mountain. Here the 2nd Battalion 95th Rifles and 1st Cacadores lost a number of men and was chiefly caused by the tardy advance of Longa's Spaniards on their left, who did not reach their ground on the flank of the redoubt in time. That work being taken, the two brigades carried all the other redoubts and entrenchments at the point of the bayonet, this success was much favoured by the advance of some battalions of the Andalusians who moved rapidly over the rugged mountains on our right taking our enemy in flank, the pass was carried and a number of prisoners made by the Light Division, but the enemy still retained an almost inaccessible mountain towering over the rest called Mont La Rhune, on the summit of which was an old ruin, on the slopes of which the French and Spaniards kept up a constant tiralade [sic] but every effort to gain the top failed, the division went into bivouac on the ground it won.

---

[286]   Lieutenant Colonel John Hunt, 52nd Foot.

9 October. The 43rd Light Infantry sent some companies at daylight to take possession of [the] Great La Rhune and enemy was also driven from the camp at Sarre on the right, but he held a lesser height called Petite La Rhune, by nature very strong and being rather advanced from the position, for the French army seems a kind of key to it, picquets on both sides were now established between the Great and Lesser La Rhune with[in] point blank musket shot of each other with mutual tranquility.

October 1813. On the night of the 12th a French brig of war mounting 16 guns came out of the River Adour on which stands the town of Bayonne and made an attempt to get round with provisions to the small fortress of Santona, where the enemy had left a garrison under General Lamash[287] and which was blockaded by Spanish troops. She was discovered at daybreak next morning by the British schooner *Telegraph*[288] who gave chase, keeping up a fire on her which was feebly returned, but soon was becalmed and finding it impossible to weather the south bank of the Adour her crew took to their boats and reached the shore having set their brig on fire before abandoning her, she drifted out to sea floating blaze for a considerable distance and at length blew up, a dense column of smoke then ascended from the spot and not a vestige of the vessel appeared on the glassy horizon. She proved to be the *Filibustier [sic]* with a crew of 160 men.[289]

On the 24 [October] the 1st and 3rd Battalions 95th Rifles encamped on the summit of [the] Great La Rhune and the ruined hermitage, the remainder of the 1st Brigade pitched their tents lower down, the 2nd Brigade occupied the ground left by that brigade. All this period the enemy worked incessantly on their position, as also on the Petite La Rhune where they constructed a square walled redoubt on the summit of the front ridge, this height consists of rocks inaccessible in most places, and where there were any openings the enemy built high walls across them and breast-works were along the slopes on the form of traverses.

1814

18 March. The French cavalry outposts in front of the Light Division were driven back by the 15th Hussars talking prisoners a captain and 25 men of the 13th French Chasseurs, the horse artillery and 95th Rifles cooperated in the affair.

---

287 General Charles Lameth was commandant at Santona.
288 *HMS Telegraph* of 12 guns was the captured American schooner *Vengeance*.
289 The French brig *Le Flibustier* had 16 guns.

Tarbes

19 March. The Light Division marched early this morning to Obrigat which stands on a low ridge (skirting an extensive plan) along these heights our road led us by Monsfort to Aget 5 leagues. At Vic [en] Bigorre, beyond the plain a sharp tiralade [sic] was going on, in dislodging the enemy's light troops from the enclosures and vineyards about the town by the 3rd Division. The communication across the plain was kept open by our cavalry, during the day the right and centre of our army closed on Vic [en] Bigorre, as Soult had collected his army between the town of Tarbes and Rabenstens [Rabastens-de-Bigorre], placing his left on the former place. Soult held Tarbes but moved his right to [Orleix] both places standing on heights.

At daylight [20 March] the Light Division advanced through Rabenstens along the high road to Tarbes, hussars in front, the advanced posts of the enemy having been withdrawn on our approach an attack was instantly by the 2nd Battalion Riflemen on the wooded height in front of the town and notwithstanding that it was occupied by a large body of voltigeurs it was carried without a check, but on reaching the summit a French column advanced at the charge-step before which as a matter quite right in warfare, the riflemen retired, but in turn this column was driven back by a rapid advance for the 1st Battalion 95th Rifles and by a close fire of a few yards literally mowed down the French officers at the head of the column with their drummers beating the 'pas de charge', the 3rd Battalion of the 95th now moved on the flank of the enemy's position by ascending on their left and the 1st and 2nd Battalions advanced along the summit, the foe was driven back from this point on their main position, a heavy tiralade [sic] was then kept up in the vineyards between the riflemen and large bodies of French voltigeurs which caused loss to us as we had no cover and could not give up any of the ground we had taken, but from the punishing fire of our Rifles the enemy lost double our number, the remainder of the Light Division now moved up and formed in support of the riflemen on this tongue of ground, this attack having succeeded, the 6th Division under Sir Henry Clinton[290] now advanced and turned the right of the enemy, and Sir Roland [sic] Hill's Corps having cleared them from the town of Tarbes arrangements were made for a general attack but Soult put his army in retreat taking the main road to Toulouse by forced marches.

22 March. General Fane's Brigade[291] of cavalry (the 3rd Dragoon Guards and 13th Light Dragoons) defeated Soult's rear guard of

---

290 Lieutenant General Henry Clinton.
291 Major General Henry Fane.

cavalry near St Gardena [Saint-Gaudens]. My entries from personal observation ceases with the action of the 20th having been very severely wounded by the fracture of the left leg, ball lodged, left at Tarbes with several brother officers 'hors de combat.'

1814 Continued

8 November. I embarked at Ramsgate with a detachment of the 95th Rifles for Ostend in the *Mary* Transport Brig, a short rough passage brought us to our destination the following morning between nine and ten o'clock having anchored in the harbour of Ostend. It is an old fortified place surrounded by a flat uninteresting country terminating at the seaward in low sand hills and canals or dikes [sic] one cut through the former on one of these sandhills eastward of the town the French threw up a work at the point where Sir Eyre Coote landed his unfortunate expedition in May 1798. We found the 44th & 2nd British Regiments and two light battalions of the King's German Legion stationed here.

10 November. Marched the detachment to Thorout [Torhout] by a paved road of 15 miles.

[Unfortunately the extracts end abruptly here]

9. FIRST LIEUTENANT WILLIAM HAMILTON LETTERS[292]

William Hamilton, of Eden, County Donegal, was born on 17 March 1788. He became an ensign in the 42nd Foot 1804 and was promoted to lieutenant in February 1807. Hamilton served with the 42nd in the Corunna campaign and assisted at the burial of Sir John Moore. At the Battle of Corunna he received a musket ball in the leg and was dragged into one of the last boats leaving. Hamilton then served on the Walcheren Expedition, where he contracted a fever and was compelled to retire from the service due to ill health.

However, Hamilton rejoined the army as a 'Volunteer' with the 95th Rifles in the spring of 1811, embarking for Portugal to join the 1st Battalion as it followed the French army's retreat from Portugal after having starved in front of the Lines of Torres Vedras. He gained a commission as 2nd Lieutenant on 26 September 1811, seeing service at Ciudad Rodrigo (severely wounded), Badajoz, Salamanca, San Millán, Vitoria, the Pyrenees, and San Sebastian (severely wounded). He did not recover from his wounds before the end of the war.

Hamilton married in August 1816 and recovered enough to enjoy a number of field sports (including horse riding, hunting, racing, fencing and boxing) but his wounds remained a near constant source of trouble. On more than one occasion, abscesses on the lungs confined him to bed for over six months. Aged 40, he caught a severe chill on his lungs and he died on 4 May 1828 in County Donegal.

To James Hamilton Esq, Eden, Nairn, Ireland
Gibraltar 5 June 1807
My dear father,

---

[292]   From The Rifle Brigade Chronicle of 1894.

I received your letter of the 1 May, which gives me great pleasure to hear you are all well. I am sorry to say we are not to be relieved by the 6th Regiment. The 1st & 2nd Battalions of the King's German Legion are going home to join the expedition for the continent. I am afraid there is not the least chance of our being relieved for some time. We have heard that General Fox[293] has applied for us to be sent up to join him in Sicily, the Expedition to Egypt has been very unsuccessful; General Frazer,[294] who commanded, sent a detachment consisting of a 1,000 men under the command of General Wauchop[295] to take Rosetta which they succeeded in doing without any loss but in the night an army of Turks crossed the Nile above the town and cut 800 of them to pieces, they consisted of 4 companies of the 78th Regiment, four companies of the 31st Regiment and a troop of the 20th Dragoons. I am afraid it is a most disgraceful business as they were taken by surprise.

General Wauchop was killed, which is very luckey [sic] for him as by all accounts had he lived, he would have been cashiered with infamy and perhaps shot, there were two other general officers wounded. Our regiment are very anxious to have [a] dash at the Turks to retrieve the honour of the highlanders as the 78th Regiment were of that nation.

I ashure [sic] you there is not a better officer in [the] service than our commanding officer and be ashured if we have an opportunity to face our enemies we shall not disgrace our country. The Marquis of Huntley[296] goes in the expedition as lieutenant general and has applied for us to go home and serve under his command. I am much obliged to you for applying to Lord Coynyngham[297] for him to try to get me a company, be ashured [sic] since I have been in the army, I have made it my particular study [sic] to learn the military science, tactics &c and if Lord Coynyngham will apply, my commanding officer will sign any recommendation necessary. My love to my mother, grandmother, sisters and brothers, my compliments to all my other friends and believe my dear father, your affectionate son, W Hamilton 42nd Regiment

To J[ames] Hamilton Esq, Eden, Nairn, County Donegal, Ireland
Shorncliffe, 3 March 1809
My dear father,
I am just arrived from hospital which I left on the 27th of February. I am sorry to say that I among many of the officers of the army in Spain, lost

---

293   General Henry Fox Commander in Chief of the Mediterranean.
294   Lieutenant General Alexander Mackenzie Fraser.
295   Major General Patrick Wauchope.
296   Lieutenant General George Gordon, Baron Huntly.
297   Henry Conyngham, 1st Marquess Conyngham.

my baggage so much so that when I arrived at Portsmouth I had not a second shirt to put on. So unfortunate was I when I lost my baggage that twenty-five pounds, which I saved in Spain was lost along with my portmanteau. The Paymaster of our regiment was so kind as to lend me twenty pounds to cloathe [sic] myself as I was perfectly naked; so completely worn out were our cloathes with lying on the ground and hard marching, that most of ye officers and I were marching without shoes or stockings, for two days before I arrived at Corunna, I had neither shoes or stockings but marched in the bare feet.

Dear father, if you could let me have thirty pounds to repay the Paymaster and ten pounds, which I owe the mess. Had it not been I was so unfortunate in Spain, I should not want a half penny from you. Dear sir, if you can let me have it, I give you my word and honor [sic] of an officer and a gentleman I shall not have occation [sic] to ask you for any more money, I ashure [you] I don't owe a farthing in the world, but that thirty pounds.

Consider what a dreadful thing for me to [be] obliged to sell out to pay thirty pounds, which I will be obliged to do if you cannot pay it. I am now 18th lieutenant in the First Battalion, I have got within these two years 18 steps and now having returned from Spain with so much credit and honor [sic] it would be most dreadful for me to go out of such a regiment.

Now my dear father, if you can for this last time save me from ruin, I promise never to have occation [sic] to write you on such a subject again. It is with the greatest regret I mention the death of Captain Duncan Campbell[298] who was mortally wounded at the Battle of Corunna and died the following morning. I must ever regret him as one of my best friends, his purse & advice were continually open to me. Poor Duncan he found an early grave beloved by his regiment and respected by every man who knew him.

Dear Sir, if you can let me have the money in about six weeks or two months, our Paymaster can transact the business with the Paymaster of our Second Battalion who is now quartered in Dublin, I will be much obliged to you to write me by return of post. My love to my mother and sisters, brothers and all friends and believe me my dear father your affectionate son. W[illiam] Hamilton, Lieutenant 42nd light Infantry.[299]

---

298   Captain Duncan Campbell, 42nd Foot, died on HMS *Resolution* on 18 January 1809. Challis does not show that he was wounded.

299   The 42nd Foot were not officially recognised as light infantry, presumably he meant light infantry company.

PS In the action I received a slight wound above the ankle, which is perfectly recovered.

To J[ames] Hamilton Esq, Eden, Nairn, County Donegal, Ireland
[With the 95th Foot]
Portsmouth, 24 April 1811
My dear father,
I am happy to say that I embarked yesterday and hope we will sail tomorrow for Lisbon. My Ensigncy has not been sold yet, nor do I care when it will [be] as I have ordered [it] not to be sold under the King's regulation. I came on shore for the purpose of writing to you, the captain is waiting therefore must conclude with my love to dear mother, sisters & brothers and believe me, my dear father your affectionate son, W[illiam] Hamilton.

You will hear from me the moment I see Lord Wellington.

Portugal, Novo de Jismehadis [?], 12 March 1812
My dear father,
We again are on the eve of a siege that of Badajoz. The army marched from the neighbourhood of Ciudad Rodrigo on the 21st last month and succeeding [to] this part of Portugal, though we do not expect to remain here any length of time, I mean our division, some of the army are now near Badajoz, we are about fifty miles from it. I am nearly recovered from the wound I received at Ciudad Rodrigo, the ball entered into the hench bone[300] and came out inside my thigh, I am still lame but as the officers of this division are all mounted, I am able to do my duty I think and that is enough for me. This next summer, we expect sharp work as the Earl of Wellington is appointed Captain General of the Spanish army which is to be officered by the British,[301] therefore by the end of 1813 not a Frenchman will be in Spain except as a prisoner. If you can get me any letters either to Lord W[ellington] or General Pakenham,[302] I may get something handsome in Spanish army as I will be well recommended from this corps as a light infantry officer, should you be able to procure me any, send them as soon as possible, no time is to be lost, I will wait your answer before I make my application. I think in course of a month you may expect to hear of the fall of Badajoz if the French raise the siege, their army must be called from all parts of Spain,

---

[300]   Scottish for haunch bone or ilium, the upper bone of the pelvis.

[301]   This was incorrect, the Spaniards did not agree to the introduction of British officers.

[302]   Major General Edward Pakenham.

as we will have about sixty-five thousand men and under his lordship we are [rest unfortunately illegible]. Your affectionate son, W[illiam] Hamilton, Lieutenant 95th Rifles

19th instant [March 1812]
My dear father,
I had no opportunity of sending off my letter until now, I have just time to tell you we opened the trenches on [the] 17th [March] just before Badajoz and we get on very well. The enemy have this moment made a sortie which we repulsed with great loss to [the] enemy. General Hill watching Marmont, Graham observing Soult [with] four divisions at [illegible[303]] in all sixty thousand men and five thousand cavalry. We shall have the place in 20 days. Your affectionate son W[illiam] Hamilton.

[The following has been discovered from family papers]

At the storming of San Sebastian, the first man up the ladder carried by the 1st Battalion Forlorn Hope men was Lieutenant Percival,[304] who was in command and who was desperately wounded. Hamilton who was second, on gaining the top of the escarp, received the bullet under his eye and fell back into the ditch, where he was speedily surrounded by many of the dead and dying who fell from the wall above. Here he lay for a long time, being rendered speechless by the nature of his wound, but never losing consciousness and feeling convinced he should live if only he could attract attention and obtain medical aid. After the town fell and those who still lived were taken out of the ditch, he was carried to a hut and the doctor upon coming to him, considering his wound mortal, remarked that it was useless to take up his time with such a case whilst so many others who might live so urgently required attention. Most fortunately for Hamilton, a doctor of the 42nd Highlanders, a Sligo man named Early [Erly],[305] chanced to come in and on seeing him said he knew Hamilton's constitution well and that so long as there was any life in him there was hope. Early [Erly] managed to extract the broken portions of bone and 'settle' his palate, then cut out the musket ball from his shoulder. For three weeks he was fed through the spout of a broken tea pot. He was reported in the San Sebastian Return as mortally wounded and the family went

---

[303] Wellington's letter of 18 March to General Hill states that Graham was at Santa Marta.
[304] Brevet Major William Percival, 95th Foot.
[305] Surgeon John Erly, 42nd Foot.

into mourning, until he appeared at his home in County Donegal. Although he survived, he was forced to retire from the service as his palate being shot away, he was unable to give commands.

Near San Sebastian, 13 September 1813
My dear Colonel,
Being on the eve of leaving the peninsula in consequence of my wounds, disabling me from further service for some time, I am anxious before I depart to perform an act of justice towards a brave officer.

Although I have every reason to feel satisfied with the conduct of all the officers of the 95th who served with me at the late assault, as they showed themselves worthy specimens of their corps, yet the behaviour of Lieutenant Hamilton, which fell under my particular observation, was distinguished by so much gallantry, zeal and activity, that I conceive my duty to report it to you.

Lieutenant Hamilton is wholly ignorant of this representation and I have felt myself prompted to make it with a hope that something might be done for him as I fear it will be very long before he will be able to serve again. Believe me, dear Colonel, very faithfully yours, J P Hunt.[306]

[Extract from John Kincaid's 'Random Shots']
At the storming of San Sebastian I happened to be the Adjutant of the regiment and on the occasion alluded to, our quota was limited to a subaltern's command of twenty-five men and as the post of honour was claimed by our senior Lieutenant [James] (Percival), it in a manner shut the mouths would not be shut; one in particular, Lieutenant Hamilton, who had already seen enough to satisfy the mind of any reasonable man, for he had stormed at Ciudad Rodrigo and he had stormed at Badajoz, not to mention his having had his share in many and not nameless battles in the interim; yet nothing would satisfy him but that he must draw his sword in that also.

Our colonel was too heroic a soul himself to check a feeling of that sort in those under him, and he readily obtained permission to be a Volunteer along with the party.

Having settled his temporal affairs, namely, willing away his pelisse, jacket, two pairs of trousers and sundry nether garments and however trifling these bequests may appear to a military youth of the present day, who happens to be reconnoitring a merchant tailor's settlement in St James's, yet let me tell him, that at the time I speak of, they were valued as highly as if they had been hundred a year in reversion.

---

[306]   Brevet Lieutenant Colonel John Philip Hunt, 52nd Foot.

The prejudice against will making by soldiers on service is so strong that had H[amilton] been a rich man instead of a poor one he must have died on the spot, for doing what was considered infinitely more desperate than storming a breach; but his poverty seemed to be his salvation, for he was only half-killed. A ball entered under his eye, passed down to the roof of his mouth, through the palate, entered again at the collar bone and was cut out at the shoulder blade.

He never again returned to his regiment, but I saw him some years after in his native country (Ireland) in an active situation and excepting that he had gotten an ugly mark on his countenance, and his former manly voice had dwindled into a less commanding one, he seemed as well as ever I saw him.

10. FIRST LIEUTENANT JOHN MOLLOY MEMOIRS[307]

John Molloy joined the 95th Foot as a second lieutenant on 17 December 1807, serving with the 2nd Battalion at Roliça, Vimeiro and Vigo. He was promoted to first lieutenant and joined the 1st Battalion in June 1809. He went to college at Great Marlow, not returning to the peninsula until 1812, seeing action at Salamanca, San Millán, Vitoria, the Pyrenees, Vera, Bidassoa, Nivelle, Nive, Tarbes and Toulon. He also served at Waterloo, where he received his only wound.

The Peninsula and Waterloo memories of an old Rifleman
Corunna Campaign
It does not seem that the Spaniards had any particular prejudice in our favour, or any remarkable confidence in our soldiers, in the early days, at all events. When the army under Sir John Moore was retreating to Corunna, some Spanish women were heard to say 'Well, they are fine men, but they are great cowards'.

Views of Wellington
Moreover, there were officers in the army who had not the same blind confidence in their great commander which they afterwards had. William Napier[308] was very critical. In the advance from Ciudad Rodrigo in 1813, he once vented his feelings thus: 'Well here we go again. We shall get so far and then have our [asses] kicked and come back here again.' We certainly had advanced into Spain and retreated three times, but on this occasion, Lord Wellington felt so much certainty in his coming success, that in crossing the frontier he cried out, 'Adieu

---

307   From the *Cornhill Magazine*, New Series Vol. III July to December 1897.
308   Major William Napier, 43rd Foot, in 1813.

Portugal', having made arrangements to shift his base of operations to Santander in the north-east of Spain.

Barba del Puerco

Our army had sometimes to contend not only with the passive opposition and indolence of the Spanish, but also with the deliberate assistance they gave to the French, against whom we were assisting them. When the English army had to retire after Talavera, owing to the failure of the Spaniards to co-operate and to hold the passes on our flank, it was transferred to the north-eastern frontier of Portugal and four companies of the 1st Battalion of Rifles were posted along the Agueda. They held the village of Barba del Puerco, opposite to which, on the other side of the river, was San Felice [San Felices de los Gallegos] held by the French and the two villages were connected by a bridge, which was the only one below Ciudad Rodrigo. Our officers used to go down to the village and dance with the girls and an old woman used to sing a song about the celebrated guerrilla:

> Don Julian Sanchez
> Con sus lanceros
> Ira a Rodrigo
> Toma los Franceses

> [Don Julian Sanchez
> With his lancers
> Shall go to Rodrigo
> To take the French]

The padre did not like all this and went and informed the French. Their commanding officer determined on a surprise. He posted 600 men in the shadow of the rocks and one night, when the dancing had gone on till twelve o'clock, the French crept across the bridge and fell on our posts higher up the hill. They were finally driven back, however, by the Rifles under Sidney Beckwith.

The French invest Ciudad Rodrigo

This was the first meeting of English and French after Talavera and was the opening of Massena's campaign of 1810. Don Julian Sanchez was in Ciudad Rodrigo when it was surrounded by the French, but cut his way out and in doing so even attacked a French cavalry force and carried off some prisoners. Those of his troopers who had wives carried them with them, and they did their share of the fighting.

Military College, Marlow

Lieutenant Molloy after this went home and joined the Military College at Marlow, where he had as a fellow student, the future Sir George Brown, who was also in the 95th.[309] His father was at the Horse Guards and one day Brown said to him 'Jack, I'm going to exchange into the [blank – 3rd Garrison Battalion as a Captain].' This was a surprise. 'Why leave the old corps?' Jack said. 'However I suppose your father knows best'. The exchange took place and the explanation soon followed, for shortly after almost all the officers were exchanged to other regiments and Brown found himself near the top of the list.[310]

Sir George Brown was a rough mannered but kindly officer. When he was Adjutant General in 1851, Colonel Molloy was sitting in his office, when an officer came in to ask for an extension of leave. 'Go back to your regiment at once, Sir,' was the answer. 'I say George, you might have been more civil; you've got a devil of a name outside,' said Molloy. The answer was 'My dear Jack, he only wants to stay among the gambling houses'.

Juanita Smith

The future Sir Harry Smith was in the Rifle Brigade.[311] The lady who was to become his wife was a native of Badajoz, and when we captured it by storm in 1812, to save herself from the excesses of the soldiery, she fled out of the town with her sister and they placed themselves under the protection of the British officers. Juanita afterwards moved with the army. She used to ride a beautiful little Arab, and she would come out to the skirmishers when they were in action and look for her husband, 'Donde esta mi Enrique?' [Where is my Henry?]. Forty years later, when Sir Harry Smith was Governor and Commander in Chief at the Cape, he wrote to his old friend Lieutenant Colonel Molloy 'Juanita is very well, but very stout; but her ankles are as beautiful as ever'. Lady Smith lived till a few years ago[312] and I remember her describing how they all hurried off from Brussels on the road to Antwerp when the news came during the day of the Battle of Waterloo, that the English were driven back; intelligence brought by some troops (Belgian I think) who took an early opportunity of retiring from the field where their lion is now so prominent.

---

[309]   He was actually in the 43rd.
[310]   This is incorrect, he transferred into the 3rd Garrison Battalion to gain his captaincy, but exchanged two weeks later into the 85th Foot.
[311]   Captain Harry Smith, 95th Foot, brigade major of the Second Brigade of the Light Division.
[312]   She died in 1872.

Bayonne

The French and English officers who came in contact with each other on outpost duty in Spain, got in the course of time on very friendly terms and were willing to avoid useless bloodshed. One day when the armies were near Bayonne, Molloy's company was separated from the French by a stream crossed by a bridge. It was necessary to cross the bridge for some purpose or other. Molloy called out to the French officer on the other side of the stream *'Je vais vous attaquer bientot'* [I will attack you soon]. The French outpost had just cooked their dinner and perhaps thought it was merely to take a rise out of them. At all events, the officer replied merely 'Ah, bah', but the Rifles did attack and the French had to bolt, leaving their dinner behind them.

Parleying

One day, when in charge of the outlying picquets in the south of France or north of Spain, a small stream separating the two armies, his sergeant came to Lieutenant Molloy while at mess and said that five French officers wanted to see him. He went to meet them on the other side of the brook. The senior of these said *'Monsieur, j'apercois que vous avez votre epee.'* [Sir I see you have your sword]. So, Lieutenant Molloy unbuckled his sword and threw it across the stream. 'Now' he said, 'you are five and I am one'. They asked for groceries and newspapers, which he got them. One of the papers contained the bulletin which had just arrived, setting forth the reverses at Leipzig which the Grand Army had suffered. 'Oh', said the senior French officer, who afterwards turned out to be Count Reille[313] *'ne parlons pas de ca, parlons d'amour'* [Let's not talk about that, let's talk about love]. So they talked of their sweethearts at Madrid and elsewhere. The pickets used to exchange little presents of delicacies of food &c and even letters to the ladies the French officers had left behind were duly conveyed to them.

Storming of Ciudad Rodrigo

After the Battle of Toulouse, the officers used sometimes to steal into the villages within the French lines. Molloy was discussing with some milliners as to some shirts they were to make him for a hundred francs each, when an orderly came up and said [that] the commandant wished to see him. He went and found it was Reille, who he had met at the outposts as just related. Reille blew him up and sent him and

---

[313]   General Honore Reille.

his friend Johnson [Johnston],[314] who had been playing billiards in the same town, back to their lines.

This Johnson [Johnston] was in point of fact, the first man to get into Ciudad Rodrigo, though he did not get the credit. He was a very active man and some days before the assault he marked a place, apart from the breach, where he would get in, he did so and some men followed. Gurwood led the Forlorn Hope of the Light Division, and his party, who came in by the breach, found Johnson [Johnston] and his party already inside, but Gurwood went straight to the commandant's house and got his sword.

Vitoria

Lord Wellington's plans for the Battle of Vitoria depended on a very wide turning movement, to be made by Sir Thomas Graham. Of the troops under his immediate command, the Light Division got first down to the river, which formed the front of the French position. They were near a bridge and were waiting for the other divisions on their left to get to their positions on the river. While thus waiting, Lord Wellington rode up and was talking to Colonel Barnard, who commanded the Rifles and seeing some of the officers looking out with their glasses, he asked Lieutenant George Simmons[315] if he saw anything, 'Yes my Lord, I see a smoke or dust in that direction'. 'Ah let me see', said he and after looking in the direction indicated, which was probably where he expected Sir Thomas Graham to emerge from the mountains in the north, he said to Sir Andrew Barnard, 'All right; get along Barnard'. So they got under arms and went down and crossed the bridge; and afterwards Picton came up and crossed it too and said his men were the first. 'But we were the first for all that', said Colonel Molloy.

In the last rush of this battle a French officer of high rank, wearing a star, was passing him and he caught him by the ribbon, which with the star came off. The star was that of an order founded by Joseph when king of the Two Sicilies and is now in my possession.[316]

After Vitoria

In the *debacle*, the men were ordered to keep the ranks and not to move, but an officer named Stilwell,[317] said to have been a natural son of the Duke of York, who went in the regiment by the name of 'Scamp', seeing

---

314   Captain William Johnston, 95th Foot.
315   First Lieutenant George Simmons, 95th Foot.
316   The Royal Order of the Two Sicilies was established in February 1808. The decoration consisted of a five-pointed, red enamelled gold star.
317   First Lieutenant John Stillwell, 95th Foot.

a strange carriage abandoned, jumped in to see what it might contain, when an officer of rank rode up and asked what he was doing there. 'I'm looking for papers, Sir', said Scamp. 'Go back to your regiment at once, Sir,' which order was of course obeyed; but Scamp went back again very soon, when the Staff officer had gone away, and found some plunder.

Some Lifeguardsmen in a hollow road a few paces from where Lieutenant Molloy was, were appropriating the contents of the military chest which was captured. Gold was so plentiful that they did not trouble to carry away the silver, which no doubt the camp followers appropriated. There were 5½ millions of dollars and none of it came into the public chest. One of the riflemen managed to get hold of a lot of doubloons and he and his wife sewed them up in a large old Portuguese saddle, which they always carried about with them. Molloy dined with the banker at Dover where they landed after the war and he told him that one of his soldiers had that day deposited 3,000 guineas in the bank. It was this man and as it was noticed that he could always command money to get drunk, it probably mostly went in that way.

Tarbes

At Tarbes, Molloy and Leach[318] and some others were lying down behind some bushes, laughing and talking, when Molloy got up to see what was going on and found a battalion of French close on them. He roused the rest and they resisted the French, who had got so near that some were killed at their feet. They then drove them back and the Rifles advanced to the foot of the hill among some vineyards, where they halted. Lord Wellington rode up and said, 'Ah, there you are as usual, just where you should be; not gone too far.'

Guard Dogs

The advanced pickets and sentries made great use of little dogs to help in warning them of the approach of any persons.

Firing in the Rear

When making an attack, it was found very useful to send a few men to fire in the opposite direction to that in which the attack was to be made, as it was found impossible to prevent men turning towards where there was firing and so their attention was taken away from the real point of danger.

---

[318]   95th Foot.

Taking Aim
Among the French, even the tirailleurs in the peninsula and at Waterloo did not trouble themselves to take aim. They would simply put in the cartridge, tap the heel of the musket on the ground, prime and fire from the hip; and the more ammunition they could fire away the better they were pleased.

Cavalry Support
In the early part of the war, the German dragoons were the only cavalry the Rifles liked to have with them in outpost work, but afterwards the 14th Light Dragoons got into the way of it. The Germans were much more intelligent as orderlies. The English would always gallop full pelt into the lines and make them suppose something was wrong and they had to turn out; but the German, as soon as he got in sight, would halt and loose his girths or do something to show there was no urgency. The Rifles at last used to let them fly at the English orderlies, as a lesson not to annoy them in that way.

New Orleans
Sir Harry Smith, who was at New Orleans, told Lieutenant Colonel Molloy that the Rifles had got into the place behind the cotton bales, when a retreat or cease firing sounded. Sir Edward Pakenham[319] refused to let the old peninsulars go at the place, saying he thought it better to blood the noses of the young dogs.

---

[319] Major General Sir Edward Pakenham commanded at New Orleans and was killed.

11. FIRST LIEUTENANT JOHN KINCAID ON THE ACTION OF SAN MILLÁN

John Kincaid joined the 95th Foot as a second lieutenant on 27 April 1809 and he became a first lieutenant in May 1811. He was present at most actions in the peninsula from 1810 to 1814, including Foz de Arouce, Sabugal, Fuentes de Oñoro, Ciudad Rodrigo (where he volunteered for the storming party), Badajoz, Salamanca, San Millán, Vitoria, the Pyrenees, Bidassoa, Nivele, Nive, Tarbes and Toulon. He also fought at Walcheren in 1809 and at Waterloo.

Note to M Moorsom, historian of the 52nd Regiment, regarding the Action of San San Millán.[320]

Undated [late 1850s?]
What happened to the leading brigade of Maucune's Division, which was exclusively disposed of by the first battalion of the 95th? What happened to the other brigade or what regiments of the Light Division were engaged in the disposal of that brigade I cannot tell, but my journal made at the time and afterwards published, stated that in this affair, our brigade came in for all the blows and the other all the baggage, which I believed at the time was literally true, and I think if you have an opportunity of examining the casualties of that day, you will probably find that except our first battalion, no other of the division had an officer or a man hit.

I had written the forgoing long explanation before I discovered that I have misread the true tenor of your description, which you of

---
[320]   Published in 1860.

course intended to be limited to the actions of the 52nd, but I think it be most help to send it you, because it clearly points out what was done by *us*, and that with the spirit of fairness which characterizes the other portions of your book, I am in hopes you will see that in the affair of that day, you cannot separate Vandeleur's Brigade from the Light Division, without giving undue importance to the actions of that brigade at the expense of the other. We all arrived on the hill above San Millan at the same time, we were about half an hour there before our battalion was ordered to attack the brigade of Maucune's Division, which was on the road below. It was probably half an hour later before the 52nd attacked the 2nd brigade of that division, which at the time our attack was made, had not arrived within sight. I must therefore submit to you whether your description does not leave it to be inferred by those unacquainted with what took place, that there had been only one brigade of Maucune's Division near San Millan and that it had been attacked and dispersed by Vandeleur's Brigade, but as the other brigade of that same division had been defeated but a few minutes before by our old 1st Battalion I think.

If you require any further information, I shall be most happy to give it.

Believe me my dear Moorsom, very sincerely yours Kincaid

12. FIRST LIEUTENANT WILLIAM BOOTH LETTERS

Booth joined the 95th Foot in September 1806 and, served at Copenhagen, Corunna and Walcheren, before transferring to the 15th Hussars in September 1809. He returned to Portugal as a captain and fought at Vitoria, Orthez and Toulouse. He landed at Ostend on 19 May 1815 from Cork and served at Waterloo, where he had his horse shot. He later became a major and retired from the service in 1824.

We only have excerpts from his correspondence, as published in the *Regimental Chronicle of the Green Jackets*[321] but unfortunately all attempts to discover the current location of the original letters has proven unprofitable.

October 1806
It is not usual to keep the officers of our regiment so long at drill as the 43rd and 52nd, the nature of our service not so particularly requiring it.

November 1806
I have perfectly made up my mind never to quit the regiment for any other infantry battalion, as long as it remains a rifle regiment. I now and then take a look at the dragoons when at squadron exercise upon the common; H who married Mrs F's sister is a captain in them and a poor insignificant ugly fellow he is; he as well as all the other officers appear loaded with hussar finery, such as would astonish a Yorkshireman. They are very capitally mounted upon rather strong horses but are allowed to be the worst disciplined in the service on account of having a bad commanding officer at their head.[322]

---

[321]   Published in the 1932 and 1933 editions.
[322]   I have not been able to identify this regiment with any certainty.

[Later he wrote]

I am situated in a particular service that I would not exchange for a first lieutenancy in any other regiment of infantry in the service, as you know how I detest all heavy slow manoeuvres. The 52nd and 43rd are both beautiful light infantry regiments and are very expert in both light and heavy movements, but yet the very nature of our service is totally different from theirs, as one of our companies is at all times supposed to act perfectly independent to any other; all other regiments but the 52nd and 43rd are called by our officers, 'gravvies'. The former are only light 'gravvies'.

Isle of Walcheren, West Souburg[323] 10 August 1809
Dear cousin,
I take this opportunity of giving you a short account of ourselves by an officer of our regiment who is returning to England in consequence of being wounded, all sick are as well as the men are returning home since their service can no longer be acceptable.

We landed in this island on Sunday evening the 30 August last without opposition, but with as much precaution as if we were to have attacked double our numbers. We remained on the sand hills all night without anything happening more than some slight skirmishing between not wiser parts of our light troops & those of the enemy firing away a great quantity of ammunition at nothing else but the thick bushes where the enemy had retired into. I must not forget to tell you though that one of our truest fire eaters, impatient of smelling gunpowder, pushed rather too forward with his regiment to attack a fort the moment he landed, which terminated (as might naturally have been expected) with his getting a complete drubbing & obliged to make a perceptible retreat. The fort has since surrendered after being bombarded by all our gun boats.

The third day after our landing was passed in skirmishing and driving in the French picquets detached from Flushing [Vlissingen] and finally arriving within the reach of the batteries of the town. From that time to this day, we have had continued skirmishing with our advanced posts & those of the enemy and am sorry to say have suffered very considerably on account of our having so very few light troops and the enemy a great number. The town has now been invested about 8 or 9 days and we are now ready to commence the bombardment which is expected will be in the course of a day or two. The French

---

[323]   2km south of Middleburgh in Holland.

general says he is determined to hold out as long as one of his men remains and to die [the] same, so that the probability is that we shall after all expend a quantity of stores and ammunition and lose a great number of useful subjects in reducing a paltry fishing town, which if we ever take possession of [at] this moment, is not worth the men we have already lost. We are totally ignorant of the intentions of our sage cabinet at home, but it is generally believed that it will be madness to proceed to Antwerp as was originally intended, as the French are now pouring an immense force [in]to that garrison. You will see by the papers that our detachment which consists only of 780 men has suffered very much, being continually on the enemy's advanced posts. We have two officers severely and one slightly wounded, the two former are gone home. Thank God I still remain with my head on & my bones unbroken though the first day was very near dishing me, as a light six pounder [cannonball] dashed through a hedge betwixt my legs, providentially doing me no more injury than tearing my loose trousers, but unfortunately killed a poor fellow of the 85th Regiment which made me first as sick as a dog, but from the continuous daily scenes of this kind since we landed, I have become almost as hardened as a cannonball. I have now seen so much of campaigning & the good effects produced by our expedition that should I come home with my limbs on I shall think it advisable to bid adieu to this *honourable profession*. Remember me to all & believe me in haste, yours very sincerely W Booth.

13. FIRST LIEUTENANT GEORGE SIMMONS LETTER ON JOINING 95TH FOOT

George Simmons joined the 95th Foot as a second lieutenant on 25 May 1809, from the Lincolnshire Militia. He received this letter one month before joining the 95th, when his application to join them had been approved.

To Ensign & Assistant Surgeon G[eorge] Simmons, Lincolnshire Militia, Hythe Barracks.
Lamerick, 11 April 1809
My dear Sir,
Painful as it is to me not to promote the gratification of the wishes of him who from the time we first became acquainted & connected in our relative military duties, has in every part of his conduct confirmed the good opinion I was predisposed to entertain & unalterably secured my esteem, I should feel more pain & consider it a far more doubtful testimony of my very sincere regard were I without extreme repugnance even at last be driven to acquiesce to them. After turning the request you have made over & over again in my mind, looking at it in every point of view I am capable of, the first impression still remains and that for you to pass the *bourne*, over which there can be no return, would in all probability expose you to more bitter disappointment than those you now are so acutely sensible of from the illiberal austerity of the Deputy Inspector, or will be likely to experience in the persevering pursuit of your profession, to the practical labour of which you have made yourself so equal, have always declared it to be your pleasure & of which the drudgery of attaining the first principles

of practise, is happily past [sic] by. All that remains for you to acquire is the *finish* that perseverance will confirm & the success which your merit deserves & your unremitting perseverance I have no doubt will without the *hair breadth escapes with imminent deadly breach,* (mind I do not use this expression in the ludicrous light sense into which some might be apt to pervert it) happily secure. You say you have been happy in the regiment & have even experienced every mark of friendship from your brother officers. Why then not be content with the happiness you are so sensible of & go to seek with all its charms the 'something impossible' & indulge the craving void *left* aching in your breast. But you lay a stress upon the *necessity* of the step & without that intrusion of its pinching & coercive violence, you had no real preference of the cutting sabre to the pricking lancets. Before I throw aside my pen or direct it to some other course, I will hope I shall cut up that plea, which strikes me to be used much in the same way & with equal right as the exclamation of the apologising pitiable unfortunate Jane Shore.[324] My poverty consents but not my will, I will leave this to you to ponder upon & request you to search your own motives & answer me when I come up to the regiment, for then it will be in good time, if you do really love its society, have pleasure in your situation & are not disgusted with your profession, there is not at the bottom some bilious affections, I would call it pique, that assuming the appearance of necessity, has unexpectedly wrought this strange passion of a change which appears to me so contrary to your interest & which I beg you to persuade yourself & not be unpersuaded by any other I have warmly at my start. You add, the consideration of being with your brother,[325] as another powerful motive for inducing you to change & but for which, would be attended with *'almost insupportable reticence'*. I have significantly marked the three last words in your sentence that you may not insignificantly pass them by & I not led to think them words of con[sidered?] prose & [*purchase hastily?*]. I like above all things the love of brothers. Yet allow me to ask you, giving your affectionate feelings all the credit they justly deserve, more than sufficiently established by the warm interest you have already taken to obtain the patronage of Colonel Beckwith in *this* favour, how long you dare rationally calculate on being *together,* whether you have

---

[324]   Jane Shore was a mistress of King Edward IV, after his death she was accused of being a harlot and condemned to do public penance in St Paul's Cathedral.

[325]   The reference to his brother is obscure. His brother Joseph did not join the army until April 1812, joining the 23rd Foot as an ensign and transferring to the 95th Foot as a second lieutenant in June 1812.

prospectively contemplated how much either would more severely feel the bitterness & the natural sorrow of separation if by climate, intrigue, in battle or from any accidental cause one or other should so circumstanced, prematurely fall. To judge of yours, by my own feelings, I would much rather serve in any other corps but that in which my brother, or a friend little less dear than a brother was. One line or little more will fill up my paper enough. I trust to convince you, I am no prosing mind & shall assert myself with my utmost strength to extract *secundum artum* [according to the practice] the stamp of necessity which has caused you all this intolerable anguish. I will beg your acceptance of 20 guineas which will help to drive the wind from your purse & if you [need more?] & shall find yourself desirous of filling up the chasm of reckons you are [suffering?] from, by the arbitrary & indiscriminating order you so unexpectedly received, do you suspect it to have originated from any insidious misrepresentation. I wish I had known it on the instant, I might possibly have counteracted it, I will with as much satisfaction as I shall do this. As soon as I set my foot within the barracks, for the same laudable purpose, be ready to repeat the dose, on this express condition, that you will not open your strifes to anyone upon this proof of my confidence in you. It will be enough to say to everyone you choose, that you had placed before me your wishes, but they had not met my approbation & 'from the many favours received at my hands, which must ever make on your mind an impression at once grateful& indelible' you cheerfully yielded your wishes to my judgement. My dear Sir, your sincere friend & faithful & obedient servant H Waldo-Sibthorp[326]

Note attached much later by George Simmons:

Colonel Sibthorp was my first commanding officer and also a very kind friend, he regretted to lose me, paying me much respect as *his* medical man, but all his kindness was of no avail, I had volunteered into the 95th or Rifle Corps as a second lieutenant and induced 150 men to follow my example. Nothing on earth could have altered my determination. My word (thank God) was ever dearer to me than life. I am forced to say I am still of this opinion in 1845!! George

---

[326]   Colonel Humphrey Sibthorpe of Canwick House, Royal South Lincoln Militia. In 1804 he took on the additional surname of Waldo following a sizeable bequest from Peter Waldo, a relative who had died childless.

14. FIRST LIEUTENANT EDWARD MADDEN LETTERS

Edward Madden joined the 95th Foot as a second lieutenant in May 1811 and was promoted to first lieutenant in May 1813. He saw service at San Millán, Vitoria, the Pyrenees, Vera, Bidassoa, Nivelle and Waterloo.

Camp near Vera, 18 July 1813
My dearest father and mother,
It is with extreme of grief I write to console with you on the loss of our dear, beloved and noble Henry.[327] You may imagine my grief and astonishment after the most favourable reports I had heard of him, at receiving a dreadful letter from his surgeon mentioning his mournful death; he was wounded through the lungs and died on 11 [July]. He thank God, did not suffer so severely as in most instances and retained his senses to the last. The pain I feel at the loss of a beloved and virtuous brother is great; but not so much so as that for the situation of his distracted and loving Charlotte.[328] However, I trust that heaven will quickly put an end to her woes and join them both in heaven; their happiness was too great for this world. I will not ask you my dearest parents to abstain from grief for it would be unnatural not to feel for the loss of such a son. But I trust you will not allow it to prey upon your minds but recollect that it is God's will and that you have to live and exert yourselves for the remainder of your dutiful and affectionate children!! Bear it with patience and resignation and bow to the will of our great and merciful creator who will repay you tenfold

---

[327] Lieutenant Colonel Henry Ridewood, 45th Foot, was his stepbrother. He had previously served in the 52nd Foot.
[328] His wife.

for your misery in this world. Oh God, the greatest misery I feel is for our dearest, unfortunate Charlotte, but let us turn from this miserable subject. We have crossed the Pyrenees and are only half a league from France. 54,000 of the French are in one of the strongest positions in the world, in front of us, who we expect to attack as soon as San Sebastian falls which is now besieged by a naval force. Of our success I have not the least doubt. I have not spirits to say more. Give my love to my dearest sisters and Wyndham[329] and trusting my dearest parents that you will bear with resignation your loss and rely on God's mercy I remain your dutiful and affectionate son, E[dward] Madden.

---

[329]   Lieutenant Wyndham Madden, 43rd Foot.

15. SERGEANT JOHN LOWE ADDRESS

The humble address of John Lowe, late Sergeant of His Majesty's 2nd Battalion of the 95th Regiment, to Field Marshal His Grace the Duke of Wellington, Commander in Chief[330]

Lamberhurst Kent, 29 January 1827

John Lowe desires to approach His Grace, the Commander in Chief, in the most respectful manner, and to solicit His Grace's attention to a statement of his humble military life, which he hopes will obtain for him his Grace's favour.

John Lowe volunteered from the Flint Militia, in which he had served about six years, to enlist in the 2nd Battalion of the 95th, in the year 1807, and first saw service against the enemy at Copenhagen. John Lowe belonged to one of the four companies of the 95th which, under the command of Major Travers,[331] were engaged at Caldas and elsewhere, previously to the Battle of Vimeiro, in which he also shared, and received a severe flesh wound, through the left thigh, which caused him to be in the hospital about seven weeks.[332]

Vimeiro

Yes, I recollect that affair. The sharpshooters were the company I belonged to. We were on picquet the night preceding the battle and Captain Leach,[333] upon visiting rounds, about nine o'clock, came up to

---

[330]   The following is a combination of excerpts from John Lowe's memorandum, with further recorded comments added which were made by John Lowe and published as notes to the published version of the address in London by the Reverend Newnham in 1827.

[331]   Major Robert Travers, 95th Foot.

[332]   He meant regimental hospital under the care of the surgeon; but not all along incapable of doing duty. He did not receive his wound till very nearly the conclusion of the firing at Vimeiro.

[333]   Captain Jonathan Leach, 95th Foot.

where I was posted and said to me 'Lowe, don't you hear the tattoo? We must be very much upon the alert, for depend upon it, it is French music, and we shall be attacked tomorrow'. It was just as the captain predicted; for I had not been long placed as advanced sentinel, early in the morning before dawn, came upon us a host of French light troops, which it was impossible for a handful of men to stand against. We consequently retired, the French light troops and column following us quickly, till we formed at last behind the 50th. And does not Sir Walter [Scott] speak of the impetuosity with which the train of French light artillery also came down, breaking even through part of the English line and almost intermixing with the British artillery? The guns were captured, every man and horse killed!

Does not Sir Walter mention the attack of another French column upon the 43rd? Did Sir W Scott[334] count half as many couples as I did, composed of a brave 43rd and Frenchman, transfixed by each other's bayonet, where they met in the vineyard and the narrow lane? Though I had often seen the thrust of a bayonet before, as I have since, I think I never saw so severe a tussle as this. The picquet of the 95th having before this event, joined the other three companies, we were ordered to reinforce the 43rd; but it had done the work; we were too late to share in the charge and had only to pursue the fugitives.

And does not Sir Walter make mention of what, besides the Duke and other officers the brave general of our division (Fane[335]) was about? Did he not see, as I saw the general, after having exerted his vigilant eye and voice like thunder in one direction, rush in a contrary one and make a desperate back blow with his sword at an English artilleryman, who it was to be feared through inexpertness, or faint heartedness or what not, was thinning the ranks of the 50th instead of the French? How well that man's place was supplied immediately; how his successor as if to repair the damage done, directed the gun so accurately, that he quickly produced a gap and a wave in the French column, which I cannot liken to anything better than the gates of a fortified town being suddenly made to turn upon their hinges and open.

Retreat to Corunna
In the retreat of Sir John Moore, our company had crossed the bridge of Benavente, the last but those who had the charge of sapping and blowing it up; and it was thought that this explosion would afford the men, exhausted in every way, a halt sufficient to serve out a ration

---

334   Lowe appears to think that Scott was an ex officer and eyewitness to the conflict.
335   Brigadier General Henry Fane.

of spirits for each. I happened to be one of those despatched for the spirits and when we returned, nearly the whole were fast asleep upon their arms; nor could we, as it seemed allowable for them to make the choice, induce more than a very few to rise and secure for themselves the precious drops. Unlucky fellows! I had but just poured my own and the share of two comrades into my canteen, when the bugle sounded to arms; the liquor moved off; and the vivacity of the sleepers was put to the test. They were up in a moment, and in the next, turned out, in the very best fashion of the 95th, to face the enemy; and I know not when they were afforded an opportunity for a nap again, several I believe, not till they slept for good.

Walcheren
In the expedition to Walcheren, John Lowe was with the 95th and there suffered severely from the ague, which continued upon him, with almost unabated violence, when orders came to Hythe for four companies of the battalion to embark for Portugal and he was deemed and declared, on parade, by his captain, to be, on account of the said ague, totally unfit to go; but the consequent distressing thoughts of being left behind his company, and his desire to embark, somehow or other, operated so wonderfully upon his constitution, that in one night, the ague quite left him and he obtained what was the object of his ambition; nor did he suffer (he believes) from that day forward to the conclusion of his services in the peninsula, any illness, saving that arising from his wounds, which compelled him to be absent from his duty a single day.

Peninsula
John Lowe, after thus embarking, was in many of the general engagements with the enemy, besides a number of affairs of less consideration in which his battalion was concerned. He can mention Salamanca, Vitoria, Vera, Toulouse and finally Waterloo.

Ciudad Rodrigo
At the siege of Ciudad Rodrigo, whilst employed in levelling the redoubt of St [San] Francisco, he received, from a splinter of a shell, a considerable cut on the head, which stunned and felled him for a time; but on being able to rise, he continued at his job, with his head bound up by one of his comrades, till regularly relieved: nor did he lie by at all after it had been bandaged by the surgeon; and at the last push, he mounted the ramparts along with his battalion.

I will tell you in private, though I would not have you state it in my memorial to the Commander in Chief, that I was one of the very first; for as I was young, healthy, strong, five feet ten without shoes and was frequently selected on account of figure, activity and adroitness, to play the flugleman[336] on parade, so I felt very unwilling to be excelled, by any of the battalion, in turning our drill to an account. You must have heard Sir, for we at least of the 95th and the whole army, had ample opportunity to know the gallantry was great of General Craufurd, who fell in the attack, within two or three yards of me. The general commanded our division and had led the advance to which I belonged, near to the walls, where the woolpacks (intended to assist us in passing the ditch) not being up, we were lying under every little cover at hand, as close as possible, for concealment sake and with the strictest orders not to utter a word. Impatient however for the arrival of the woolpacks, the general himself quickly broke through this silence and cried out for Colonel Elder[337] and the Portuguese cacadores, in whose charge they were, in a too audible voice, besides manifesting his gallant spirit and disappointment, by the utterance of words which I will not mention. A moment after this, a fireball, from the walls, being thrown near us, was followed by a discharge of small arms and the general fell, only saying 'I am done for'. The Portuguese, for what reason I know not, not being now up, we crossed the ditch without the use of woolpacks and easily passed the breach, it neither being well defended, where we attacked by chevaux de frise, other contrivances or men. The infantry who had lined the walls retired for the purpose, as it turned out, of making a stand in the streets, where the 95th, covered by the 3rd Division, had a sharp encounter with them; and it may be excusable perhaps for me, who am out of the battalion now, yet as fond of its good character as ever, to add that as we were pushing on, I heard the colonel of the 88th say to his men 'Come on my noble Connaught Rangers, the 95th, the glory of your country is in your front!' At length, when the 95th and other regiments got to the market place, they found none inclined to bargain for any more firing and the British Colours soon became visible and respected on a post, where a skilful enemy had contended that none but the French should be suffered to wave.

Badajoz

At the siege of Badajoz he was one of the six volunteers from his company for the Forlorn Hope, of which six, only two survived the storm. Whilst

---

336   A soldier who leads the way or demonstrates drill.
337   Captain Sir George Elder of the 95th Foot had joined the Portuguese Army in 1809 and had risen to the rank of lieutenant colonel, commanding the 3rd Cacadores.

nearly upon the lowest round [rung] of a ladder, in descending into the parapet, he was brought roughly to the ground, close to and at the same instant as, Lieutenant Manners,[338] by a severe wound in his left shoulder, from a splinter of a shell; and he trusts it will be permitted to a grateful soldier to express here, without giving any offence, the much greater impression this wound (which inflamed and sloughed quite down to the elbow) made upon his mind, since it led to his seeing, whilst in the hospital at Elvas, His Grace the Commander in Chief condescending to stand by his bedside, to enquire carefully into the nature of his wound, and the state of his appetite and to order him an additional allowance of two measures of wine per day. What a gallant young officer [Manners]! What a determined leader on! Never a follower if he could help it! Always so good tempered! So beloved by the men!

As the night was dark, I could see, but very indistinctly, the ladder I descended, except during the flashing of guns; but there was such a splendid illumination, such a plentiful supply soon, of this sort of light, that I have no excuse, in respect of absence of sunshine, or moonshine, for being inaccurate about the hollow or ditch into which I came tumbling.

As I was not in a condition to go on myself, it seemed to me to be prudent to retire the way I came; but retirement from such a situation was not easily effected. Who there were by and around me in an equal or worse condition, I did not very well know, saving that I quickly recognised Lieutenant Manners. Shall I say that I did so by his condemning his leg for failing him in such a moment, in terms not usual for him to utter and not recommended for common use? He rose to go on, but again he laid it all to the fault of his ineffective leg and fell. Upon this, we chose a little rising ground near at hand, as a place of rest and observation. It was from this spot that I witnessed explosions of mines, not far off, one of which is supposed to have carried up Major O'Hara of the 1st Battalion 95th,[339] of whom nothing afterwards was found but a part of one leg in his Wellington boot. It was from this spot I could hear further on, noise indescribable arising from the desire of our brave Forlorn Hope to be admitted through the breach and the determination of the enemy to keep them outside. It was on this spot I had the mortification to listen to the bugle sounding their retreat! And what more reached my ears? Whilst we were sitting, a part of the 4th Division marched by to supply the place of the Forlorn Hope in the attack and one from the ranks (very probably a brave man only too

---

338   First Lieutenant Henry Manners, 95th Foot.
339   Major Peter O'Hara, 95th Foot.

jocular, yet possibly a jester whose tone lowered as he approached the difficulties) cried out 'Well Light Division, never boast any more, since you can't take the town!' What! To be taunted with boasting and ill success at such a moment! This speech was to me, my other shoulder out of socket! Lieutenant Manners quite growled!

On the 4th Division went! … that they also were not called off, till they had given ample proofs, besides the loss of life and limb, of most determined courage! By this time some assistance was procured for Lieutenant Manners, from some of the retreaters of the Forlorn Hope. He was conveyed up the ascent and thence to the surgery. Which of us was first wounded it is impossible to say. My legs however, gave me the advantage over him and I was a moment before him at the surgery. When therefore the surgeon said 'Now Lieutenant Manners, I am ready to attend upon you Sir!' He replied 'My turn is not yet come, that man has been waiting longest' and he insisted upon my wound being first dressed. When it had been dressed I was not yet incapable of moving, and with my arm in a sling, I felt an eager wish to visit the town, principally to survey the breach. This I did, and there I saw the huge chevaux de frise! And I am not, here also, engineer enough to describe what various other defences a brave and skilful enemy had prepared; but this I know. That I well noticed, close by the breach, a mass of bodies, clothed in green jackets and trousers, and with a black feather in their cap, with hardly room between them, for many yards together, sufficient for the observer to rest his foot!

The French
Fine troops the French, Sir! How admirably have I often seen them behave, as well when matters were going on well with them, as when they were quite out of luck.

The first day that I was capable of taking a very slight share of duty, after my wound at Vimiera, was when the French gave up to us the citadel at Lisbon; and in a leisure hour, I was invited by some French soldiers to accompany them to a wine shop which I did. 'Let us be friends' said they 'whilst we can, there will be plenty of opportunities to give each other cross looks, and hard blows, when we meet again, in the field under our respective officers.' And after the Battle of Vitoria, whilst San Sebastian and Pamplona delayed the advance of the army, I have, when on picquet on the cold Pyrenees, more than once been sent out on a foraging party, with two or three companions, for a little wood, to be collected from some old deserted dwelling and a like or a larger number of Frenchmen have entered for wood also, when we each procured our burthen, working on quite close to the strangers, not merely without offering or experiencing molestation, I might rather say with sociability and good humour. But the smartest and most agreeable fellow, the most intimate friend I picked up among them on the Pyrenees, was when I was placed sentry, one most stormy night, within a few yards of a large chestnut tree, a French soldier being as far off on the other. For some time we were silent, and stationary, but upon the rain increasing, we both looked at the tree and seemed mutually to be of opinion that it was unwise not to make its branches serve as our umbrella and in doing so conversation began, and we did not separate till we had interchanged the civility of drinking from each other's canteen.

The quantity [of the two measures] should be stated as about two pints. The wine was but light wine and our cases required further support. I believe too, that in the 95th I was considered a tolerably temperate man; and above all, I endeavoured to be as much as possible upon my guard against the destructive use of spirits. But I ought to bear testimony to the advantage of an allowance of your brandies and rums, and gins to a soldier, when disposed to use them properly. Many a time have I been nearly exhausted, when a few drops of one or the other, and nothing but a few bits of biscuit, have set me quite right, brought me back from a state of second childhood to manhood, made me fit for a soldier's work again!

Bidassoa
At the Battle of Vera, on the 7th of October, after the 52nd and 95th had established themselves upon the heights, and whilst they were following the enemy from post to post, John Lowe received a severe wound in his right hand, which once more compelled him to be sent to the hospital; but he was fortunately up with his company again three days before the Battle of Toulouse.

Promotion
It was sometime before the Battle of Vitoria, that John Lowe was made a corporal; and he was further advanced to the rank of sergeant, when about to embark for the continent, previously to the Battle of Waterloo.

Waterloo
In this great engagement, after various skirmishes, he had, in an advance, the misfortune to be driven, along with two lieutenants and several more of the 2nd Battalion 95th, by an overwhelming column of the enemy's lancers, as prisoner into a sort of straw yard, to the

rear of the enemy's line,[340] where they were at one time questioned by a general, (understood to be Bonaparte) and his aides de camp; but profiting at last from a temporary confusion among the enemy, John Lowe, as all unanimously attempted to do, succeeded in rejoining his battalion, and remained with it till between six and seven, (as far as a soldier so engaged could judge) when he received, in the act of charging a brigade of light artillery, a grapeshot, which, entering his body under his left ribs, passed close to his backbone, and then out of his right side. This shot caused him to fall, and he remained in the field, without assistance, two nights, one whole day and part of another day, (quite sensible all the time) when he was picked up by two Hanoverians, and removed to the hospital at Waterloo, and thence passed, successively, to Brussels and Gosport,[341] and he ultimately rejoined the depot of the 95th at Shorncliffe.

Reduction and Pension

Upon the reduction of the 95th, (then under orders for Ireland,) John Lowe had served in the 2nd Battalion 95th a period of 11 years 4-12ths, which, with the addition of the two years graciously allowed by his Majesty to the troops at Waterloo, amounted to 13 years 4-12ths.

Above all, John Lowe knows how deservedly he might incur reprehension were he to presume to observe here, that if Colonel Norcott,[342] under whom he served so long, had been present at the reduction; or if he, John Lowe, had been in possession (which he was not) of sufficient certificates of his services and wounds, to have exhibited his case fully to his then commander, Colonel Gilmour,[343] under whom he marched so little, and who could know nothing of him but by report; and if, when before Sir D. Dundas[344] and the rest of the Board at Chelsea, he had had the same certificates to produce; it would be very inexcusable indeed, John Lowe is convinced, for him to endeavour to express to his Grace the Commander in Chief, that then, though the reduction happened (some have said somewhat unfavourably for him) eight months previously to the completion of his second period of service, his country might possibly have thought

---

[340] This would appear to have occurred between 4.30 and 5 pm when the squares of the brigade were arraigned along the front face of the allied ridge to break up the cavalry charges.

[341] The Naval Hospital at Haslar.

[342] Lieutenant Colonel Amos Godsill Norcott commanded the battalion at Waterloo.

[343] Lieutenant Colonel Dugald Gilmour.

[344] General Sir David Dundas was Governor of the Royal Hospital Chelsea from 1804 until his death in 1820.

him not undeserving of something more than his Waterloo medal and a pension of sixpence per day.

… John Lowe, thankful for the provision of six pence per day … retired from the 2nd Battalion 95th to the village of Lamberhurst in Kent (the native place of his wife) where he has ever since resided (now the only Waterloo medal man) struggling to obtain a livelihood by working as a cordwainer, whilst his wife undertakes the education of a few young children. In working however, with the tools of his trade, he often feels considerable inconvenience and sometimes experiences almost a complete hindrance, from the wound received on the back of his right hand on the 7th of October, at Vera, the ball having first struck him close to his wrist, then in its course, partially destroyed both veins and tendons, till it reached and tore away nearly the whole of the main knuckle of the third finger, rendering that finger quite useless, whilst it almost as badly crippled a second and stiffened a third. From the act of stooping, also necessary in his trade, as well as from the change of weather, the wound through his body (which at all times makes him, when standing, less upright in his shoes than when he marched to Waterloo) often causes him considerable pain and stiffness; and John Lowe, having already a family of four young children to maintain, cannot but sometimes allow the reflection to cross his mind, how ill his wife and children would be off, were either, his stated wounds seriously to inflame and his application to his tools to be thus long, necessarily interrupted. In a word, he cannot but suppose he might be subject to be compelled, in order to relieve the Parish of Lamberhurst from the burthen, to be driven from his present home, and the possibility of resuming his little established trade, to the Parish of Mold, in the County of Flint, which he has never visited since he entered the 95th and where he believes he has no remaining relations or friends, there perhaps only to obtain in the poor house what would, with his pension of sixpence per day, be barely sufficient to maintain so young and large a family …

John Lowe will now, after soliciting His Grace's pardon for so long an address, only venture further to add, that if any testimony to his military behaviour in the 2nd Battalion 95th be wanting, he has the confidence to think that Colonel Norcott and other officers under whom he served, would be far from unwilling to speak in his behalf; and further, that if enquiry should be made at Lamberhurst, whether John Lowe has not disgraced his Waterloo medal, but on the contrary conducted himself throughout, peacefully civilly, soberly and honestly, there will not be wanting many respectable inhabitants of the village to vouch for this likewise.

16. PRIVATE ROBERT HOWARTH LETTER REGARDING COPENHAGEN[345]

Letter to his father, September 1807

I shall give you an account of what has happened since I left England. I embarked on board the *Urania* transport, at Harwich on the 25th of July and remained in harbour till the 1st of August, when we set sail and arrived safe on the coast of Denmark on the 9th and anchored close under Elsinore Castle,[346] one of the strongest places I ever saw in my life. We remained there till the 16th, when we landed within a few miles of Copenhagen and marched up the country. Early the next morning, the 17th, we came within about two miles of the city, when we were ordered to halt at some small villages to get some refreshment. About two o'clock, our regiment was ordered to advance upon their outposts, which were about one mile from the town. We marched down upon them without firing one shot; but when they perceived we advanced, they began to fire upon us with their artillery very smartly, but without effect. We gained our position within one mile of the city and remained there till the 21st, during which time the enemy kept up a brisk fire from their battery upon us, and we had severe skirmishes with their outposts and picquets; but early in the morning of the 21st, our regiment was ordered out to drive them all into the town if possible. We marched down upon them with as little noise as possible and was ordered not to fire till we came close to them, when we fired a few shot at them. When they perceived us, they gave

---

345   From the Historical Manuscripts Commission, 14th Report Appendix part IV, The Manuscripts of Lord Kenyon (1894).

346   Kronborg Castle.

way and we took up our position over the first drawbridge and drove them over the second.

On the 25th the whole of the army was ordered under arms, about two o'clock in the afternoon and received orders to advance upon the town. We all thought that we were going to make the grand attack, but we only drove them all from their batteries and made them to fly into the city, the only place left them to go to, for we had the possession of the suburbs and the action lasted about two hours, during which time the enemy lost a great number of men killed, wounded and prisoners. Our regiment had only one man wounded and none killed, for we have always the best chance, although we are always in front of the rest of the regiment [army], being riflemen. On the 26th, the Light Brigade, consisting of 9 companies of our regiment,[347] the 43rd, 52nd, 92nd and two brigades of artillery, with four troops of the German Legion light dragoons, was ordered to the rear of the army to attack an army of the enemy that we heard was coming to attack our army in the rear; their strength was reported to be between 8,000 and 9,000. We marched three days and could hear nothing of them till late on the 28th. On the 29th we marched early in the morning to a town called Kioge, where we were informed the enemy was. About ten o'clock we came in sight of the town, where we halted and sent the artillery and light dragoons in front of the town. When the enemy perceived them, they began to fire on them from their batteries. We were then ordered to fall in and marched up to the town. Our five companies of the First Battalion, which I belong to, were ordered out to the front of the other regiments. The action began a little before eleven o'clock and continued till about five in the afternoon. When we began to advance upon the town they fired very smartly both great and small guns. When we came within 50 yards of the enemy, our five companies that were in front, were ordered to the rear of the other regiments to let them charge, but they would not go, so we gave three cheers and charged them ourselves, with three companies of the 92nd and two troops of light horse. We drove them all out of the town with great loss on the enemy's side. We pursued them for two or three miles into the country.

When all was over, we found ourselves in possession of 9 pieces of cannon, besides a great number of ammunition and provision waggons and fifteen hundred prisoners. That day and the two following days, their own account of their killed, wounded and prisoners are 840 killed

---

[347]   Most records show that there were five companies each of the 1st and 2nd Battalion, 95th, present, making ten companies in all.

and wounded and 3,100 prisoners. On the 6th of September, the city of Copenhagen surrendered, after being burning two days and nights and the same day there was a great quantity of money taken that they were sending away. The whole amount of money taken is twenty-one millions and some thousands, but you will hear more in the papers than I am able to tell you in a letter. Do not write again, as we expect to leave this place in a short time as we have nothing more to do here, and British soldiers must not lie idle at this time.

17. WILLIAM SANKEY
MEMORIES OF HOSPITAL[348]

He commenced serving as an army surgeon in the Peninsular War, attached to the Rifle Brigade. On one occasion he related that he was in charge of a field hospital arraigned on the hill above the fortified town of Alicante, where on the occasion of a battle he had a second experience. Being short-handed and overwhelmed with the number of wounded men brought in, he sent his sole Assistant [Surgeon] down to Alicante to seek help, but instead of securing it, the Assistant himself was kept in the town all night, the gates having been closed while he was delivering his message.

Mr Sankey, deprived of all his usual help, had to work all night single-handed. In those days it was the practice after extracting a ball to put a linseed poultice on the wound. The great pot of linseed and water had to be kept hot and stirred and as young Sankey could not stir the pot and extract bullets, he had to elicit some of the least hurt patients to stoke and stir, while he went from man to man extracting bullets, which dropped one by one into his pocket, so that before his task was done his pockets were full and the linseed pot was empty. Mr S[ankey] served as Surgeon with the army under Sir John Moore in Spain & Sicily and after four years at the front he was invalided home, attached to the Rifle Brigade at Shorncliffe in the early part of the year 1814 attached to the Light Division.

The Battle of the Nive
This ground had not been long occupied before the enemy attacked the allies; and the first attempt appeared to have been directed against this central position. The French army advanced along the summit ridge from Bayonne, bring up their masses of infantry very near and opening a battery of cannon at about five hundred yards only from the church

---

[348]   Published in the *Dover Express* of 11 January 1907.

[at Arcangues]. I deserves [sic] here to be recorded, that the outposts of the 52nd Regiment had been so well fortified by a captain (Captain George Barlow[349]) of that regiment, that the pickets had no occasion to retire until they had fired their sixty rounds of ammunition. This officer had taught himself how to strengthen posts by barricades and other temporary expedients and he deserved the support he always received from the Engineers, who supplied him with what he required from their small depot of entrenching tools. The pickets being thus enabled to hold their ground without risk for a considerable time, the troops for the defence of the main central position had full time to assemble (for it was in December and they were scattered in houses) and to deploy on the position, the greater part being somewhat retired behind the slope of the ground. There was nothing in the defences which impeded the usual formation and everything was prepared to maintain this ground offensively. The enemy not choosing to attack here, moved in the afternoon to their right.

---

[349]   George Barlow was only a lieutenant in the 52nd Foot. He became a captain in the 69th Foot on 30 December 1813.

18. BRIGADIER GENERAL ROBERT CRAUFURD LETTERS[350]

The Light Division was most famously commanded by the irascible Brigadier General Robert Craufurd (Black Bob), who was both admired and hated in equal measure by his men.

Robert Craufurd joined the 25th Foot in 1779; by 1787 he was a captain in the 75th Regiment and fighting against Tipoo Sahib from 1790 to 1792 in India. He was deputy assistant adjutant general to General Lake during the Irish Rebellion and served in the Helder campaign in 1799 on the Staff. He served at Buenos Aries as a full colonel in 1806, on his return he was placed under Sir David Baird as part of his reinforcement of Sir John Moore's army. Craufurd was given command of a brigade consisting of the 1/43rd, 1/52nd and 2/95th, which during the retreat marched to Vigo as a flank guard rather than Corunna. Craufurd returned to the peninsula in May 1809 with his brigade but just missed the Battle of Talavera. The Duke of Wellington retained him in command of the Light Brigade and the subsequent Light Division, despite the fact that he was merely a colonel. His record under Wellington was, however, erratic and he drew a great deal of criticism from his subordinates. He was killed at the storming of the fortress of Ciudad Rodrigo. His family correspondence shows a different side of the man.

His son Charles wrote to him in his best handwriting and had clearly been helped by his mother [March 1810?]:

My dear Papa,
I am very glad you asked me to write to you because it seems as if you like to read my letters. I should not have doubted the buttons were

---

350   From Winchester Archives Reference D/4512

silver if Mama had not thought so, so pray Papa do not be affronted with me. Mama received a letter from you a few days ago, it gave her very great pleasure and I was very much obliged to you for the little bit which you sent to me. Mama says that the day after she is settled, she will send to the tailor and order jackets to be made for our buttons. Bob and I are very impatient to wear them, but much more so to have you see us wear them. Al is very much grown since you was at home, I wish you could see how much. I love you very much and am your affectionate sone [sic] C[harles] H[enry] Craufurd.

Craufurd sent him a personal reply addressed 'To Charles Henry Craufurd from his father in Portugal' and dated 1 April [1810?]:

To Mrs R [obert] Craufurd,[351] Brighthelmstone,[352] Sussex

My very dear Car,
I was very much pleased at receiving your letter & I assure you that you cannot wish to see me more than I wish to be with you and your dear Mama and my nice little Boody & Lou and little Al, whom I hardly know. I think I shall be quite surprised when I come home & find him walking about. I have got a poney [sic] but he is rather too large and too frisky and jumps too much for you. But if I cannot get a very nice one here, I certainly will buy one when I come to England for you. It shall be yours and dear Boody shall have a *Donty*. And what shall we give to our nice little Lou? I believe a very pretty *Tap*. As for Al, he will be easily suited, I suppose he will prefer some barley sugar to anything else. But is a pity he should wait so long for it and therefore tell your dear mother that I beg she will give you five shillings to make a feast. I think we shall have some fine games at hide & seek next winter.

God bless you my dearest Car. I love you all very very much. I cannot possibly tell you how much. I am and shall always be, your most affectionate father, Robert Craufurd.

Letter from Robert Craufurd to *The Times* regarding the Action on the Coa, published 21 November 1810

Marshal Massena, not content with the gross misrepresentations which were contained in his first official account of the action of the 24th of July near Almeida, has in a subsequent despatch reverted to it

---

351   He was married to Mary Frances (nee Holland).
352   An old name for Brighton.

in a tone of boasting wholly unjustified by the circumstances; assuring the War minister that his whole army is burning with impatience to teach the English army what they taught the division of Craufurd in the affair of Almeida.

Brigadier General Craufurd has therefore determined to give this public contradiction to the false assertions contained in Marshal Massena's report of an action which was not only highly honourable to the Light Division, but which positively terminated in its favour, notwithstanding the extraordinary disparity of numbers. A corps of 4,000 men remained during the whole day in presence of an army amounting to 24,000. It performed, in the presence of so superior a force, one of the most difficult operations of war, namely a retreat from a very broken and extensive position over one narrow defile. It defended, during the whole of the day, the first defensible position that was to be found in the neighbourhood of the place where the action commenced; and in the course of the affair, this corps of 4,000 men inflicted upon this army of 24,000 a loss equal to the double of that which it sustained. Such were the circumstances of the action in which Brigadier General Craufurd's corps was opposed to the army commanded by Marshal Massena and Ney on July 24; and it is therefore indisputable that they had the best of it.

From Marshal Massena's official despatch, containing a statement of the force to which we were opposed, it appears that the cavalry consisted of the 3rd Hussars, 15th Chasseurs, 10th, 15th and 25th Dragoons and that the whole of Ney's corps was present, except one regiment of the division of Marchand. The infantry of Ney's corps was present, except one regiment of the division of Marchand. The infantry of Ney's corps according to the intercepted official returns, amounted at that time to upwards of 22,000 effectives and the cavalry regiments were certainly between 600 and 700 each. It therefore appears that the force with which Marshals Massena and Ney advanced to attack the Light Division on the morning of 24 July, consisted of 20,000 infantry and between 3,000 and 4,000 cavalry; to which were opposed three English battalions (43rd, 52nd and 95th) two Portuguese battalions (1st and 3rd Chasseurs) and eight squadrons of cavalry, making in the whole, a force of about 3,200 British and 1,100 Portuguese troops.

Almeida is a small fortress situated at the edge of the declivity forming a right bank of the valley of the Coa, which river runs from the south to the north, and the bridge over which is nearly an English mile west of the town. From 21 July to 24th the chain of our cavalry outposts formed a semi-circle in front of Almeida, the right flank being appuye to the Coa, near As-Naves [Naves], which is about three miles above this place, and the left flank also appuye to the river near Cinco-Villa [Cinco Vilas], which is about three miles below the fortress. The centre of this line was covered by a small stream; and on the principal roads by which it was expected the enemy would advance, namely on the right and centre of the position, the cavalry posts were supported by piquets of infantry. The only road which our artillery and the body of our cavalry could make use of, to retreat across the Coa, was that which leads from Almeida to the bridge. The nature of the ground made it difficult for the enemy to approach this road on our left, that is to say, on the north side of the town; and the infantry of the division was therefore placed in a position to cover it on the right or south side, having its right flank appuye to the Coa above the bridge, its front covered by a deep and rocky ravine and its left in some enclosures near a windmill, which is on the plain, about eight hundred yards south of the town. The governor had intended to mount a gun upon the windmill; and one was actually in it, but quite useless, as it was not mounted. Another gun, also dismounted, was lying near the mill. These are the guns which Marshal Massena says he took in the action.

On the morning of the 24th the centre of our line of piquets was attacked, namely that which occupied the road leading from Almeida to Val de la Mula [Vale da Mula], which village is about four English miles east of the fortress. These piquets were supported by the 14th Light Dragoons and two guns; but when the head of a considerable column, with artillery, presented itself and began to form on the other side of the rivulet, the piquets were withdrawn. The enemy then passed the rivulet, a cannonade took place and they formed a line of fifteen squadrons of cavalry at a distance of about a mile from the above mentioned windmill, with artillery in its front and a division of about seven thousand infantry on its right. Other troops were seen, though not so distinctly, advancing upon our right.

It being now evident that we were opposed to such a force as to render it impossible for Brigadier General Craufurd to prevent the investment of the place, he determined to cross the Coa. He ordered the artillery and cavalry to move off by the road leading from the town to the bridge and the infantry to follow, retiring across the vineyard in the same direction. The infantry were directed to move in echelon from the left, it being necessary to hold the right to the last, in order to prevent the enemy approaching the bridge by a road coming from Junca and which runs along the bottom of the valley close to the river. Some companies, which formed the left of the line, were in a vineyard so completely enclosed by a high stone wall, that it was quite impossible for cavalry to get into it; but the preceding night had been excessively severe and some of the troops stationed in the vineyard had unfortunately pulled down the wall in many places, to make use of the stones to form a shelter against the violent rain. This wall, which Brigadier General Craufurd had considered as a complete defence, was therefore, no longer such; and after our artillery and cavalry had moved off, the enemy's horse broke into the enclosure and took several prisoners.

Our total loss in prisoners and missing amounted to about sixty, after all those who were at first returned as such had contrived to rejoin their regiments. The 43rd Regiment, having been on the left of the line, was the first that arrived near the bridge. The Brigadier General ordered some companies of it to occupy a height in front of the bridge and the remainder to pass on and form on the heights on the other side of the river. Part of the 95th Rifles and the 3rd Battalion of Chasseurs [Caçadores], who arrived next, were formed on the right of those companies of the 43rd Regiment that were in front of the bridge. This position was maintained until everything was over and until one of the horse artillery ammunition waggons, which had been overturned in a very bad situation, was got up and dragged to the other side by the men. During the remainder of the day the bridge was most gallantly defended by the 43rd and part of the 95th Regiments and after it was dusk, we retreated from the Coa.

To retire in tactical order over such ground, so broken, rocky and intersected with walls, as that which separated the first position from the second, would have been impossible, even if not under the fire of the enemy; and the ground on the other side of the river was equally unfavourable for reforming the regiments. Whoever knows anything of war, knows that in such an operation and upon such ground, some derangement of regular order is inevitable; but the retreat was made in a military, soldier-like manner and without the slightest precipitation. In the course of it the enemy, when he pressed, was attacked in different places by the 43rd, 52nd and 95th Regiments and driven before them.

With respect to the enemy's loss, it is of course, difficult to say what it was, because we know that from the commencement of the Revolutionary war, no French official report has ever contained true statements on this point. Upon this occasion Marshal Massena says 'we have taken one stand of Colours, four hundred men and two pieces of cannon; our loss amounted to nearly three hundred killed and wounded.' He took no Colours; the cannon were the two dismounted guns belonging to the fortress, which were lying in and near the windmill; and instead of four hundred prisoners, he took only about sixty, supposing every one of those we returned as missing, to have fallen alive into the enemy's hands. Now if in the same paragraph in which he states his own loss at three hundred, he calls sixty prisoners four hundred, we may fairly infer that he is not more accurate in the one statement than in the other; and this circumstance as well as the usual practise of their service and the probability of the thing. From what we could observe, fully justify us in assuming to have been from six to seven hundred. Ours amounted in killed, wounded and prisoners, to three hundred and thirty.

Such is the true account of this affair, upon which the Marshal prides himself so much, but in which it is certain that the advantage was on our side. We could not pretend to prevent the investment of the place; but in our retreat, we did not lose a gun, a trophy, or a single article of field equipage; and we inflicted on the enemy a loss certainly double that we sustained. The account contained in the commencement of the Marshal's despatch, of what had passed on July 21, is equally contrary to the truth. He talks of having forced the passage of the little rivulet that runs between Almeida and Val de la Mula [Vale da Mula] on the 21st; whereas our picquets remained there, and not a single Frenchman passed it until the morning of the 24th. He says that many of our sharp-shooters fell into their hands on the 21st; the truth is that they did not take a single man. The retreat of the 14th Dragoons from Val de la Mula [Vale da Mula] was conducted in the most slow and regular manner and all our intentions with respect to Fort Concepcion was completely fulfilled. Robert Craufurd Brigadier General.

El Bodon, 15 January 1812

My beloved Fanny,[353]

In my last I informed you that we were going to besiege Ciudad Rodrigo. The Light Division was the first employed and a detachment of it distinguished itself very much in taking an advanced work in almost ten minutes, which the enemy had expected would delay us several days. Our batteries began to fire upon the town yesterday evening, so that the worst of it is over, for hitherto the firing has been all on the side of the enemy. There are four divisions employed in the siege, one each day; and when relieved we return to our quarters. I have received your letters up to the 30th of December very regularly. I have not yet heard of the stands for the side dishes, which were sent so long ago, but I have no doubt I shall hear of them. The things you have sent me by the packet, I am sure to get; they are probably now at Lisbon. Do

---

[353]   Robert Craufurd was married to Mary (nee Holland) at St Saviour's in February 1800.

not imagine, my dearest Fanny, that I am always out of spirits, because I occasionally write as if I was &c. It is only now & then. I occupy a part of almost every day in coursing. Colonel Beckwith writes me word from Lisbon that he has got 3 greyhounds for me. Pray tell Charles that the mares arrived here two days ago perfectly sound & well and that I like 3 of them very much. I will write to him by next post, but have not time today. God Bless you my beloved Fanny, give my kindest love to our dear little ones and believe me ever, with the purest love, your most tenderly affectionate husband RC.

To General Charles Craufurd[354] from Lord Stewart,[355] Gallegos 26 January 1812
My dear friend,
I have to entreat you to summon to your aid all that resignation to the will of heaven & manly fortitude which I know you possess, to bear with composure the sad tidings this letter is doomed to convey. I think you must have discovered that from the first moment I did not encourage sanguine hopes of your beloved brother, whose loss we have alas! now to deplore. But my dear friend, as we all must pass through this transitory existence sooner or later to be translated to a better, surely there is no mode of terminating life equal to that which providence ordained should be *his*. Like Nelson, Abercrombie, Moore & inferior to none (if his sphere had been equally extensive) your much-loved brother fell, the shouts of victory were the last he heard from the gallant troops he led and his last moments were full of anxiety as to the events of the army & consideration for the Light Division. If his friends permit themselves to give way to unbounded grief under this heavy calamity, they are considering themselves rather than the departed hero, the army & his country have the most reason to deplore his loss. For as his military talents were of the first calibre, so was his spirit of the most intrepid gallantry. There is but one universal sentiment throughout all ranks of the profession on this subject and if you and those who loved him dearly (among whom God knows! I pity most his angel wife & children), could but have witnessed the manner in which the last duties were paid to his memory by the whole army, your tears would have been arrested by the contemplation of what his merits must have been to have secured such a general sensation & they would have ceased to flow, by the feelings of enemy such an end irresistibly excited.

---

[354]   Lieutenant General Sir Charles Craufurd, brother of Robert Craufurd.
[355]   Major General Charles Stewart Marquis of Londonderry

As I fervently trust that by the time you receive this letter you may be so far prepared for this afflicting stroke as to derive consolation even from sad details & as I really am unequal to address Mrs Craufurd at present, I think it best to enter at large into everything with you, leaving it to your affectionate & prudent judgement to unfold events by degrees in the manner you deem best.

You will perceive by Staff Surgeon Gunning's[356] report (Lord Wellington's own surgeon) upon an examination of the wound (which I enclose) that from the nature of it, it was impossible Robert should have recovered. The direction the ball had taken, the extreme difficulty of breathing and the blood he brought up gave great grounds of alarm. But still, it was conceived the ball might have dropped lower than the lungs & as there have been instances of recovery from wounds in the same place, we were suffered to entertain *a hope*, but alas! that was all. Staff Surgeons Robb[357] & Gunning who were his constant attendants & from whose anxiety, zeal & professional ability, everything was to be expected, were unremitting in their exertions. His ADC's young Wood[358] & Lieutenant Shaw[359] of the 43rd, showed all that affectionate attention, which even his own family could have done to him; the former I must say evinced a feeling as honourable to his heart as it must have been gratifying to its object. To these I must add Captain William Campbell[360] whose long friendship for Robert induced him never to leave him and he manifested in an extraordinary manner his attachment on this occasion. If my own duties had permitted me, you may believe I never should have absented myself from his bedside. As it was, feeling like a brother towards him, my heart led me to act as such to the utmost of my poor abilities. The 3 officers I have above named & his surgeons alternately watched & attended him from the evening of the 19th until 10 o'clock on the morning of the 24th when he breathed his last. On the 22nd he was considered easier & better, the medicine administered had all the effects desired, he conversed some time with me principally about the assault & he was most anxious as to news of the enemy. He was so cheerful that his mind did not revert, as it had done before to his wife & children & I was anxious to keep every subject from him that might awaken keen sensations. I knew well from many conversations I have had with him the unbounded influence & affection Mrs Craufurd's idea was attended with & his ardent anxiety as to the education & bringing up of his children. These thoughts I was anxious, while a ray of hope existed,

---

[356]   Staff Surgeon John Gunning.
[357]   Staff Surgeon John Robb.
[358]   Lieutenant Charles Wood, 52nd Foot, was an aide-de-camp to Robert Craufurd.
[359]   Lieutenant James Shaw, 43rd Foot, aide-de-camp to Robert Craufurd.
[360]   Captain William Campbell, 23rd Foot, deputy assistant quartermaster general.

not to awaken it, being of the utmost moment he should be kept free from agitation & I trust this will be a sufficient reason to Mrs Craufurd & yourself, for my being unable to give you those last sentiments of his heart, which he no doubt would have expressed, had we felt ourselves authorised to acquaint him, he was near his end, I do not mean to say he was ignorant of his situation, for when he first sent to me, he said he felt his wound was mortal & that he was fully prepared for the will of heaven. But I think subsequently he cherished hopes, he obtained some sleep on the night of the 22nd & the 23rd. He was to all appearance better, at two o'clock in the morning, William Campbell wrote me a most cheering account of him. He had been talking of his recovery & every pleasing prospect and he fell into a comfortable sleep as those around him imagined; but alas! From that sleep he never awoke again, his pulse gradually ceased to beat, his breath grew shorter and his spirit fled before those near him were conscious he was no more, so easy was his passport to heaven. If in detailing so mournful a recital, I can derive the smallest consolation, it arises from knowing his last words united his affection for his wife & his friendship for me in one train of thought in which he closed his eyes. Having thus acquainted you, as well as my present feelings enable me with the last scene, I shall now assure you that no exertion was wanting to prepare everything for the mournful ceremony that was to follow, with the utmost possible regard & respect to his memory. Lord Wellington decided he should be interred by his own division near the breach, which he has so gallantly earned.

The Light Division assembled before his house in the suburbs of the San Francisco convent at 12 o'clock on the 25th. The 5th Division lined the road from his quarters to the breach. The officers of the Brigade of Guards, cavalry, 3rd, 4th, & 5th Divisions together with General Castanos[361] & all his Staff, Marshal Beresford & all the Portuguese. Lord Wellington & the whole of headquarters moved in the mournful procession. He was borne to his place of rest on the shoulders of the brave lads he led on, the field officers of the Light Division officiating as pall bearers and the whole ceremony was conducted in the most gratifying manner, if I may be permitted such an epithet, or such a heart-breaking occasion. I assigned to myself the mournful task of being chief mourner & was attended by Captain Campbell, Lieutenants Wood & Shaw & the Staff of the Light Division. Care has been taken that his gallant remains can never be disturbed and he lays where posterity will commemorate his deeds!!

All his worldly affairs here I shall not neglect. His papers, writing cases, books &c & everything which I conceive may be [in] the least gratifying as remembrances or important, shall be carefully sealed packed up &

---

361   General Francisco Castanos, 1st Duke of Bailen.

sent by one of his most confidential servants to London as soon as possible, his horses & campaign furniture of every description shall be disposed of by public auction to the best advantage as is usual in similar cases. An exact inventory of the whole shall be taken & forwarded, any demands that may be against him shall be liquidated & his servants paid & discharged & the Paymaster General's account & the whole of the above shall be remitted in proper form without delay to you.

I must apprise you that Lord Wellington has declared his intention of writing to Mr Perceval[362] very strongly to do everything possible for Mrs Craufurd & his children and to commemorate his memory as he so richly deserves & I entertain a perfect confidence that the most gratifying arrangements will be made on this head.

Alas! my dear friend of our small party of five who were headed by you & first knew each other in 1796, how many are gone! & how cruelly have others suffered; poor Anstruther[363] & Robert!! & yourself who have gone through so much. Proby[364] & myself alone remain & while we lament over our two invaluable lost friends, the conviction of their merits & the force of their examples should never be absent from our thoughts. I hope you know me sufficiently to believe, what I must suffer on the present occasion, if I have been silent as to myself, it is because I will not intrude my own affliction on those so heavily borne down. But when shall I find so invaluable so inestimable a friend again!

Excuse me my dearest friend, I will not now add to this but write again shortly, when we shall all be more composed. Believe me as ever, your most affectionate & ever obliged, Charles Stewart

29th I have nothing material to add since I wrote the above, except that the effects are selling today at a very high value.

To Sir James Craufurd bart [Baronet], Downing Street, 2 April 1812
Dear Sir,
I have to communicate to you the result of such further consideration as I have been enabled to give to the case of your much lamented brother's widow and children; but I must, first, desire that you will not for a moment suppose that I could ascribe your frequent applications to me upon this subject to any other motives than those which the circumstance that has occasioned them very naturally excites.

---

362   Spencer Perceval was Prime Minister. He has the unenviable fame of being the only Prime Minister to be assassinated.

363   Brevet Colonel Robert Anstruther, 3rd Foot Guards, died at Corunna.

364   Brigadier General Anstruther died from pneumonia brought on by exhaustion on 14 January 1809 at Corunna.

You will I am sure do me the justice to believe that were I at liberty to indulge my individual feelings, unrestrained by any other consideration, I should readily yield to the impulse of those feelings by recommending a larger grant in the present case, as well as in many others, than I could feel myself justified in advising under the reflection that what is done in one instance, is always looked to and quoted as a precedent in future cases. With this reflection I do not feel that I can make any further distinction between the cases of General Craufurd and General Mackinnon,[365] than what may be due to the consideration of the unprovided state of General Craufurd's family, his superior command and his former services; and after very mature consideration of those circumstances, I have been induced to recommend that in addition to the pension which has been granted to Mrs Craufurd, further annuities of one hundred pounds should be granted to each of her children.

I trust that you will feel that I have not been wanting on the present occasion, in giving every possible consideration to the case upon which I have had to determine and that if the provision is short of what you could desire, you will ascribe it to the proper motives, arising from the restraints imposed upon me by my public duty, rather than to any indisposition to meet the wishes which you so naturally feel and have so earnestly expressed, on behalf of your brother's widow and children. I am, dear Sir, yours very truly, Spencer Perceval

To Sir William Fraser [grandson of General Craufurd's brother Daniel], Bath, 13 June 1861[366]
Sir,
In reference to your letter to me from Paris in April and to that of last month, I send addressed to you by this post, a copy of Lord Fitzclarence's work on outpost duties[367] which has as an appendix a letter from me and extracts from a diary which I kept of Craufurd's operations between the Coa & Agueda. I happen to have two copies and shall be obliged if you will be so good as to let Mr Robert Craufurd[368] have the copy I now forward to you, begging his acceptance of it, as I understand from his letter to you that you were good enough to send me that he wishes to possess a copy. According to your request I now proceed to give you some accounts of General Craufurd's death.

---

365   Major General Henry Mackinnon was killed at Ciudad Rodrigo.
366   Published in From *Coila's Whispers by the knight of Morar* by William Augustus Fraser, published London 1872.
367   Lord Frederick Fitzclarence's *A Manual of Outpost Duties*, published 1851.
368   Robert Craufurd's second son.

Captain James Shaw 43rd Foot, General Craufurd's ADC, on the death of Robert Craufurd[369]

Ciudad Rodrigo was stormed on the 19 January 1812. There were two breaches reported practicable on that day; the greater destined to be assaulted by the 3rd Division commanded by General Picton; the lesser by the Light Division commanded by General Craufurd. The 3rd Division was in the trenches and the Light Division and Pack's Brigade were ordered to march from the villages which they occupied to take part in the assault. For this purpose the Light Division crossed the Agueda by a ford three miles above Rodrigo and marched from that ford by a considerable circuit to approach the place from the ford. I was sent forward by General Craufurd to report to Lord Wellington the approach of the division and to ask his orders as to how the division was to approach the place and as to the position it was to keep up. I found Lord Wellington's Staff near to the Convent of San Francisco and asked for His Lordship whom they pointed out, sitting near the convent and at some distance and alone, but they said I could not speak to him, as he was writing the orders for the assault. But this I had nothing to do with and went immediately up to him and informed him of the orders which I had received from General Craufurd. He stopped writing, listened attentively to what I said, gave the most clear and distinct orders as to the division and then returned [to] writing. This anecdote is characteristic of Wellington; here we find him totally alone, sitting in the open air, within range of the guns of the place, unassisted by maps or plans, or any person to refer to and at the last stage of the operations, when the assault was about to made, writing a full clear and distinct order for an assault involving considerable complication.

Craufurd having placed the Light Division according to Wellington's orders near to the Convent of San Francisco, made his dispositions for the divisions assaulting the lesser breach at 7 o'clock pm. About that hour the division advanced to the assault in the following order three companies of the Rifles moved to the right to enter the ditch between the greater & lesser breaches. And the main column consisting of the 43rd and 52nd Regiments [&] part of the Rifles, marched directly for the lesser breach, preceded by a forlorn hope under Lieutenant Gurwood[370] and 800 men as a storming party under Major Napier.[371] The 43rd and 52nd Regiments were formed in columns of sections and were abreast of each other; the 43rd formed the right-hand column of sections, the 52nd the left-hand column of sections.

---

369 From Winchester Archives Reference D/4512
370 Lieutenant John Gurwood, 52nd Foot.
371 Major George Napier, 52nd Foot, commanded the Forlorn Hope at Ciudad Rodrigo.

The 43rd column of sections was formed right in front, the 52nd left in front. The 43rd was ordered on entering the breach to proceed in its column of sections along the rampart, towards the greater breach, the 52nd in the opposite direction towards the Salamanca gate. Thus the 43rd, when it wheeled to the left & the 52nd to the right when on the rampart would form a line facing the town. The leading sections of the 43rd and 52nd it will be observed were abreast of each other, they were led respectively by Lieutenant Colonel Macleod[372] & Lieutenant Colonel Colborne the commanders of those regiments, who in their advance followed up closely the storming party. While the column, as above described, advanced to the assaults, General Craufurd, keeping to the left of the column, proceeded directly to the crest of the glacis, about sixty yards to the left of where the column entered the ditch and from that spot, at the highest pitch of his voice, continued giving instructions to the column. This brought upon him an intense fire of musketry from the opposite parapets of the fausse braie and rampart and at a very short distance, for the ditch of the fausse braie was very narrow and even the main ditch was very narrow and the place had no covered way. He was thus exposed to a double fire of infantry at a very short distance, the superior slope of the parapet of the fausse braie being in the same line as the slope of the glacis, he could not remain many minutes where he was without being hit, accordingly he was struck by a musket ball, which passed through his arm, broke through the ribs, passed through part of the lungs and lodged in or at the spine; and he not only fell, but the shock was so great that on falling he rolled over down the glacis. There was not a soul with him but myself, there was no one even near us. I immediately took hold of him and half dragged and half carried him to where there was an inequality of ground in which he was out of the direct fire from the place. After lying for a few minutes in this situation, he said to me that he was mortally wounded and that he felt that he was just dying. I expressed my grief that he had such a feeling and a hope that he was mistaken, in answer to which he reiterated his opinion that he was just dying. I then asked him if I could do anything for him. To this he replied that I could not, as all his affairs were fully settled. I then asked him if he had anything to communicate to Lord Wellington. After considering a little he said that he did not recollect anything that he had to communicate to Lord Wellington and that there was only one thing I could do for him, which was to 'say to Mrs Craufurd that he was quite sure that they would meet in heaven'. After this he lay for some time quiet and

---

[372]   Lieutenant Colonel Charles McLeod, 43rd Foot, was killed at Badajoz.

without speaking, recovering himself in some measure from this quiet, he said that he felt a little better. I then proposed to attempt to raise him and that if possible he should proceed to the suburb. To this he agreed and leaning heavily upon me he succeeded in getting to the convent of San Francisco, on our approach to which we met a medical officer of the Rifles who made enquiry as to the wound and thought that the arm alone was injured and he pointed out the place in the San Francisco where General Craufurd should be taken for examination. There he was taken and examined by some medical officers. During that examination, I had gone to look for a house to which he might be taken and on my return, met one of the surgeons who had examined the wounds; he said that the wounds were so serious as to leave no hope of the general's life being preserved. From the San Francisco he was removed to a house very near it.

General Craufurd was wounded at say, eight o'clock pm on the 19th and died at say, ten o'clock am on the 24th. That is, he lived one hundred and ten hours after being wounded, during which time, I regret to say, his sufferings were very great indeed, arising from feverish irritation and great difficulty of breathing. He was not without hope of recovery, but expressed a wish that if death was to be the consequence of his wounds it might occur speedily as his sufferings were very great.

By accident I met Lord Wellington at the Salamanca gate, on the morning of the 20th and he asked most anxiously for Craufurd. I gave him an unfavourable report of his state. His Lordship called afterwards and saw Craufurd and they conversed together, for some time. Craufurd congratulated Lord Wellington on the great advantage he had gained by taking Ciudad Rodrigo, to which his lordship replied in these words, 'Yes, a great blow, great blow indeed'.

General Craufurd had the advantage of the opinions of several senior military surgeons, but the case was in charge of and was managed by Doctor Walker, then Assistant Surgeon of the 52nd Regiment.[373]

The funeral of General Craufurd took place on the 25th, the grave being in the ditch of the place near to the breach. Lord Wellington, Marshal Beresford, General Castanos and the Headquarters Staff were present; the ground was kept by the 5th Division. The escort consisted of the whole of the Light Division. I beg to remain, your obedient servant, J[ames] S[haw] Kennedy.

---

[373]   Assistant Surgeon Thomas Walker, 52nd Foot.

19. LIEUTENANT JAMES SHAW, AIDE-DE-CAMP JOURNAL

James Shaw was born on 13 October 1788 and was commissioned an ensign in the 43rd Foot in 1805. He was promoted to lieutenant on 23 January 1806. He served with his regiment at Copenhagen in 1807, in the Corunna Campaign of 1808–09, and returned with his regiment to the peninsula in 1809. He was appointed General Robert Craufurd's aide-de-camp on 19 November 1809. While in that position he was the de facto intelligence officer for the Light Division. He was seriously wounded at the Coa on 24 July 1810 and returned to Great Britain. After recovering from his wound, Shaw served as an extra-ADC to Craufurd from November 1811 until Craufurd's death in January 1812. He was promoted to captain on 16 July 1812 and appointed an extra-ADC to Major General Charles Alten, the commander of the Light Division, on 6 November 1812. He went home to Great Britain in November 1813. He was a deputy assistant quartermaster general during the Waterloo Campaign. After the occupation of France, he became a staff officer in England and eventually organised the Royal Irish Constabulary. In 1854 he was promoted to lieutenant general and in 1862 to general. He died in 1865 at the age of 77. He changed his name to Shaw Kennedy in 1834.

The Journal of Lieutenant James Shaw, 30 January–23 July 1810
The journal when originally published was littered with vast notes and jumped about with regard to chronology. To make it easier for the reader to follow, it has been rearranged in chronological order.

Pinhel, January 1810
Tuesday, 30 January
I left Pinhel early this morning and proceeded to reconnoitre the River Coa, from the bridge of Pinhel down to where it joins the Douro.

174

After passing through the villages of Bogalhale [Bogalhal] and Azeva [Azevo], I arrived at Citadella [Cidadelhe], which is three leagues from Pinhel and there passed the night.

Wednesday, 31 January
I this morning passed the Coa and visited the villages of Quintan [Quintã de Pêro Martins] and Val de Francina [Vale de Afonsinho] on the right bank; after which I repassed the river and crossing the Masueme, remained for the night at a village called Santa Comba, which is only one league from Citadella [Cidadelhe].

Thursday, 1 February
After following the Coa from where it is joined by the Masueme, I passed through the village of Monohega [modern Chas?] and made Villa Novo [Vila Nova de Foz Côa] my quarters for the night. It is three leagues from Santa Comba.

Friday, 2 February
I this day crossed the Coa and visited Castell Melhoe [Castelo Melhor] on its right bank; after which I passed the Douro and proceeded to Torre de Moncorvo, where I remained the night and found Finlay, the commissary there.[374]

Saturday, 3 February
Yesterday I crossed the Douro by the Barcade Almendra and today re-crossed it by a boat half a league further down; after passing Villa Novo [Vila Nova de Foz Côa] and Monohega [Chas], I again reached Santa Comba.

Sunday, 4 February
Proceeded from Santa Comba by the villages of Bormura [Barreira] and Getieroe [Gateira], Azeva [Azevo] and Bogalhah to Pinhel. The principal results of my reconnaissance of the Coa, were to discover that below the bridge of Pinhel there are sixteen places at which it is possible to cross the river. From the bridge to where the Coa joins the Douro is between six and seven leagues. The banks of the river, from the bridge to Azeva [Azevo] are very rugged and difficult; from thence, to where it is joined by the Masueme, its banks are singularly high, rugged, rocky and perpendicular; from that to the Douro they are high, but not so rocky. Upon the whole, that part of the river may

---

[374]   Deputy Assistant Commissary General John Finlay.

be defended by a very few men. Villa Novo [Vila Nova de Foz Côa] and Torre de Moncorvo are two very good towns; the former is close to where the Coa joins the Douro.

Monday, 5 February
Was employed in making out the report of my reconnaissance.

Tuesday, 6 & Wednesday, 7 February
Went out with Lloyd[375] and Wells[376] to Villa Torpin [Vilar Torpim] and remained all night with Wells.

Thursday, 8 February
Returned to Pinhel by the villages of Reygada [Reigada] and Cinqua Villa [Cinco Vilas]. This afternoon appeared the commencement of wet weather.

Friday, 9 February
This day continues wet and cloudy. Received a letter from Duffy.[377]

Saturday, 10 February
Wrote a letter to my father and sent a bill for Prize money.

Sunday, 11 February
Today positive information was received from several quarters that the enemy, after having collected his force in the neighbourhood of Salamanca, had moved towards Ciudad Rodrigo; he yesterday occupied Saint Martin del Rio [San Martin del Castanar] and Tamames; his force not accurately known, but computed at 15,000 men. Captain Runian[378] states in his reports, that the enemy had only 18,000 men at most in Castille. There are accounts of their also having troops in Leon, Benavente &c &c. Today we received information that Soult had reached Xeres and that some English regiments had sailed from Lisbon for its support, under General William Stewart[379] 95th. The garrison of Ciudad Rodrigo consists of 3,000 or 4,000 men and the Duke de Parque[380] has 13,000 fighting men. His headquarters are at Saint Martin in the Sierra de Gata.

---

[375]   Captain Thomas Lloyd, 43rd Foot.
[376]   Captain Joseph Wells, 43rd Foot.
[377]   Captain John Duffy, 43rd Foot, who was on home leave.
[378]   Captain Lewis Ruman, 97th Foot, was a deputy assistant quartermaster general and often served as one of Wellington's exploring officers.
[379]   Major General William Stewart.
[380]   Lieutenant General Vicente María Canas y Portocarrero, 7th Duke of Parque.

Monday, 12 and Tuesday, 13 February
A French corps,[381] having only field artillery, scattered themselves round Ciudad Rodrigo and kept up a fire upon the town and summoned it to surrender; but receiving a determined answer of resistance from the governor, they left the place and marched to San Felices [de los Gallegos].

Saturday, 16 February
The last of Ney's corps left San Felices [de los Gallegos] this morning, directing their march towards Salamanca, Ledesma and Zamora &c &c. A few of them had on the 15th crossed the Agueda and entered Barba de Puerco. Yesterday the general met General Cole[382] at Castanheiro [Castanheira] to confer with him upon what was best to be done and recommended that the Third Division should move up to the Coa and that the brigade from Trancosa [Trancoso] should move to Pinhel. To this proposition General Cole dissented. I accompanied the general part of the way to Castanheiro and then turned off to Almeida for information.

Saturday, 17 February
Remained all day in the house.

Sunday, 18 February
Visited the quarters of the 43rd and returned by Lamegal, Manegotta [Manigoto] &c.

Monday, 19 February
The quarters of the [3rd] Division were now as follows viz:

> 43rd Valverde, Azinbal [Azinhal], Peva, Chevethos [Chavelhas], Treixe [Freixo], Aldea Nova [Aldeia Nova].
> 52nd Pinhel
> 95th Villa Torpin [Vilar Torpim], Reygada [Reigada], Cinqua Villa [Cinco Vilas].
> 45th Louroperez [Souropires], Varcaverde [Vascoveiro], Manegotta [Manigoto], Boqua [Roque], Lanieiris [Lameiras] and Barragao [Bogalhal?].
> 88th Lanegal [Lamegal], Freixinho, Attalaya [Atalaia], Carvalhal [de Atalaia] and Vendada

---

[381]   These troops were from Marshal Michel Ney's 6th Corps.
[382]   Major General Galbraith Lowry Cole was the commander of the 4th Division.

Troop of artillery[383] Pinhel
Troop of hussars[384] Aldea Bispo [Aldea del Obispo]

Information was received that the enemy were very near to Badajoz with a corps and that a very considerable one was collected near to Placencia [Plasencia]. The weather has been remarkably fine for some days and seems set in for the fine season.

Tuesday, 20 February
A spy who had been sent by the Duke de Parque to see what men entered Spain from France, gave the following account:

On the 29 of January, he met on this side of Barjos [Burgos] 1,400 conscripts; on the 30th, at Mariando [Miranda] de Ebro, he met a corps of 8,000 men; and on the 1st and 2nd instant he met Junot's corps,[385] consisting of 24,000 men at Toloso [Tolosa]. He remained from the 3rd to the 6th at Bayonne. On the 6th 15,000 of the infantry [of the] Guard had arrived and Bonaparte was expected from Bordeaux that evening and to set off for Spain next morning.

Wednesday, 21 February
I went this morning by Villa Torpin [Vilar Torpim] to Castello Rodrigo [Castelo Rodrigo] and returned by [blank – Bizarril?]. Castello Rodrigo [Castelo Rodrigo] is situated on the Sierra de Marofa and from it you have a very extensive view over a great plain towards Spain. I understood from the people here and it was confirmed by other accounts, that the French were only three and a half leagues from San Felices [de los Gallegos], occupying Bitagudinia [Vitigudino], Yecla [de Yeltes], Bogaga [Bogajo] &c, with about 2,000 men and patrolled near to San Felices. There are the remains of a castle and wall at Castello Rodrigo [Castelo Rodrigo]; both were destroyed by the Spaniards in 1762.

Thursday, 22 February
Information was received today, that the corps of the enemy at Talavera and that at Placencia [Plasencia] had crossed the Tagus and were proceeding towards Badajoz. Also, that a part of the Andalusian army had marched some time ago towards Badajoz. King Joseph was in Seville with 4,000 men.

---

383   Captain Hew Dalrymple Ross' Royal Artillery Troop.
384   1st King's German Legion Hussars.
385   General de Division Jean Junot's 8th Corps.

Friday, 23 February

There was now a new distribution of the army, which was in order as follows.[386] By private letters it appeared that the works which had been worked at for a month past at Torres Vedras &c were now ordered to be razed and new ones begun nearer to Lisbon at Mafra &c. It is also known that General Hill's[387] division had passed the Tagus and marched towards Elvas, but for what purpose is not ascertained.

Monday, 26 February

The weather very fine for some time past; today sultry and blowy.

Tuesday, 27 February

The officer[388] of hussars at Aldea Bispo [Aldeia do Bispo] and the officer of the 95th stationed at Barba del Puerco reported that the enemy had returned to San Felices [de los Gallegos] about 3,000 strong and had pushed forward a party to Barba del Puerco.[389] These reports were received between one and two o'clock this morning and the officer of the 95th added that there was a considerable number of the enemy reported to be in the villages in the neighbourhood of San Felices. Received my father's letter of the 10 January and my aunt's from Liverpool.

Wednesday, 28 February

Yesterday a company of the 95th marched to Escarrigo [Escarigo] and 20 men went to the bridge of San Felices [de los Gallegos], where they saw about 30 cavalry and 200 infantry pass. The 20 men retired to Escarrigo [Escarigo] and had a slight skirmish with the enemy near Barba de Puerco, which place the French took possession of. No despatch having been received today from Lieutenant Colonel Beckwith[390] I set off between three and four in the afternoon for Villa Torpin [Vilar Torpim] and being informed that the enemy had retired from Barba del Puerco to San Felices I returned to Pinhel at 7 o'clock.

Thursday, 1 March

The general went to visit the outposts today and was to sleep at Malpartido [Malpartida] where I went to meet him; from whence

---

386	Interesting Lieutenant Shaw did not mention that the same order created the Light Division.
387	Lieutenant General Rowland Hill commanded the 2nd Division.
388	Captain Wilhelm Aly, 1st King's German Legion Hussars.
389	Present day Puerto Seguro.
390	Lieutenant Colonel Thomas Beckwith, 95th Rifles.

I went to Almeida, which is only half a league and was informed by the governor that the Duke de Parque had gone to Lisbon and that his army was at Albuquerque for the protection of Badajoz; also that the French had suffered a repulse in their advance upon Cadiz.

Friday, 2 March
The general [Craufurd] having remained at Villa[r] de Ciervo all night, I came home early this morning. Today we got English letters and papers to the 13th ultimo, but no letters for me. I wrote to William Kennedy by Tylden[391] today.

Saturday, 3 & Sunday, 4 March
Today Captain Muller's[392] troop of hussars arrived, being on their way to join Captain Ally's[393] troop at the outposts. It is now known positively, that our troops under General Stewart[394] had entered Cadiz and were well received. It is reported that preparations are making at Salamanca for the arrival of Bonaparte there and that he has ordered all arrears due to his army in Spain to be immediately paid to the soldiers.

This is a wet blowy day and appears the commencement of bad weather. The people still expect rain and unsettled weather at this season of the year. The following is reported to be the corps of Marshal Ney viz; 6th and 25th Light infantry; the 8th, 16th, 27th, 32nd, 69th, and 76th Regiments of the Line; the 15th and 25th Dragoons; the 15th and 25th Chasseurs and the 3rd Hussars.

Monday, 5 March
Rained nearly the whole day. I wrote today to my father. No news today of the enemy.

Tuesday, 6 & Wednesday, 7 March
Information was received today of about 200 of the enemy having marched into Barba del Puerco from San Felices [de los Gallegos]. They only remained there two hours. The Field officers[395] 52nd all dined with the general.

---

391   Captain John Maxwell Tylden, 43rd Foot, was returning to England soon.
392   Either Captain Georg von Müller or Captain Moritz von Müller, both of the 1st King's German Legion Hussars.
393   Captain Wilhelm Aly, 1st King's German Legion Hussars.
394   Major General William Stewart.
395   Lieutenant Colonel Robert Barclay and Majors Hugh Arbuthnot and Henry Ridewood.

Thursday, 8 & Friday, 9 March

Today the whole of the enemy's force[396] at San Felices [de los Gallegos], about 1,500 men passed the bridge and advanced upon Barba del Puerco, Escarrigo [Escarigo] and Villa[r] de Ciervo. After plundering these villages of all the provisions they could get, they returned to San Felices. Our hussars were driven back from Villa[r] de Ciervo to Val de Cuelha [Coelha] and lost a man who was wounded and fell from his horse. They had also a horse shot. As soon as the information of the enemy's advance was known here, I went out to the hussars at Val de Cuelha and remained there during the night. For these five days past we have had heavy rain, so that most of the rivers were not fordable, but they now fall rapidly.

Saturday, 10 March

I started from Val de Cuelha [Coelha] about 8 o'clock this morning and proceeded first to Aldea Bispo [Aldea del Obispo] and from that to Barba del Puerco, where I met the general and Campbell.[397] The enemy have a sentry on the bridge and picquet on the hill. While we remained at Barba del Puerco, a Spanish detachment arrived there from Ciudad Rodrigo. I returned to Pinhel by the villages of Boisa [La Bouza], Escarrigo [Escarigo], Vimiosa [Vermiosa] and Villa Torpin [Vilar Torpim]. From Escarrigo I sent two companies[398] of the 95th to occupy Barba del Puerco by order of the general and one company is to occupy Boisa [La Bouza] tomorrow morning.

At the time that Marshal Ney advanced his corps to Ciudad Rodrigo, no distinct orders had been given to General Craufurd or to General Cole (the latter was at Guarda) in what manner they were to act. They met to consider of the best measures to be taken and did not altogether agree in their opinions as to the distribution of the outposts. General Craufurd therefore, being anxious to have more explicit instructions, wrote to Lord Wellington upon the subject and stated to His Lordship the matter as it appeared to him; and particularly pointed out, that while our outposts were on the Coa and the enemy on the Agueda, with the support to the right brigades as far back as Guarda and Celerico [Celorico da Beira], that it could not be in His Lordship's option the defence of the Coa, as the enemy might pass before our force could be brought up. In answer to this, Lord Wellington stated that it had long been his intention to bring up the divisions at Celerico and Guarda

---

396   General de Brigade Jean-François Ferey's Brigade of the 3rd Division of Ney's Corps.
397   Captain William Campbell, 23rd Foot.
398   Four companies actually went.

to the villages near the Coa as soon as the weather would admit of their being in such quarters; and stated that he was anxious to have the defence of the Coa in his power, as it would enable him to save Ciudad Rodrigo if the enemy approached with a force that he could cope with. His Lordship said that the outposts must all be under the direction of one person and that the person must be General Craufurd.

Accordingly next day a memorandum[399] to Generals Picton, Cole and Craufurd (from Lord Wellington) was received, by which the whole of the outposts were put under General Craufurd's directions and the regiment of hussars, First German Legion, was put under his orders. Generals Picton and Cole also were directed to move up to their divisions for the defence of the Coa, upon General Craufurd's suggestion and to afford him what assistance he at any time wanted of infantry. The general therefore moved the regiment of hussars near to the Agueda and occupied a line extending from Escalhon [Escalhao] to [El] Payo. The infantry were also brought across the Coa and Barba del Puerco was occupied by the 95th; they had also some companies in Boisa [La Bouza], Escarrigo [Escarigo] and Almofallo [Almofala]. The 52nd were in Malpartida, Val[e] de Cuelha [Coleha] and Val de [da] Mula. The two Portuguese battalions[400] were at Coimbra on their way to join. The Light Brigade can bring about two thousand five hundred men into the field and the hussars four hundred. The four guns[401] were moved across the Coa to Aldea Bispo [Aldeia del Obispo].

By the most authentic accounts it appears that the enemy had now a force collected in the vicinity of Salamanca of about 20,000 men under Marshal Ney. Besides this collected force, they had detachments in Ledesma, Bitigudinia [Vitigudino], San Felices [de los Gallegos] and also in Tamames and in the Sierra de Francia, to within three leagues of Ciudad Rodrigo. Constant garrisons are kept in Zamoro [Zamora], Toro, Valladolid, Leon, Benavente and all the principal towns. Kellerman[402] and Loison[403] appear certainly to serve under Ney, in his corps collected at Salamanca; but the information is contradictory and uncertain respecting Junot. The governor of Almeida[404] has intelligence from Braganza which he gives credit to, that Junot was before Astorga about the 10th instant,

---

399   The memorandum was dated from Viseu 11 March 1810. It is to be found in Volume V of John Gurwood's *Duke of Wellington's Dispatches, 1799–1815* pp.565–6 (1837 edition).

400   1st and 2nd Caçadores.

401   At this time Captain Ross only had four of his 6-pounder guns with him.

402   General de Division François Kellermann.

403   General de Division Louis Loison commander of the 3rd Division of Ney's Corps.

404   Colonel William Cox.

with 5,000 or 6,000 men and occupied the same points which Loison had done (Loison appears to have made three attacks on Astorga about a month ago and was repulsed by General Garxia,[405] who is in the place with about 900 Spaniards and 20 pieces of artillery) and that 5,000 more were expected to join him. A French corps of about 15,000 men occupy a position from the vicinity of Badajoz to Merida. General Hill is between Portalegre and Elvas with 10 British battalions of infantry and some regiments of cavalry; he has with him two brigades of Portuguese infantry and a regiment of cavalry under General Hamilton[406] with two brigades of British and one brigade of Portuguese artillery. General the Marquis of Romana is in Badajoz; and the army which was under the Duke de Parque is now under Romana (about 13,000 men) and near to Badajoz. The governor of Ciudad Rodrigo says that General Blake[407] has an army in Andalusia of 20,000 Spaniards, this is exclusive of the garrison of Cadiz, which is certainly upwards of 20,000 men. The garrison of Ciudad Rodrigo consists of 5,000 men commanded by Don Andres de Herrasti. The wall of Ciudad Rodrigo is very old, high, nearly perpendicular and almost circular in its form, with small square projections as flanks, upon each of which three guns are mounted. The work therefore is weak inasmuch as it has been constructed not according to the modern system, with proper flanks &c its glacis is also very bad. There are no bomb proofs and there is a hill higher than the works of the town within 600 yards of the ramparts. It has however, a double ditch. The division of the ditches is a considerable rampart, in which is the covert way and which is well covered by the glacis. The garrison is also very large, in proportion to the periphery of the wall of the place, which is mathematically small from its circular form. The governor is also commander of the province of Castille. It appears by the account of a deserter from the enemy, that the corps of Ney consists of the following regiments, viz: 6th, 25th, 27th, 39th, 50th, 59th, 69th and 76th, with two regiments of dragoons, one of the chasseurs a cheval and one of hussars. Each regiment of the line consists of three battalions and each battalion of 4 companies of the centre, 1 of grenadiers and 1 of chasseurs. Each regiment has one colonel and three commandants of battalion; each company has 1 captain, 1 lieutenant, 1 sub lieutenant, 1 pay sergeant, 4 sergeants and 8 corporals; each battalion of about 500 at present, but when complete of 120 per company. The advance guard of the Spanish army is now at Coria, where it was forced to in consequence of the advance of the French into the Sierra

---

405   General Garcia Velasco.

406   Major General John Hamilton was a British officer who served in the Portuguese Army.

407   Lieutenant General Joaquín Blake.

de Francia. It is under the command of General Carrera[408] and is about 3,000 strong. The Marquis of Romana's army consists of five divisions, the first is at Campo Mayor [Maior], under General Pol; the second at Elvas under General O'Donald;[409] the third is commanded by Ballesteros;[410] the fourth is under Garxia [Garcia] in Astorga and the Asturias; and the fifth is in Badajoz commanded by the Marquis de Contrafuerte. It appears that the Fourth Division under Garxia [Garcia] has marched into the Asturias, leaving only a garrison in Astorga.

From where this river falls into the Douro, which it does about two leagues and a half north-east of Castello [Castelo] Rodrigo, to within half a league of Ciudad Rodrigo, its banks are very high, rugged and difficult to pass, with the exception of three or four of the fords. From Ciudad Rodrigo upwards, its banks do not form any serious obstacle, also for half a league below it, they are quite low and flat. After heavy rain, it is impossible to ford the river from the bridge of Navas Frias [Navasfrías] (which is about two leagues south east of Alfaiates) to its mouth and from thence to the Douro there are only three bridges, viz, that of Villar, which is about a league below Navas Frias and that of Ciudad Rodrigo, which is under the guns of that place and that of San Felices [de los Gallegos], which is so exceedingly difficult to pass, from the banks of the river being uncommonly high and inaccessible, so that a small number of men may defend it against a large force. Our position extends from Escalhon, which is near to the mouth of the river, to Gallegos [de Argañán] and from that by parties of hussars to the bridge of Villar [de Flores] and at Payo, a small party and an officer is stationed to get information. While the river is not fordable, this position, although a very extended one, is pretty strong and well calculated to give the army an opportunity of relieving Ciudad Rodrigo, in case of its being attacked; and this is positively Lord Wellington's intention, if the enemy appear before it with a force which he can cope with. When the river becomes fordable, we do not occupy Barba del Puerco with infantry, but only watch it with cavalry; and the infantry occupy Villa[r] de Ciervo and back to Malpartida. Behind Barba del Puerco and Villa[r] de Ciervo runs the Duas [Dos] Casas River, the banks of which behind Barba del Puerco are very difficult and would be a good position for defence. The hussars and horse artillery are in the villages between Villa[r] de Ciervo and Gallegos [de Argañán] when the river is fordable.

---

[408]   Major General Martin Carrera commanded the Spanish troops in Coria, about 100km south of Ciudad Rodrigo.

[409]   General Enrique O'Donnell.

[410]   General Francisco Ballesteros.

Monday, 12 March

I left Pinhel before the general and passing through Villa Torpin [Vilar Torpim], got to the Convent of [blank [Santa Maria de Aguiar] (which is within cannon shot of Castello [Castelo] Rodrigo) about 5 pm. The general, Campbell and Bell[411] arrived about 7. Here we remained for the night.

Tuesday, 13 March

We left the convent about 9 o'clock this morning and passing through Almafallo [Almofala] to Escarrigo [Escarigo], we found Colonel Beckwith at the latter place. Captain Creagh's[412] company of the 95th entered Almafallo [Almofala] as we passed through. While we remained at Escarrigo [Escarigo], the governor of Almeida arrived there and accompanied the general to Barba del Puerco. From this I went directly to Villa[r] de Ciervo. The general and Campbell arrived soon after. We took up our quarters in the priest's house.

Wednesday, 14 March

We set off after breakfast and visited the fords of Valdespino [Molino de Valdespino], Attalaya [Atalaya] and Cupero [Molino de Copero]; from thence we went through Martillan and Sexmeiro [Sexmiro] to Gallegos [de Argañán], where we remained the night. The enemy patrolled this morning to the ford of Valdespino.

Thursday, 15 March

Campbell went off early this morning for Pinhel. The general visited the fords of the Agueda between Sexmeiro [Sexmiro] and Ciudad Rodrigo, while I went straight to Ciudad Rodrigo and called upon the governor with whom I dined. The general got to Ciudad Rodrigo about 4 o'clock and returned to Gallegos [de Argañán] to dinner.

Friday, 16 March

The general went to Villa[r] de Ciervo this morning and I went to Ciudad Rodrigo to ascertain the truth of the report which had reached us that the enemy were approaching Ciudad Rodrigo with twenty five thousand men. The governor disbelieved it; but said they had collected 20,000 near to Salamanca. I returned to Gallegos [de Argañán] in the evening and the general remained at Villa[r] de Ciervo. The day was very wet accompanied by thunder. The 12th, 13th, 14th and 15th were very fine days & hot.

---

411   Lieutenant John Bell, 52nd Foot, was assigned as the deputy assistant quartermaster general in August 1810.

412   Captain Jasper Creagh of the 1st Battalion, 95th Rifles.

Saturday, 17 March

I wrote last night to the general the substance of the information given by the governor of Ciudad Rodrigo. This day was very wet and the general did not arrive at Gallegos [de Argañán] as I expected. A little before two o'clock therefore, I left Gallegos [de Argañán] and proceeded to Villa[r] de Ciervo, which is two leagues from Gallegos. The road passes through Burlada [Hurtada], Villa de Puerco [Villar de Argañán] and Barquilla. Burlada [Hurtada] is a single house. Upon my arrival at Villa[r] de Ciervo, I found that the general was out looking at the fords and I went on towards Val de Cuelha [Vale de Coelha] to see after my horses, which had not yet arrived and met them a short way from it and returned with Campbell. I sent my luggage to Pinhel to proceed to Gallegos [de Argañán].

Sunday, 18 March

This was likewise a very wet day. The general went towards the Coa to see the road by which he might retreat in case of necessity from the Agueda and we met at Gallegos [de Argañán] to dinner. Rowan[413] remained at Villa[r] de Ciervo. Captain Krauchenberg's[414] squadron of hussars arrived at Gallegos today, with a sergeant's party at Guinaldo [Fuenteguinaldo].

Monday, 19 March

Campbell returned this morning to the quarters of the brigade to regulate the quarters and provisions. The general, Cornet Cordemann[415] and I left Gallegos [de Argañán] about one o'clock for Guinaldo [Fuenteguinaldo]. The direct road is through Especa [Espeja] and Campilla [Campillo de Azaba]; but we lost the road and got to Carpeo [Carpio de Azaba], which is on the right bank of the Azava [Azaba]. When you cross the river, there is a single house on the left bank. From this we proceeded to Especa, which in a direct line does not appear more than three-fourths of a league from Gallegos [de Argañán]. Here we got a guide and proceeded to near Campillo, which is on the right bank of the river. We did not cross to Campillo, but continued to proceed up the river to Ituera [Ituero de Azaba], where there is a bridge called Ponte de Ituera [Ituero]. From

---

413   Captain Charles Rowan, 52nd Foot, was the brigade major to General Craufurd's brigade. When the Light Division was created in February 1810, he continued to serve as the brigade major but on the division's staff because the division had no brigades at the time. He would become the brigade major of Lieutenant Colonel Robert Barclay's Brigade in August 1810 when the infantry assigned to the division were placed within two brigades.

414   Captain Georg Krauchenberg, 1st KGL Hussars.

415   Cornet Ernst Cordemann, 1st KGL, was assigned as a liaison officer to the division's HQ.

Ituera to Guinaldo [Fuenteguinaldo] is a short league. From Gallegos [de Argañán] to Ituera, we found the country quite different from that which is between the Coa and the lower Agueda, being flat and much wooded. The country round Guinaldo [Fuenteguinaldo] is quite open and flat. The Azava [Azaba] is the same river which you pass between Gallegos and Ciudad Rodrigo and which runs near to Marialva [Marialba]. Carpeo [Carpio de Azaba] is only half a mile above the bridge at Marialva.

The villages on the Azava, beginning with Marialva and going upwards are Marialva, Carpeo, Campillo [Campillo de Azaba], Ituera and [blank – Puebla de Azaba?]. [On the] opposite side of the river and [opposite] to Carpeo, is a house called Aldeguala. From this country you see that very high conical hill of the Sierra de Marofa, which are two of the most conspicuous objects of the whole country. Guinaldo [Fuenteguinaldo] is a large village and the country about it very abundant. It is five leagues from the Sierra de Francia, which the enemy at present occupy. The people told me that there are 250 inhabited houses in Guinaldo.

Tuesday, 20 March
We started from Guinaldo this morning, for the purpose of visiting the bridge of Villar [de Flores]. Cornet Cordemann and three dragoons[416] accompanied us. For half a league we passed through quite an open country, with the Agueda about half a league to our left; we then entered a wood, through which it is a league and a half more to the bridge. From the road, we saw upon our right, the village of Castillas dos [Casillas de] Flores and to our left, on the opposite bank of the Agueda, Penhoparde [Penaparde]. We crossed the bridge of Villar [de Flores] and from thence proceeded to [El] Payo, which is one league distant from the bridge of Villar. Here the general took post horses and proceeded to Porto de Perales [Perales del Puerto], which is one league from [El] Payo. On his return, we immediately set off and returned to Guinaldo, where we found seventy Spanish dragoons. About 9 o'clock pm, the general received a letter from Campbell, informing him that the enemy had at 11 o'clock pm attempted to pass at the bridge of San Felices [de los Gallegos]. They were opposed by the four companies of the 95th which were at Barba del Puerco, under Colonel Beckwith. The enemy were driven back with the loss of two officers and fifteen men killed and made prisoners. The 95th lost Lieutenant Mercer[417] and two men killed and seven or eight wounded. The enemy passed about 1,500 men and had 1,000 more on the

---

416 The 1st KGL Hussars were also called the 1st KGL Light Dragoons.
417 1st Lieutenant James Mercer, 95th Foot.

other side. This information caused the general to leave Guinaldo, which he did at 10 o'clock and arrived at Gallegos [de Argañán] at 1 in the morning of the 21st, where we found Campbell. Rowan had not arrived.

Wednesday, 21 March
The general and Campbell went this morning to Barba del Puerco and I went to Almeida to speak to General Cox.[418] I returned to Val de [Vale da] Mula and slept in Dalzell's[419] quarters.

Thursday, 22 March
Set off pretty early with Johnson[420] this morning and went to Malpartido [Malpartida], where I breakfasted with Colonel Gifford.[421] Then proceeded through Val de Cuelha [Vale de Coelha] to Villa[r] de Ciervo. Found the general and all out, but his luggage and servants [are] here. Two companies of the 52nd were now at Barba del Puerco with the four of the 95th. For these two days there has been no rain. For a fortnight before, we have had rain every day. This has caused the rivers to swell so much, that the Agueda and Coa are quite impassable, but by the bridges. They will both become fordable with four days' drought.

About 10 o'clock this night the companies of infantry were withdrawn from Barba del Puerco and a troop of hussars sent there. The infantry were recalled from Barba del Puerco in consequence of information being received, that 4,000 or 5,000 of the enemy were moved near to it and that it was their intention to force the post, also because the river was falling rapidly and it was supposed that the fords would be passable in the morning. About a league from Villa[r] de Ciervo there are three fords called Valdespino [Valdespino], Attalaya [Atalaia] and Cupero [Copero]; there were infantry picquets at these fords, which were recalled tonight and those fords were watched by the hussars. The enemy placed picquets opposite to these fords this evening and reconnoitred them about 4 o'clock in the afternoon with about 300 men.

Friday, 23 March
I went to Barba del Puerco early this morning and found all quiet; the enemy's picquets as before. In the afternoon I rode into Almeida to

---

418   Lieutenant Shaw is mistaken. William Cox was only a colonel. In 1818 he was promoted to brigadier general in the Portuguese Army and his date-of-rank was backdated to 1811. Shaw probably changed the rank in the diary prior to its publication in 1851.

419   Captain Robert Dalzell, 43rd Foot.

420   Lieutenant George Johnson, 43rd Foot. Sometimes his name is spelled Johnston.

421   Lieutenant Colonel William Gifford, 43rd Foot, commanded the battalion until June 1810.

speak to the governor about intelligence of the enemy and the means of sending reports. Got wet in going in.

It appears that the enemy retired from the Sierra de Francia and marched towards Tamames and the French have drawn in their troops from Ayamonte.

Saturday, 24 & Sunday, 25 March

It appears that the enemy's force in Bitigudinia [Vitigudino], Guadriamiro [Guadramiro], Yecla [de Yeltes], San Felices [de los Gallegos], Banobares [Bañobárez] &c, amounts to about 6,000 or 7,000 men and 4 pieces of artillery. It is certain that a part of Ney's corps from Salamanca had passed the Puerte de Banos and that thus reinforced, the enemy have approached Coria from Placencia [Plasencia], which had obliged Carrera, who was there with 3,000 Spaniards, to fall back upon Celleras [Caceras?]. Mortier's corps[422] has been withdrawn from Zappa [Zafra] to Santa Ollala [Olalla] and the enemy's troops at Merida have gone towards Trujillo. Battering cannon have entered Spain from France and are, they say, to be brought in advance of Burgos. This information is got by intercepted letters. Blake is said to have collected between 20,000 and 30,000 men in Murcia.

Since the affair of Barba del Puerco (for which Lieutenant Colonel Beckwith and the companies there, were handsomely thanked by Lord Wellington) the division has been distributed as follows viz:

43rd Malpartido [Malpartida], Val de Mula [Vale da Mula] and Val de Cuelha [Vale de Coelha]
52nd Castellejo [Castillejo de Dos Casas] and Alameda [La Alameda de Gardón]
95th Villa[r] de Ciervo

The four guns are in Barquilla and a farmhouse (Burlada [Hurtada]) between it and Villa[r] de Ciervo. A sergeant and 8 hussars at Escalhon [Escalhao]; a troop at Barba del Puerco; a squadron at Villa[r] de Ciervo; troop at Villa[r] de [la] Yequa; a squadron at Barquilla; a squadron at Serenilla [Serranillo] &c; and a squadron at Gallegos [de Argañán], one troop of which is in Ituera [Ituero de Azaba] with parties at Guinaldo [Fuenteguinaldo] and [El] Payo. There are beacons along the chain, which are to be lighted if the enemy should pass in any force. The 43rd are to be brought more near to the Agueda; and the two Portuguese battalions to occupy the villages which the 43rd leave.

---

[422] Marshal Edouard Mortier commanded the 5th Corps.

All the information now received of the enemy, showed that heavy artillery had arrived at Salamanca, viz 5 mortars, 5 guns of 24 lbs, 8 of 18 lbs and others of different calibre, amounting in all to 40 pieces, large and field.

It appears certain that Ney can collect a corps of 20,000 besides Junot's, which is 10,000 or 12,000; but the accounts differ as to Ney's being at Astorga or Valladolid. The French corps which was before Badajoz retired some time ago to Caceres and took up a position behind the Labor [Guadiloba?] River. It marched from that position on the 31st ultimo and took the direction of Merida. General Carrera has about 4,000 Spaniards at Coria. General Blake has an army between Malaga and Ronda of 2,000 men according to accounts. The French have taken possession of the Puerto de Banos with 3,000 men and 3 or 4 pieces of artillery; Generals Ney and Mermet[423] are in Salamanca and Loison in Ledesma. Ney's own corps consists of two divisions. The 6th Regiment has only one battalion at present. The brigadiers who serve under him are Marchand,[424] Maucune,[425] and Mauconnia.[426]

A division consists of 12 battalions, each battalion of 6 companies, each company of 120 men, consequently a division, if complete, would be 8,640 men. To each regiment is attached a four or eight pounder and a howitzer; they have twelve pounders in the park. At present their battalions do not average above 500 and as the 6th have but one battalion, that would make Ney's own divisions about 11,000 men.

Loison's Division occupies Ledesma, Bitigudinia [Vitigudino], Tamames, Yecla [de Yeltes], San Manos [San Muñoz], Bonobares [Bañobárez], San Felices [de los Gallegos] &c and is about 7,000 strong. The other division is commanded by Kellerman[427] and is 5,000 and is between Alba and Peneranda [Peñaranda de Bracamonte]. By this it appears that Ney's corps is 23,000 men. Carrera continues at Coria; and defeated a party of the enemy on the 9th at Aldea Nueva [Aldeanueva del Camino], with he says 200 men. The corps of the enemy which was near to Badajoz and which, as already stated, took up a position

---

[423] General de Division Julian Mermet commanded the 2nd Division in Ney's Corps.

[424] Shaw's intelligence is wrong. General de Division Jean-Gabriel Marchand commanded the 1st Division.

[425] General de Brigade Antoine-Louis Maucune commanded a brigade in the Marchand's Division.

[426] General de Brigade Pierre Marcognet commanded a brigade in the Marchand's Division.

[427] Kellerman was the commander of a dragoon division and the Military Governor of Valladolid and Palencia.

behind the Sabor (which it quitted on the 31st and marched towards the Guadiana) is commanded by General Regnier[428] and has marched by Medelin [Medellín], towards Cabazade Bues [?] and is supposed to be moving upon Cordova [Cordoba], which seems as if they intended to attack Blake, who is between Malaga and Ronda with 20,000 Spaniards.

Monday, 26 March
Today I went with the Spanish captain of horse to the governor of Ciudad Rodrigo to get information &c and returned late to Gallegos [de Argañán], where the general, Campbell and I passed the night.

Tuesday, 27 March
Today I went from Gallegos to Villa[r] de Ciervo and returned to Gallegos.

Wednesday, 28 March
The whole of us returned to Villa[r] de Ciervo. Yesterday the two battalions of Cacadores (Portuguese) which are attached to this division, the first and second, arrived at Pinhel and are to be brought up immediately to the frontier villages of Portugal. They are together about 800 or 900 rank and file. We have had little or no rain for the last three days and the Agueda is fordable today at Valdespino [Valdepino] and Cupero [Copero].

Thursday, 29 March
Today and yesterday have been good, but the wind cold and northerly.

Friday, 30 March
Went this morning to Almeida.

Saturday, 31 March
The 52nd, who occupied Alameda [La Alameda de Gardón], marched from it this morning, in consequence of a fever which was in the place. I went to Ciudad Rodrigo and the general went to Valbom. We all slept at Alameda.

Sunday, 1 April
The general went this morning to Castellejo [Castillejo de los Casas], thinking it would be a good quarter for him, but found it would not do and returned immediately.

---

[428]   General de Division Jean Reynier commanded the 2nd Corps.

Monday 2, Tuesday 3, Wednesday, 4 April
Remained at Villa[r] de Ciervo.

Thursday, 5 April
The general went to Villa Torpin [Vilar Torpim], accompanied by Rowan and myself to see the two Portuguese battalions of Cacadores attached to the division. They had altogether, about 700 men in the field.

Friday, 6 April
About 10 o'clock this morning Colonel Arentschildt[429] came to report that considerable bodies of the enemy's cavalry and infantry were on the river. The hussars and 95th were turned out and the general and Staff went down to the river. We found parties of the enemy at each ford. They had in all, about 200 cavalry and 300 infantry. The infantry remained near the ford, while the cavalry went on to San Felices el Chico [Saelices el Chico] and after taking some provisions, the whole retired to San Felices [de los Gallegos] and Banobares [Bañobárez]. We followed them with about 110 hussars (by passing at the ford of Cupero [Copero]) as far as the small River Granao [Granja]. Today we had snow and rain.

Saturday, 7 April
A very wet day and we remained all day in the house.

Sunday, 8 April
Continued wet.

Monday, 9 April
I went this day to the governor of Ciudad Rodrigo. Cornet Cordemann of the hussars accompanied me from Gallegos [de Argañán]. There were some showers in the forenoon and very heavy rain in the evening.

Tuesday, 10 April
Remained at home all day. A little rain, but trifling.

Wednesday, 11 April
No rain. Remained at home.

---

429   Lieutenant Colonel Friedrich von Arentschildt was the commander of the 1st KGL Hussars.

Thursday, 12 April
Fine day. We received this evening letters from England up to the 24th ultimo. I had one from my father of the 16 March, by which I found all idea of getting Deshon's[430] company to tally at an end. Today Captain Runian of the 97th called on the general; he is employed as a spy and returned to the Sierra de Francia, after getting some money, for which he came.

Friday, 13 April
A fine day. I wrote to my father, in answer to his of the 16 March. Only took an hour's ride with the greyhounds.

Saturday, 14 April
Fine day.

Sunday, 15 April
A rainy day.

Monday, 16–Tuesday, 24 April
These were all very fine days. We removed to Villa[r] de Ciervo and all quiet.

Wednesday, 25 April
Today I went to Gallegos [de Argañán] and returned in the evening, rainy.
    Very early this morning we had a report of the enemy's having advanced to Seradilla and Zamarra.

Thursday, 26 April
Went at 1 o'clock in the morning to Val de [Vale da] Mula with the despatch, returned at 4. Set off with the general at 10 am and went to Gallegos [de Argañán]. Campbell went on to Ciudad Rodrigo. We got back to dinner at Villa[r] de Ciervo at 6 o'clock pm.
    By the officer sent to Ciudad Rodrigo, it was reported that the enemy appeared before the place last evening with 4,000 men and six light guns. Campbell went there today and the governor said there were only 2,000 men before the place.

Friday, 27 April
The general went today to Gallegos [de Argañán], where he took up his quarters. Visited by Governor Cox.

---

430   Captain Peter Deshon, 43rd Foot.

Upon Lord Wellington's receiving intelligence of the enemy's advance to Ciudad Rodrigo, he moved from Viseu and arrived today at Celerico [Celorico da Beira]. The First Division of the army also moved to Celerico and its neighbourhood and the Portuguese troops and English cavalry were put in motion from Coimbra. The information of the enemy's force &c near to Ciudad Rodrigo is very uncertain. A great many cars were seen on the Salamanca road, but certainly no heavy artillery has even moved from Salamanca. The enemy occupied Zamarra. His headquarters were on the 29th at San Martin de Trebeja [Trevejo]; his corps altogether is not more than 3,000 effective men. The following is at present the distribution of the Light Division:

Regiment of hussars extend along the Agueda from Barba del Puerco to Campillo [de Azaba];
First Cacadores and six companies of the 95th in Gallegos [de Argañán];
Third Cacadores[431] and two companies of the 95th in Espeja;
Second Cacadores in [blank];
Seven companies of the 43rd in [La] Alameda [de Gardón] and three in San Pedro [São Pedro de Rio Seco].

Saturday, 28 & Sunday, 29 April
Were wet days and nothing particular occurred. On both days we were turned out by patrols of the enemy crossing the river below Ciudad Rodrigo, but they immediately returned to the right bank.

Monday, 30 April
I went this morning to Almeida and after returning from that, went to meet the Spanish General Carrera at Espeja, as he had promised to come to Gallegos [de Argañán] from San Martin de Trebeja [Trevejo]. He arrived at Gallegos in the evening and remained till next morning.

Tuesday, 1 May
Went to Espeja with General Carrera.

Wednesday, 2 May
Continued rainy and the Agueda not to be forded.

---

[431]   The 3rd Caçadores were assigned to the Light Division in late March.

Thursday, 3 May

The general went today to see the country near the Agueda on the left bank, higher up than Ciudad Rodrigo. I went to Villa[r] de Ciervo. A fine day.

Friday, 4 May

Today we had some heavy showers. No movement of the enemy. The river not quite but nearly impassable. Rowan went into Ciudad Rodrigo. The enemy remained as before.

We now had intelligence that the enemy had taken Astorga on the 22nd ultimo and that they had reinforced their corps in Estremadura. They still occupy Zamarra and in Martiajo [Martiago], they have 2,500 men. Today General Carrera moved his headquarters to Puebla de Azava [Azaba] and he has two battalions of infantry in Guinaldo [Fuenteguinaldo]; he occupies Robledo [Robleda], Campillo [de Azaba], Ituero [de Azaba] &c with cavalry. His division could only be calculated upon at between 3,000 and 4,000 men in the field. It was now agreed upon between General Craufurd and General Carrera, that if the enemy attacks us, the Light Division should, in the first instance, assemble in the wood behind Espeja; and if the enemy's force was superior to that of the Light Division, that it was to fall back and join that of General Carrera at Nave de Aver [Haver], where the two divisions would wait the attack, if the enemy was not very superior; in which latter case, the two divisions would retire to Villa Mayor [Maior].

The following information was given by the officer mentioned in the journal of date Friday 18th instant. Marshal [André] Massena, the Prince d'Essling has been announced in the orders of the French army as commander of what is called the Army of Portugal. This army consists of the Second, Sixth and Eighth Corps of the army of Spain. Massena arrived at Salamanca on the 15th instant. The French army is divided into corps, the corps into divisions, and the division into brigades. The brigades consist of two regiments each; and the regiments, some of two, and some of three battalions. Each battalion has six companies and he averages the battalions at between 500 or 600 men each. Of the Second Corps he knows nothing. The Sixth is commanded by Marshal Ney and the Eighth by Junot. The Sixth Corps consists of three divisions and the eighth of two. The following is the detail of the divisions, brigades and regiments of the Sixth or Ney's Corps.

First Division, Commander Marchand,[432]
6th and 69th Regiments of Foot, Brigadier General Mauchunle [Marcognet]
39th and 50th Regiments of Foot, Brigadier not known
Second Division, Commander Mermet
25th and 27th Regiments of Foot, Brigadier General Fere [Ferey]
59th and 76th Regiments of Foot, Brigadier General not known.
Third Division, Commander Loison
66th and 82nd Regiments of Infantry, Brigadier not known
32nd and another not known, not the brigadier, but supposed the 26th.

There are before Ciudad Rodrigo three hut camps; and in each camp there is one brigade and one regiment of cavalry, amounting to about 3,000 men in each and making the whole encampment 9,000 men. In the centre camp are two regiments of cavalry.

The following is the detail he gives of the regiments in each camp:

First, in their right camp, which is on the Val[e] de Carros road, there are the 66th and 82nd Regiments of Foot and 15th Chasseurs a Cheval; he thinks that the proper commander of this brigade, is General Larcha,[433] but that he is absent and it is now commanded by a colonel.

Second, in their centre camp are the 25th and 27th Foot, the 10th and 25th Chasseurs a Cheval and two four-pounders commanded by Fere.

Third, their left camp, which is at Pedro de Toro [Pedro Toro], consists of the 6th and 69th Foot and 3rd Hussars, two four-pounders and a howitzer. He says that Mermet commands the camp. He is not certain of what artillery was in each camp, but believes there are three in each; in all nine. Junot's Corps consist of only two divisions.

The following is the establishment of a regiment of two battalions complete:

1 Colonel, Gros Major
2 Chefs de Battalion
2 Adjutants Majors
36 officers

---

432   General de Division Jean-Gabriel Marchand.
433   General de Brigade Matthieu Labassée.

In each battalion there are six companies and to each company, one sergeant major, four sergeants and eight corporals. The company is 120 rank and file when complete. Regiments of the Ligne have four companies du centre, one du grenadiers and one du voltigeurs. The light infantry battalions have:

4 companies du centre, 1 company du carbinier, 1 du voltigeur.

Besides the regiments mentioned above as forming Loison's Division, he has also the Legion du Midi, or First Legere infantry and the Fifteenth Legere infantry. By a deserter from the 3rd Regiment of cavalry, it appears there is a foreign division commanded by Colonel Daniel and composed of the following regiments, 3rd and Regiment of Baden (cavalry) and two regiments of infantry, the 3rd Dutch and Paluca Regiments, By another deserter, it appears, that a portable bridge had arrived at St Espiritou [Sancti Spiritus] from Salamanca. Massena remained only a very short time at Salamanca and was understood to have returned to Valladolid, accompanied by Junot. Another corps of the army of Spain was also mentioned as forming part of the Army of Portugal, viz the 4th.

Saturday, 5 May
Went this morning to Val de [Vale da] Mula, from whence the priests of Toras [?] were marched prisoners to Gallegos [de Argañán]. A wet day.

Sunday, 6 May
Wrote home today. The Agueda impassable this morning.

Monday, 7 May
The regiments of this division changed quarters this morning and were assembled on the road between [La] Alameda [de Gardón] and Espeja.

Tuesday, 8 May
The day of Alameda fair, which I went to see with Mr Fraser.[434] Fine day.

Wednesday, 9 May
The 43rd marched this morning to Espeja, the 52nd to Villa [Vilar] Formosa and the 95th and 3rd Cacadores to Fuentes de Onoro [Oñoro]. I went into Ciudad Rodrigo.

---

[434]   Paymaster David Fraser, 43rd Foot.

Thursday, 10 & Friday, 11 May
Went into Ciudad Rodrigo.

Saturday 12 May
The weather very bad.

Sunday, 13 & Monday, 14 May
Continued bad wet weather. Today the general and Campbell set off to visit the upper Coa.

Tuesday, 15 May
Wet day. Wrote to Campbell, to Captain Bouverie,[435] to Captain Ellis.[436]

Friday, 18 May
A French officer, who deserted from the 6th Regiment Light Infantry, was examined today. He gave himself up at Ciudad Rodrigo yesterday and arrived here late last night. He had wounded his captain in a duel and was afraid of being shot for it. Went to Villa[r] de Ciervo in the evening.

Saturday, 19 May
The weather hitherto so very wet and unsettled, now become quite fine.

Sunday, 20 May
Went this evening with Lloyd to see the ford of Molinos Flores [?]. We saw there a French party of infantry and spoke to the officers across the water. Yesterday the French attempted to try if the ford was passable, but were prevented by our hussars. The general and Campbell returned this evening.

Monday, 21 May
A very fine day. Went with Lloyd to Cismeiro [Sexmiro], Martillan &c and returned by the ford.

Tuesday, 22 May
Went to Villa[r] de Ciervo and saw the priest of Garuy Ruy [?], the person in the habit of giving information. Tonight we were turned out by a false alarm of the enemy having passed the river at Molinos Flores [?].

---

[435] Captain Henry Frederick Bouverie, Coldstream Guards, was an ADC to the Duke of Wellington.
[436] Captain Conyngham Ellis, 40th Foot.

Wednesday, 23 May
This morning we got English papers to the 3rd instant. I received no letters. Some rain.

Thursday, 24 May
Today the general went to Puebla de Azava [Azaba] to see General Carrera. Fine day. Rode in the evening with Lloyd to Palacios [?] and towards the ford of Pezerel to see the enemy's camp.

Friday, 25 May
Rain.

Saturday, 26 May
A very wet day. In the forenoon the servants of Lord Wellington and Marshal Beresford arrived at Gallegos [de Argañán] and told us that the two marshals would arrive in an hour, which they accordingly did. They had slept at Almeida last night and came by Fort Concepcion, Villa[r] de Ciervo and Villa de Yequa [Villar de la Yegua]. They were attended by General Cox, governor of Almeida, a general of the Portuguese army and Captain Bouverie, aide de camp. After remaining at Gallegos [de Agañan] about an hour, they went to the bridge of Pontecilla [?] and returned to dine at Almeida. The general, Campbell and I went as far as the Dos Casas with them. The Agueda was 7½ feet high, owing to today's rain.

I was informed by the Adjutant General of the Portuguese troops, that there are now between Celorico [da Beira] and Almeida, two Portuguese brigades and immediately behind Celorico three more; these five brigades including officers and everything, amount to 16,600, fit for duty, including four brigades of artillery. Marshal Beresford's headquarters are about two leagues from Celorico. The artillery is commanded by a Major Arentschildt.[437] There are also two brigades of infantry and two brigades of artillery with General Hill, commanded by General Hamilton. He says that the Portuguese regiments have each two battalions and are considerably upwards of 1,000 per regiment, upon an average.

Sunday, 27 May
Wrote No.3. Went this evening with Lloyd and dined at Espeja with McKenzie.[438] Wet day.

---

[437] Major Victor von Arentschildt, King's German Artillery.
[438] Lieutenant Thomas McKenzie, 43rd Foot. He returned to England shortly afterwards.

Monday, 28 May
Wet day. Remained in the house.

Tuesday, 29 May
The cast horses of the hussars were sold today and we went to the sale at [La] Alameda [de Gardón]. This is a fine warm day.

Wednesday, 30 May
This is Ferdinand the Seventh's birthday. The general, Campbell, Rowan, Lloyd and myself went into Ciudad Rodrigo and dined with the governor. There were three rounds fired by all the guns of the place in honour of the birthday. We went out after dinner with Don Julian[439] and his guerrillas and passed along the French line of vedettes.

Positive intelligence was received this evening by the governor of Ciudad Rodrigo that the enemy's battering cannon left Salamanca on the 28th instant. Captain Ally, the officer of hussars at Martillan, reported that he saw a column of 3,000 infantry and 400 horse pass through San Felices Chico [Saelices el Chico] this afternoon and take the road towards Ciudad Rodrigo. Lights were seen this night on the hill called Biban Rey [Ivanrey] and the enemy established a camp there, which appeared to be a brigade of infantry, with cavalry and two field pieces. The enemy established himself also on the right of the town, by a camp, the left of which was at the Convent of La Caridad[440] and fronting the town.

Thursday, 31 May
The general went today to [La] Alameda [de Gardón] and slept there.

Friday, 1 June
This forenoon we rode to Gallegos [de Argañán] and after doing some business there, went on the road to Ciudad Rodrigo with Krauchenberg. We found that some of the enemy's parties had come down to the ford of Carbaneros [Molinos Carbonero] and were skirmishing with the guerrillas. This induced the general to go on and having got pretty near the place, we went into Ciudad Rodrigo and dined with the governor. After dinner, we went up to the belfry of the cathedral to see the enemy's position. As there appeared something like a work being in progress at the Convent of La Caridad and as we saw a considerable body of men there, we proceeded with Don Julian and 20 or 30 guerrillas to

---

439   Don Julien Sanchez Garcia.
440   It is about 5km south of Ciudad Rodrigo and is where Massena set up his HQ.

reconnoitre them and found upon getting near to the convent, that the enemy had already commenced a bridge and had a body of cavalry on the left bank of the river. General Carrera whose parties watched this part of the river, had not reported either of these circumstances, nor did the people in Ciudad Rodrigo know anything of a bridge having been commenced. We returned to [La] Alameda [de Gardón], which we reached about 12 o'clock at night.

Saturday, 2 June
The general wished to see what progress the enemy had made with their bridge and to see if they had taken up a position on this side of the Agueda; for that purpose we went to Gallegos [de Argañán] in the forenoon and all the hussars in Gallegos and Espeja (amounting to 200) were ordered to march to Fonseca [?]. An officer was sent into Ciudad Rodrigo to beg that Don Julian would come out with his party. We proceeded across the country and by keeping [to] the hollows got pretty near to the hill on the left bank of the Agueda opposite to La Caridad without being perceived. Upon our arrival, we found that the enemy had all gone back to the right bank and that their bridge was completed. Don Julian and all his party joined us and we went with him into Ciudad Rodrigo and dined with the governor. Returned to Gallegos at midnight. Had a fall from my horse in mounting! Since the 29th ultimo, which I mentioned as being a fine day, we have had quite settled weather and very hot. We slept at Gallegos.

Sunday, 3 June
Wet day and nothing done.

Monday, 4 June
I went this forenoon with the general to Carpeo [Carpio de Azaba], where he met General Carrera by appointment. After remaining a short time at Carpeo, we went upon the Ciudad Rodrigo road to near Conaje [Sanjuanejo?]; about a mile and a half below which place, at the ford of Carbaneros [Molinos Carbanero], we found the enemy carrying materials to the water's edge for the construction of a bridge. General Carrera dined at Gallegos [de Argañán] with the general and went home in the evening.

Tuesday, 5 June
Some of the enemy's cavalry passed the Agueda this morning by the bridge of La Caridad and came to our posts at Marialva [Marialba] and Manzana [?], where they skirmished with our hussars. The general had

201

ordered the hussars and two pieces of artillery to be at the hill above the enemy's new bridge at Carbaneros [Molinos Carbanero] before daylight this morning to interrupt them in its construction; but a very wet night prevented their marching and in the morning we found that the enemy had brought artillery for the protection of the bridge and that the hill on which our guns must have been brought was within musket shot, I went with the general by Mansanilla [?] &c and returned by Carpeo [Carpio de Azaba].

Wednesday, 6 June
Went today to Almeida and returned by Val de Cuelha [Vale de Coelha], Villa[r] de Ciervo, Barquilla &c. Don Julian dined at Gallegos [de Argañán] today.

Thursday, 7 June
There was a false alarm this forenoon which caused our being turned out. I rode out in consequence with the general towards Mansanilla [?] and returned by Carpeo [Carpio de Azaba] &c. The enemy had completed their bridge at Carbaneros [Molinos Carbanero] this morning.

Recapitulation by Shaw
On the 1st of June the enemy commenced to throw a bridge over the Agueda a little above La Caridad and completed it on the following day. This bridge was made with 15 chevalets and capable of bearing cannon. It was protected by the camp of infantry at La Caridad (which appeared a brigade) a considerable force of cavalry and some field pieces. A deserter informed us that the following six regiments of dragoons were encamped near the bridge, viz 3rd, 6th, 10th, 11th, 15th and 25th, making a force of 2,500 or 3,000 cavalry. The same deserter stated positively that Massena reviewed the troops in the camp on the 3 June. On the morning of the 4th the enemy encamped a body of cavalry between the camp of Biban Rey [Ivanrey] and the ford of Carbaneros [Molinos Carbanero]. This morning the enemy commenced to bring to the ford of Carbaneros the materials for the construction of a bridge. The Agueda is here divided by a small island. On the 5th they threw the bridge over one of the divisions of the river and completed it on the 7th. From the ford of Carbaneros the Agueda begins to make a bend towards Ciudad Rodrigo, so that the situation of the enemy's bridge is very favourable for taking in flank an enemy approaching the town. The bridge at Carbaneros was similar in its construction to that at La Caridad. The enemy's cavalry have sometimes passed the bridge at La Caridad, but did not yet take up any position on the left bank of

the Agueda. The weather being so extremely wet, makes the roads so deep as to delay the march of the enemy's battering train, which was now said to be near San Munos [Munoz]. Besides the six dragoon regiments mentioned above, the enemy are said to have in their camp, the 3rd Hussars and 15th Legere[441] regiments of cavalry. The enemy now occupy all the villages near to the camp and the villages on the right bank of the Agueda, from Ciudad Rodrigo to the Douro. The troops in the camp and those in the neighbourhood, are certainly Ney's (or the 6th) Corps of the army of Spain. The whole of this corps is certainly before and in the neighbourhood of Ciudad Rodrigo and it appears that Junot's (the 8th) Corps of the Army of Spain is on its march to Ciudad Rodrigo. About the 27th of May, Junot arrived at Salamanca and 3,500 of his infantry. It appears very certain, therefore, that the corps of Ney and Junot, under the command of Massena, are destined to undertake and cover the siege of Ciudad Rodrigo. Junot's Corps will of course be diminished by the garrisons which he must have left in Astorga, Valladolid and that neighbourhood. Nothing whatever has been heard of the division of Martinier[442] since the account given of it by Mr Jackson, a person calling himself son to the commanding General Jackson[443] of our troops in Sicily. He was made prisoner in Germany and made his escape by entering the Irish Brigade. He states that in April, a division commanded by Martinier and which belongs to the 2nd Corps, was on its march between Vitoria and Valladolid, which place its advance entered on the 26th of April. This division consisted of the following regiments and was said to be on its march to Ciudad Rodrigo, viz:

2nd and 17th Light Infantry, 8th, 45th, 46th, 54th, 64th, 103rd, 115th, 122nd, and 96th of the Line, making in all 23 battalions. Also the 1st and 3rd Chasseurs a Cheval and 3rd Dragoons. As this division did not approach Ciudad Rodrigo and nothing since having been heard of it, Martinier [Merle] must have either joined the 2nd Corps on the Tagus or marched into Aragon and Catalonia, if any such corps existed.

Sir Brent Spencer,[444] who was appointed Second in Command of the troops serving in Portugal, joined the army about this time and took the command of the 1st Division of the army. General Payne,[445] our former Second in Command went home on the plea of bad health.

---

441 15th Chasseurs.
442 There was no division in the 2nd Corps commanded by a Martinier. It was likely General de Division Pierre Merle.
443 There was no General Jackson serving in the British Army in June 1810.
444 Major General Brent Spencer commanded the 1st Division.
445 Lieutenant General William Payne commanded Wellington's cavalry.

General Hill continued on the south of the Tagus. The Spanish General O'Donnel, who was stationed at Albuquerque, having been threatened with an attack by Regnier [Reynier], General Hill advanced to his support and the enemy retired. After this, the enemy threatened Badajoz and General Hill moved towards Elvas. The Spanish General Ballasteros, having advanced in the direction of Seville, was attacked by Marshal Mortier, Duke of Treviso and totally defeated. The following is a statement of Ney's Corps, taken from accounts given by the deserters; and as there have been deserters from every infantry regiment, it may be considered as pretty correct as to the regiments composing the corps and the number of battalions. The corps consists of three divisions.

1st Division (Marchand)		
Brigadier	Regiments	No. of Regiments
Mauchune [Maucune]	6th Legere	2
	69th Line	3
Blank	39th Line	3
	50th Line	3
2nd Division (Mermet)		
Basset[446]	25th Legere	2
	27th Line	3
Blank	59th Line	3
	76th Line	3
3rd Division (Loison)		
Simon[447]	15th Legere	1
	26th Legere	3
	32nd Legere	2
Legion du Midi		
Fere	66th Line	3
	82nd Line	4
	Hanoverian Legion	2

Making in all 37 battalions of infantry; and calculating the battalions at 500 each, makes a force of 18,500 men. The cavalry, with a corps, forms always a separate division of itself and the following regiments are mentioned by the deserters as being with Ney's Corps and I suppose form a division commanded by General Millet; Kellerman formerly commanded the cavalry of this corps, but has not been with it since

---

[446] General de Brigade Martial Bardet.
[447] General de Brigade Edouard Simon.

the Battle of Alba. The regiments of cavalry and their strength is stated as follows by the deserters, viz:

	3rd Hussars	600
	15th Dragoons	600
	25th Dragoons	800
	10th & 15th Chasseurs	600
General Milet[448]	3rd Dragoons	800
	6th Dragoons	600
General Carrier[449]	10th Dragoons	400
	11th Dragoons	500
Total		**4,900**

By this calculation the cavalry and infantry of the corps amount to twenty-three thousand four hundred men. We have no account of the number of artillery and engineers; but by a state of Victor's Corps last year, it appears that with his corps, they amounted to 2,100 and supposing this corps to have the same establishment, it would make it upwards of twenty-five thousand men. Scarcely a day passed, without some skirmishes between the garrison and the besiegers. On the 6th there was a very heavy cannonade during the greater part of the day, in consequence of the enemy's endeavouring to possess themselves of some mills near to the town; in which the governor stated the enemy to have lost 200 men. As already stated, the enemy had on the 7th completed his bridge over the Agueda, at Carbaneros [Molinos Carbanero]; and as the operations of the siege became at this period more interesting, they are hereafter given in the form of a journal, commencing on the 8th.

Friday, 8 June
Were turned out this forenoon by a report of the enemy's having crossed the river. Went with the general to Mansanilla, looked at their bridge and saw a column of infantry halted on the side of the river.

The enemy passed the Agueda today, by their bridge at Carbaneros [Molinos Carbanero], with infantry and cavalry and established themselves on the left bank of the river, near to the bridge. The Agueda has been for some days and still continues to be, quite unfordable and was so much swelled on the 7th, that the enemy was obliged to discontinue his work at the bridge, but which he had completed today.

---

[448]   General de Brigade Jacques Milet.
[449]   General de Brigade Jean Carrie de Boissy.

Saturday, 9 June
Nothing particular occurred today. Rode in the afternoon with the general and Rowan to the river.

An infantry picquet consisting of one company was placed today at Marialva [Marialba].

Sunday, 10 June
The general employed today in regulating, with the officers of hussars, the different picquets and stations of vedettes, their duties at the beacons &c. Rode in the afternoon to the hill above Mansanilla and saw the enemy busily employed in the construction of what appeared three distinct redoubts, which seemed to serve as a *tete de pont* to their bridge at Carbaneros [Molinos Carbanero]. Rodrigo was now completely invested, the French having placed picquets on all the roads and occupied the heights of Maria Mayor [?] and Pedrotelho [Pedro Toro]. An attempt was made to send some ammunition into the town at night, but they could not get in.

Monday, 11 June
Remained at home all day. Wrote No.4. For the last four or five days the weather has been unsettled; but the rain not heavy. The Agueda, however, continues impassable at the usual fords.

The enemy continued his works near Carbaneros. The river not fordable.

Tuesday, 12 June
I set off with the general early this morning, who went out with the intention of regulating the posts at Marialva [Marialba], Carpeo [Carpio de Azaba] and Manzana [?]. At Marialva there has been a picquet of one company of infantry since the 9th. Yesterday the picquet was augmented by twenty-four of the 95th, given from the company at Gallegos [de Argañán]. The general made them build up the entrances from the front of both Marialva and Carpeo. While we remained at Carpeo a flag of truce arrived: it brought a letter for Lord Wellington from Ney. The person who brought it said he was colonel[450] of the 3rd Hussars. A company of infantry happened to be in Carpeo at the time the flag of truce came; they were drawn up so as to be seen at the entrances of the village and the French party brought far enough to see them. From Carpeo we proceeded to Manzana [?] and found there a Spanish picquet and near to it some of our vedettes,

---

450   Colonel Louis Laferriere-Levesque.

given from Captain Grubin's[451] picquet at Aldea Nueva. Passing Manzana, we went to within half a league of El Bodon and returned by Aldea Nueva [Aldeanueva de Portanobis] and the quinta of Aldequela. This afternoon the French took possession of Palacios [?] and the height to its left, between the fords of Capilla [?] and Pezerel [?]. The general ordered tonight that the 52nd should go to the hill in front of Gallegos at daylight tomorrow morning and 43rd, 95th, and 1st Cacadores to be formed on the heights behind the village at five o'clock in the morning.

In the evening, the enemy took possession of Palacios [?], which he occupied with cavalry; and the hill between it and the river with infantry.

Wednesday, 13 June
Remained in the house most of the forenoon. Rode with Colonel Elder[452] to Marialva [Marialba] and from the height above it, saw the French very busily employed in the work near to their bridge at Carbaneros [Molinos Carbanero].

A heavy cannonade from the town this morning, but the cause of it not known. No information has been received of the arrival of the enemy's battering train. The fords of the Agueda were passable this morning with difficulty. The guerrillas appear to have become active in Castille, since the French troops were withdrawn from it. The following account was received of Junot's Corps, the only information we have of it:

Stations	Salamanca	3,000
	Toro	2,000
	Zamora	4,000

He has left a garrison of about 1,500 men in Astorga and the remainder of the corps is in the neighbourhood of the above places. On this day, 28 pieces of the enemy's heavy artillery were said to be at San Munos [San Muñoz] and 4 mortars, 1 large and 3 small; 11 howitzers and ammunition left San Munos on the 10th and took the road towards Ciudad Rodrigo. This information and that respecting Junot's Corps rest on the authority of a spy, who was went to Salamanca.

---

[451]   Captain Philip Moritz von Grugen, 1st KGL Hussars.
[452]   Lieutenant Colonel George Elder, 95th Rifles, was the commander of the 3rd Caçadores.

Thursday, 14 June
Went this forenoon to [La] Alameda [de Gardón] and from thence with Booth[453] to Barquilla, to see Hamburgh's[454] horses &c and returned by Villa Puerco [?]. The field officer of the 52nd, also Ross and Jenkinson[455] &c dined with the general today. After dinner, there being some mistake about the instructions given to the sentry at the general's door, the officer who was on guard was sent for by the general and upon the general's asking him whether or not he had received any particular instructions from the officer whom he relieved, as to the orders of the sentries, he replied that he had not and that he had a general idea, but not a particular knowledge of the orders which the sentries had. The officer who had been relieved this evening was next called for and gave much a similar answer. Both were put under arrest and the general declared he would bring them both to a court martial. The officer on guard was Lieutenant [blank]. Lieutenant [blank] stated that he had not visited his sentries since coming on guard, which was at sunset. It was about eight o'clock pm when the general spoke to Lieutenant [blank]. The general's reason for putting these two officers under arrest was their not having received and not knowing the particular orders of the sentries of their guard. The weather is now uncommonly fine and appears quite settled. The Agueda quite fordable. One of our hussars on vedette at Valdespino [Valdepino] spoke yesterday to General Loison who was then reconnoitring. Two of our hussars deserted last night. Received this morning a joint letter from Mary Kennedy and Helen. Also received No.1 from Helen alone. The enemy did not continue to occupy Palacios [?], nor the hill between it and the river.

Friday, 15 June
Remained in the house all day. The day rather cloudy, with some thunder and lightning, but very hot. This morning Lieutenants [blank] and [blank] were released. A great deal of firing during the night.

By the information of deserters, the enemy appear to have begun their first parallel tonight, on the height of San Francisco.

---

[453] This could be either Captain Charles Booth, 52nd Foot, or Lieutenant Henry Booth, 43rd Foot. They were brothers and both were with the Light Division at this time. It is likely Henry, who was in the same regiment as Shaw.

[454] Cornet Christian von Heimbruch, 1st KGL Hussars, returned to England in June 1810.

[455] 2nd Captain George Jenkinson, Royal Artillery, was in Captain Ross' Royal Horse Artillery Troop.

Saturday, 16 June
Went this morning to the hill on the right of Marialva [Marialba] and saw the enemy's parallel on the height of San Francisco. The morning was wet and hazy.

A very heavy fire from the town, which commenced last night, continued till after daybreak this morning; a corroboration of the enemy's having opened his trenches.

Sunday, 17 June
Remained in the house all forenoon. Bought Hamburgh's grey mare. Rode to Marialva [Marialba] in the afternoon. The field officer of the Portuguese battalions dined with the general. A battery, capable of holding about ten guns, was observed in front of the enemy's parallel today. They also had a work extending from the hill to the river.

The enemy's first parallel was today distinctly observed from the height above Marialva, it could not be seen yesterday owing to the haziness of the day. This parallel of the enemy ran along the crest of the height of San Francisco and extended from thence to the river, on which its right rested. No other parallel was necessary, for from this one, they were not more than 500 yards from the wall of the town and saw nearly to the bottom it. The wall of the town is nearly circular, having no flanks, but three small projections, carrying 3 guns each; but it is secure against assault by the height of the wall and by its having a double ditch. Upon its great wall were mounted 41 pieces of very good, heavy artillery, about 24 of which could bear on the height of San Francisco. The governor, Don Andreas Harrasti [Herrasti], was a brigadier general in the regular army of Spain, previous to the present war. The garrison was sufficiently supplied with provisions and ammunition and although there were not in the place bomb proofs sufficient to hold the powder, yet very considerable exertions had been made to put one of the churches into such a state, that it proved a secure magazine during the siege. The garrison of the place consisted of about 6,000 armed people.

Monday, 18 June
Rode this afternoon to Molinos Flores [?], to inquire respecting the march of columns of the enemy and some guns which were seen in motion on the opposite side this morning. Was told by the officer on picquet, Captain Crampton[456] 95th, that about 1,000 men and 80 waggons entered Felices Chico [Saelices el Chico] and another column

---

[456]   Captain Jeremiah Crampton commanded No. 8 Company, 1st Battalion 95th Rifles.

marched towards Castelligo [Castillejo de Dos Casas]. We supposed this to be the arrival of the advance of Junot's Corps.

Two columns of the enemy and about 8 field pieces and 80 waggons were seen this morning from Molinos Flores [?]. One of these columns, about 1,000 strong together with the guns and waggons, entered San Felices Chico [Saelices Chico] by the road from Banovares [Bañobárez]; the other column, which appeared of about the same strength, marched towards Castellejo. This was the arrival of the first of Junot's Corps come to join Ney's, which two corps under Massena, Prince of Essling, now formed the siege of Ciudad Rodrigo. The Spanish General Carrera, who since the enemy came before Ciudad Rodrigo, has had his corps (which consists of the light troops of Romana's army and consisting of between 2,000 and 3,000 men) between the Puerto de Perales and our division was now at Almadilla [La Alamedilla]. By General Craufurd's advice, he had come to Espeja.

Tuesday, 19 June
Went to [La] Alameda [de Gardón] early this morning and got a bill from Fraser[457] on Greenwood and Cox[458] for fifty-five guineas, which I gave to Hamburgh for the grey mare. Felt unwell today and upon speaking to Robb,[459] he said I had some fever and advised me some medicine.

Wednesday, 20 June
Was worse today and continued all day in bed. The day very hot. The enemy continue to work hard in the trenches and fired some rounds of howitzers into the place today. Some of our officers saw them take three guns into the trenches. Nothing [else] particular occurred.

Thursday, 21 June
Was alarmed this morning about 10 o'clock and the infantry brigade formed behind the hill in front of Gallegos [de Argañán], on the Ciudad Rodrigo road. This proved only a foraging party, at which we fired seven rounds from one of the six pounders. As if alarmed by this, about two hours after the enemy advanced upon Marialva [Marialba] and Carpeo [Carpio de Azaba] with four regiments of infantry. Our picquets retired behind the Azava [Azaba]. The enemy retired again about 4 o'clock in the evening. This advance of the enemy caused

---

457   Paymaster David Fraser, 43rd Foot.
458   Greenwood and Cox were the regimental agents for the 43rd Foot.
459   Surgeon John Robb, 95th Rifles.

the brigade's being again marched out in front of Gallegos. Captain Mellish[460] and Mr Fitzclarence[461] came here last night; the captain is to stay with the general for some time.

General Carrera encamped his division on the road from Gallegos to Fuentes de Onoro [Fuentes de Oñoro] and near to the great road leading from Aquilla [Barquilla?] to [La] Alameda [de Gardón]. This evening the enemy advanced with 4 regiments of cavalry and two battalions of infantry upon Marialva [Marialba] and Carpeo. Our picquets retired behind the Azava. The enemy withdrew from Marialva and Carpeo in the evening.

Friday, 22 June

Our picquets occupied Carpeo and Marialva early this morning. All was quiet today and I remained nearly all day in bed.

The enemy was observed to be carrying his parallel more to his left towards the suburbs of the town and to be constructing many batteries in front of his parallel.

Saturday, 23 June

Nothing particular occurred today. Being better, I rode in the evening to General Carrera's camp on the Fuentes road.

At one o'clock this morning the famous chief of the guerrillas, Don Julian Sanchez, made his escape from Ciudad Rodrigo with 190 of his men, he galloped through the enemy's line.

Sunday, 24 June

On the morning of the 23rd, Don Julian Sanchez with about 190 men, sallied from Ciudad Rodrigo and cut their way through the French picquets; he now joined Carrera. Today Carrera and his Staff dined with the general. Colonel d'Urban[462] came to Gallegos [de Argañán] tonight & Captain [blank], aide de camp[463] to General Beresford.

During today nothing particular occurred, till soon after dark, when a heavy fire commenced from the place.

Monday, 25 June

A heavy fire was heard all this night from Ciudad Rodrigo and at daybreak the enemy opened their batteries against the place. The fire

---

460 Captain Henry Francis Mellish, 87th Foot.
461 Lieutenant George Augustus Frederick FitzClarence, 10th Light Dragoons, was the illegitimate son of King William IV. He was created the 1st Earl of Munster in 1831.
462 Colonel Benjamin D'Urban, 2nd West India Regiment, was the quartermaster general of the Portuguese Army.
463 Captain William Henry Sewell, 16th Light Dragoons.

from the place during the night must of course have been in consequence of the enemy's bringing their battering guns into the trenches. The enemy's fire from the trenches was extremely heavy, but returned by the garrison with great spirit. During the middle of the day the firing was not brisk, but again became heavy in the evening. Being now nearly quite recovered from my slight feverish attack, I rode out with the general to see the place from the hill above Marialva [Marialba] and to examine the enemy's batteries &c. I soon returned, but while the general remained there (till about half past 7 o'clock) the enemy advanced with a considerable body of cavalry and took possession of Marialva and Carpeo [Carpio de Azaba], from which places our picquets retired behind the Azava [Azaba]. We lost two horses and no men. During the forenoon there were three explosions of powder. The first of these was the most considerable and happened when we had possession of the hill above Marialva, and the people there saw plainly that it was in the enemy's principal battery. Where the other two happened could not so distinctly be seen. The French showed no disposition to leave Carpeo and Marialva and continued there with a very considerable force of cavalry. A considerable body of the enemy, supposed near to 3,000 cavalry and infantry, were seen about 7 o'clock tonight, marching as if coming from San Felices [Saelices el Chico] and proceeded on towards Ciudad Rodrigo. This we supposed to be more of Junot's Corps.

The firing from the place continued all the morning and at daybreak the enemy opened his batteries against the town. The heavy firing from the place must of course, have been in consequence of the enemy bringing his guns into the batteries. The fire from both sides continued to be extremely heavy from three o'clock in the morning until midday. During this time two explosions took place in the enemy's batteries, one of which was so great as to entirely destroy one of their principal batteries and of course killed many people in it. The firing ceased in a great measure during the heat of the day and recommenced to be heavy in the evening, when it was kept up about five hours, making the whole continuance of heavy fire during this day, about fourteen hours.

At 8 o'clock this morning, the enemy advanced upon Carpeo and Marialva, with strong bodies of cavalry and threw some cannon shots into Marialva from a field piece, which they brought to the hill on the right bank of the Agueda, above the ford of Marialva. Our picquets retired immediately behind the Azava and occupied the strong ground on its left bank. The enemy now occupied permanently the villages of Marialva and Carpeo and in fact, the right bank of the Azava.

Tuesday, 26 June

At daylight went out with the general to the Azava. Lord Wellington and Sir Brent Spencer came to Gallegos [de Argañán] this forenoon and rode to the picquet at Molinos [Casillas de] dos Flores, from which they looked at Ciudad Rodrigo. After this, they returned to Gallegos and after waiting here a few minutes proceeded to Almeida, which was now made the headquarters of the army. General Beresford's headquarters were now [at] Trancoso; his aide de camp Captain Suel[464] and his Quarter Master General, Colonel d'Urban, have been here for several days. There was nothing particular occurred today.

Don Julian Sanchez surprised a strong party of the enemy's cavalry this morning, consisting of 4 officers and 80 men, all of whom were either killed or made prisoners.

Wednesday, 27 June

A man arrived here this morning with a note from the governor of Ciudad Rodrigo, he came from the town last night. The following is the principal information brought by him;

The wall of the town has been knocked down about six feet, the breadth about eight yards. In all, from 800 to 1,000 killed and wounded in the town. About three houses have been burnt. One small explosion took place on the rampart and destroyed 14 people. One mortar and two guns of the town can no longer fire. Says they have still 28 pieces, which they can fire on the enemy's works. The people continue determined. The explosions which took place on the 25th, were all in the enemy's trenches and the first of them entirely destroyed (at least totally silenced) their chief battery. They constructed a new one behind it. The enemy have 11 guns and 5 mortars bearing on the town; they have 5 batteries. They have also a great many grenades and howitzers. Says the town is much in want of provisions and place their entire hope on our relieving the town.

This man returned in the evening with a letter from Lord Wellington to the governor. I was at Molinos dos [Casillas de] Flores with the general, received Lord Wellington's letter and returned to Gallegos [de Argañán] and sent the man off.

The fire from the town was kept up with great vigour during the whole day, as well as that from the cannon batteries which, by the bye, was not thought to be with such heavy metal, since the explosion of yesterday and the wall of the town (which we could see distinctly with glasses from Molinos dos [Casillas de] Flores) had not been materially injured.

---

[464]   William Sewell.

The town was two or three times on fire during the day, but it did not seem to extend.

Information from Barba del Puerco and from the enemy's deserters, agreed in proving that the troops which were seen entering the enemy's camp, as before mentioned, were of the corps of Junot, the 8th of the Army of Spain. It appears certain, indeed that the march of the corps was so regulated that its advance should arrive at the camp before Ciudad Rodrigo, at the same time that that the battering train did.

The fire from the enemy's batteries was considered heavier today than it had been the previous ones, but was returned from the place with the greatest spirit. The information given by the man sent by the governor was pretty correct except in his statement of the loss sustained in the place, its want of provisions and the injury done to the wall, all of which are much exaggerated and supposed to be done with the view of inducing Lord Wellington to afford immediate relief to the besieged. Ever since the enemy placed themselves before Ciudad Rodrigo, they have kept possession of the Pass of Banos by a detachment of infantry and cavalry. They have not occupied Plasencia, but have sometimes entered it; they however constantly occupy Almaraz and Arzobispo and at the former place they have constructed a *tete de pont*. They generally have troops in Talavera. The occupation of Almaraz and Arzobispo is necessary to them for the communication of their corps on the north and south of the Tagus. The French General Regnier [Reynier], whose corps (the 2nd of the Army of Spain) has still kept upon the Guadiana and which has made a great variety of movements between Trujilla [Trujillo] &c and Badajoz (and which has been kept in check by General Hill and the Marquis de Romana) appeared now to be collecting nearer to the Tagus and showed an intention of passing it. General Hill's force consisted of the 2nd Division of the British army, a division of Portuguese infantry under General Hamilton and the 13th British Dragoons and a brigade of Portuguese cavalry under Fane;[465] the Marquis de Romana's force was estimated at 13,000 men, exclusive of garrisons. Regnier's [Reynier's] Corps was not computed at more than 16,000 or 17,000 men.

Thursday, 28 June
Some French papers having fallen into our hands, the general sent them by a flag of truce to Marialva [Marialba] this forenoon. The sergeant of the 1st Hussars who took it, met Junot near the village; he conversed with him for some time and sent his compliments to Lord Wellington and General Craufurd by him.

---

[465] Brigadier General Henry Fane.

There was a total suspension of firing for about four hours today and people were seen walking perfectly exposed upon both the walls of the town and the enemy's trenches. This induced a belief that the place had surrendered; but the firing commenced with great vigour on both sides about 6 o'clock pm and continued the whole night.

Friday, 29 June
A general officer (supposed to be Ney) reconnoitred the bridge at Marialva [Marialba] this morning: this caused a false alarm; and I rode out to the bridge with Colonel d'Urban and from thence to Molinos dos [Casillas de] Flores. In the evening, we again rode to Molinos dos [Casillas de] Flores, from which we saw very plainly a breach in the wall of Rodrigo.

A French general officer, supposed to be Marshal Ney, reconnoitred the bridge of Marialva at noon.

The following is the copy of a letter received from Don Andres Herrasti, the governor of Ciudad Rodrigo addressed to General Carrera and dated Ciudad Rodrigo 28 June, 4 o'clock pm.

'La brecha esta ya formada, y en desposition de asaltarse. El Puebla todo se halha en ruina, e en cendido pr varios partes. La guarnicion no pueda ya con la fatiga y empieza a caer de animo a la visto del abandona en que se la dexa. En estas circumstancias, o venir, luego, luego, luego a secorrer esta plaza, O no contra con ella si asi no de executa, porque imposible no se devan pretender.' [The breach is already practicable and is fit to be assaulted. The town is in ruins and is burning in several places. The garrison can no longer endure the fatigue and its morale is beginning to give way, on account of a feeling that it is being abandoned. In these circumstances, either you must come immediately to relieve this place or you cannot count on it [holding], because we cannot aim for the impossible.]

The fire from the trenches continued during the whole of today.

Saturday, 30 June
Set off at four o'clock this morning and rode as usual to the hill above Gallegos [de Argañán]. Finding all quiet, we proceeded to [La] Alameda [de Gardón], which the general made now the headquarters of the division. We passed the infantry which had marched in the night from Gallegos and now remained in the wood, a little in front of Alameda, where the whole of the infantry of the division halted. General Carrera's Division was now halted behind Alameda, on the right bank of the Dos Casas. Soon after our arrival at Alameda, an

alarm took us back to Gallegos, where I remained till between four and five o'clock in the evening. The enemy now placed a regiment of infantry behind the Azava [Azaba].

The whole infantry of the division which had been collected for some days past, in and near to Gallegos, retired before daybreak this morning to the wood immediately in front of Alameda and hutted themselves there. The cavalry and a picquet of three companies and a half of infantry remained at Gallegos. The enemy placed picquets of infantry on the Azava this evening.

Sunday, 1 July

It was reported to the general early this morning that our picquet at Molinos dos [Casillas de] Flores had been all taken, except the sergeant and officer. This however, proved totally a mistake. The corporal who went out with the relief stayed for an hour and [a] quarter, upon which the officer, without farther enquiry, galloped off and reported that his picquet was taken. There was only one relief, his vedettes having been increased late last night; their situation also had been changed and he did not show the corporal where they stood, so that the corporal lost his way and this caused his being so long out.

We dined at Gallegos [de Argañán] today and went to Molinos dos Flores in the afternoon. Nothing particular occurred today. The place continues to fire very well; but letters from the governor prove that he must soon surrender. We returned in the evening to [La] Alameda [de Gardón].

The following letter was received today, from the governor of Ciudad Rodrigo, directed to General Carrera and dated yesterday.

'Repito por ultimo vez, que luego, luego, luego manana mismo en el dia, ó no contar que puedo tirar mus tiempo el enfermo, porqueel mal ha tomado un encremento que ya no Alcanzan los remedios y es preciso contra lo que raiz.' [I repeat for a last time that very soon, even by tomorrow the 6th, you can no longer count on my ability to obtain more time for the patient, because the disease has become so severe that no ordinary remedies can be effective, and it will be necessary to proceed to more drastic measures.]

Today however, although the fire from the enemy's batteries continued during the day, the number of shots was inconsiderable and must have been occasioned either by want of ammunition, or some accident in their batteries.

Monday, 2 July

Set off about four o'clock am, with the general for Gallegos [de Argañán]. Just as we got to the beacon in front of Gallegos we saw a regiment of the enemy's cavalry march to and form with their right upon Marialva [Marialba]. Six or eight pieces of cannon came near to Marialva and halted behind the village. A chaise also entered the village. The regiment halted and remained permanently at Marialva; the guns were withdrawn. By a deserter we found this is the 1st Dragoons and belongs to the 8th Corps. We went to Molinos dos [Casillas de] Flores from which we returned to Gallegos and the general wrote to Lord Wellington. Got to [La] Alameda [de Gardón] about ten pm. The general went again to Molinos dos Flores in the evening and took Cotton[466] with him, who joined us two or three days ago as Assistant Adjutant General to the division, in place of Graham,[467] who is gone to [blank – England] sick. I passed the evening with the 43rd and saw Fergusson,[468] who joined today from England. The weather continues very fine and not oppressively hot.

The enemy's fire continued to be trifling during today. A sergeant who deserted from the enemy's Irish Brigade, gave the following account of Junot's Corps (the 8th Corps of the Army of Spain). The whole corps formed the siege of Astorga. It consists of three divisions. Did not know the commanders of the 1st and 2nd, but the 3rd, in which is the Irish Brigade, is commanded by General Sallinack.[469] The Irish Brigade is commanded by General Torny.[470] The Irish Brigade has two battalions and about 350 men in each and the 70th Regiment was brigaded with it. The whole strength of the corps, at this time effective, he conceives to be 25,000 souls. The regiments of which he recollected the numbers were 15th, 41st, 70th, 92nd and 95th. The corps is composed of native French, except a regiment of Prussians. [He] states that there is a 9th Corps of the Army of Spain, of which he saw two regiments at Valladolid which belongs to it, viz a Swiss regiment and the 65th of the Line. Junot's headquarters were at San Felices [Saelices] Chico on the 1st. Immediately after the fall of Astorga, the whole corps moved by Salamanca &c, towards Ciudad Rodrigo and the 4 regiments of Swiss belonging to the 9th Corps, were put into Astorga as a garrison. The following and further particulars of the regiments composing the 8th Corps, according to the account of deserters.

---

[466]   Captain Willoughby Cotton, 3rd Foot Guards.
[467]   Captain Henry Charles Edward Vernon Graham, 26th Foot.
[468]   Captain James Fergusson, 43rd Foot.
[469]   General de Division Jean Solignac commanded the 8th Corps' 2nd Division.
[470]   The Regiment Irlandaise was commanded by Colonel Daniel O'Meara.

22nd Regiment, 4 battalions, 600 per battalion
2nd, 7th and 15th Dragoons
4th and 10th Hussars
17th Chasseurs

The deserters generally state that there are 8 regiments of cavalry with Junot's Corps. The 22nd forms a brigade commanded by Godarvo.[471] A regimental provisor and a regiment of the line, formed the other brigade and these two brigades a division.

Another account of the 8th Corps was given as follows by a deserter, who appeared to be very intelligent.

1st Division
36th Regiment, one battalion, 600 strong
46th Regiment, one battalion, 600 strong
50th Regiment, one battalion, 600 strong
75th Regiment, one battalion, 600 strong
This is the 2nd Brigade and is commanded by General Lopem[472]
19th Regiment, one battalion, 600 strong
25th Regiment, one battalion, 600 strong
38th Regiment, one battalion, 600 strong
34th Regiment, one battalion, 600 strong
This is the 1st Brigade and is commanded by General [blank]
2nd Division
1st Brigade 22nd Regiment, 4 Battalions, 2,000 strong
2nd Brigade 65th Regiment, 4 Battalions, 2,000 strong
3rd Division
1st Brigade 70th Regiment, 4 Battalions, 2,000 strong
2nd Brigade
Irish Brigade, 2 Battalions, 700 strong
Polish Brigade, 1 Battalion, 500 strong
Bavarian Regiment, 600 strong
Total 3,800

But it is evident that many regiments which belong to Junot's Corps, are altogether omitted in the above statements of it. Three men of the 1st Prussian Regiment stated that their regiment belongs to the 2nd Division of the 8th Corps, of which division they gave the following account.

---

[471]   General de Brigade Roch Godard.
[472]   General de Brigade Eloi Taupin.

	Strength
1st Prussian Regiment	1,300
Irish Brigade	600
52nd Regiment of Line	1,800
58th Regiment of Line	1,800
Total	**5,500**

And state that the division is commanded by General Sallina.[473] By the accounts most to be depended upon, it appeared that the cavalry of their corps consisted of the 1st, 2nd and 3rd Regiments of Provisional, which amounted in all to about 5,000 men.

Ney's corps the Sixth

This corps is certainly underrated previously by averaging the battalions (of which there are 37) at 500 per battalion, as the whole corps when before Ciudad Rodrigo, did certainly not amount to less than 22,000 infantry. The following statement of the 6th Corps does not differ very materially from that made earlier but it does somewhat as to the distribution.

1st Division (Marchand)
Brigade of Manenule[474]
6th Legere 2 battalions
69th line 3 battalions
Brigade of Marconnier[475]
39th Line 3 battalions
76th Line 3 battalions
2nd Division (Mermet)
Brigade of La Passet[476]
25th Legere 2 battalions
27th Line 3 battalions
Brigade of Berte[477]
50th Line 3 battalions
59th Line 3 battalions
3rd Division (Loison)
Brigade of Simon
26th Line 3 battalions
82nd Line 4 battalions

---

[473]   Solignac.
[474]   Maucune.
[475]   Marcognet.
[476]   Labassée.
[477]   Bardet.

Legion du Midi 1 battalion
Brigade of Ferre
32nd Line 2 battalions
66th Line 3 battalions
Hanoverian Legion 2 battalions

Also the 15th Legere [of] 1 battalion is in one of General Loison's Brigades. The statement of the cavalry attached to this corps recorded previously is confirmed by the accounts of deserters and that it appears that Lancé[478] commands one of the cavalry divisions.

The two above stated corps (6th and 8th) together with the 2nd, which is commanded by Marshal Regnier [Reynier],[479] were avowedly those intended for the conquest of Portugal and were called the Army of Portugal, of which Massena was commander. Of this last (the 2nd Corps), we had but little information, but it was supposed to consist of from 15,000 to 17,000 men in cavalry and infantry. This corps passed the Tagus by a bridge of boats on or about the 13th, 14th and 15th of July between Almaraz and Alcantara. It marched immediately after crossing the river, upon Coria and Marolejo [Moraleja], and its advanced parties extended themselves as far as Azevo [Acebo] (which is close to the Puerto de Perales) on the eighteenth. At the same time that Regnier [Reynier] crossed the Tagus, General Hill made a corresponding movement, by crossing the Tagus at Villa Velha [Vila Velha de Ródão] and marching to Castello [Castelo] Branco.

General Hill afterwards occupied the passes of the Sierra de Pedrigao, which is a chain of mountains running from the Villa Velha on the Tagus, in a north-west direction to the River Zezere. In this chain there are only two passes, that of Alvito, which is about two miles broad and that of Perdigao which is more narrow and difficult. From the above statements of the situation and numbers of the enemy's 2nd, 6th and 8th Corps, it appears that very soon after the fall of Ciudad Rodrigo they could collect (by two or three day's marches) on the frontiers of Portugal, an army of (supposing the 2nd Corps, infantry 15,000, cavalry 2,000; the 6th Corps, infantry 22,000, cavalry 4,500; the 8th Corps, infantry 20,000, cavalry 5,000), 57,000 infantry and 11,500 cavalry: but it is to be considered, that out of this force Ciudad Rodrigo must be garrisoned and also Almeida if they succeed in reducing that fortress. The enemy's force did not at all diminish during the siege of Ciudad Rodrigo. The deserters agreed universally in stating,

---

478   General de Brigade Auguste Lamotte commanded the 6th Corps' cavalry brigade.
479   Reynier was a general de division.

that detachments were joining the regiments continually; that these detachments were very considerable and came from France. Besides these three corps, the enemy had some troops under Kellerman, in and about Leon, of which province as the Asturias, Kellerman appears to have the command; but it appears that his force had quite enough to do to keep the two provinces in subjection, without attempting any offensive operations either in Galicia or the North of Portugal. There was certain information of three battalions of the Imperial Guard having arrived at Burgos some time ago, but they never joined Massena. The enemy's 5th Corps under Marshal Mortier continued in the Sierra Morena; and it appeared quite doubtful whether or not this corps would act in conjunction with Massena in his future operations against Portugal. Such was the disposition of the enemy's force on the frontiers òf Portugal at the middle of July.

Tuesday, 3 July
Went early this morning to Gallegos. Found the enemy exactly in the same position as yesterday and the place continuing to fire. We returned to [La] Alameda [de Gardón] about 10 o'clock am and again went to the out picquets after dinner. On our way we met a hussar who brought a report that the enemy were advancing. Upon getting to the bridge of Marialva [Marialba], we found that this report was occasioned by a small party of the enemy having carried off one of the cars which were laid across the bridge, so as to obstruct the passage. Returned to Alameda rather late.

Wednesday, 4 July
Immediately after daylight this morning, about 100 of the enemy's cavalry crossed the Azava [Azaba] immediately below the bridge and proceeded in full speed to the top of the hill in front of Gallegos [de Argañán], to where our beacons stood, driving before them a small picquet of the 16th [Light] Dragoons[480] commanded by Mr Thomson.[481] Here he halted and skirmished with them for a few minutes. Columns of the enemy's cavalry having now passed the Azava, they advanced in three bodies and a line of skirmishers in their front. One of the enemy's columns entered Gallegos, while two others turned it upon either flank. Our cavalry and guns withdrew gradually and kept up a constant skirmish with the enemy. Behind Gallegos there is a small

---

[480] Two squadrons of the 16th Light Dragoons were attached to the Light Division in late June.
[481] Lieutenant William Tomlinson.

stream, with a stone bridge over it; the enclosures here obliged the enemy's centre column to pass by the bridge. Our skirmishers had got over and Captain Krauchenberg of the 1st Hussars had about half his troop formed behind the bridge. The enemy advanced rapidly over the bridge in considerable numbers. At the moment they were passing, Krauchenberg charged them and drove them back with loss. The general was on a height immediately above the bridge and from it he made the artillery give them two or three shots, admirably directed by Macdonald,[482] but the enemy did not regard them and advanced steadily to the bridge with his centre column, while his two other columns turned our flanks and obliged us to withdraw. The enemy advanced rapidly and we withdrew, giving them now and then a shot from the artillery and continuing the skirmish. Upon getting near the camp we were much disappointed to find that the infantry, in place of being formed, were advancing upon the road in columns; the 43rd and 52nd were halted and the 95th formed in line in front and extended a little. The Cacadores were formed in line on the left of the 95th. Our squadrons of cavalry formed in line with the infantry, also two pieces of artillery. A squadron of the enemy came very close to our left and received the fire of the 3rd Cacadores, upon which the squadron retired. We remained for some time in this situation, but the general having determined not to make a stand here, the 43rd and 52nd and Cacadores were ordered to march off and form near to the bridge, on the strong ground, on the left bank of the Dos Casas River. The enemy now began to turn our right and the whole were withdrawn through [La] Alameda [de Gardón]. The enemy received some destructive shots from our artillery, both when we were in front of Alameda and when they were advancing into the village. After the whole division had crossed the Dos Casas, the enemy's skirmishers came close to the river and shortly after withdrew to Alameda. The enemy soon after retired from Alameda and only left a picquet in Gallegos, with their vedettes towards Alameda. The infantry of our division marched to Fort Concepcion and the cavalry kept the line of the Dos Casas. The troops which were in Fort Concepcion (the 9th Portuguese Regiment and 4 companies of the 45th) marched upon our arrival to their division; also 18 guns which were in the fort went to Almeida. A picquet only occupies the fort and there is an engineer[483] in it ready to blow it up upon the advance of the enemy. Our left is in Val de [Vale da] Mula and our right extends to the right of the village. Our right is prolonged

---

482   Lieutenant Alexander MacDonald was part of Ross' RHA Troop.
483   Captain John Burgoyne, Royal Engineers, was responsible for blowing up the fort.

by General Carrera's Division, who marched here with us from his camp on the Dos Casas. We saw Don Julian today; he withdrew his party from Martin Hernando [?] upon the advance of the enemy and is now in front of Fuentes [de Oñoro]. The general made Val de Mula his headquarters. Colonel Pakenham,[484] Colonel Hardinge[485] and Major Warr[e][486] were with us all day. We had five men wounded. We made one prisoner, but it was impossible to ascertain the enemy's loss. Krauchenberg killed one officer and wounded two when he charged at the bridge. The fire from Ciudad Rodrigo continued today.

Thursday, 5 June

Went with Colonel Pakenham, Colonel Hardinge and Major Warr to Barquilla this forenoon and returned by Villa[r] de Ciervo. The inhabitants had fled from all these villages. The enemy occupy Gallegos [de Argañán] with a picquet only, but had entered it at noon day with a considerable body, probably to forage. A small party of the enemy was in Villa de Yequa [Villar de la Yegua] last night, also in Serranilla [Seranillo] and Martillan, but they did not remain in these villages. The appearances were sufficiently melancholy during our ride today. We met the unfortunate inhabitants flying from their homes and the whole of the people of some of the villages encamped in the fields, having with them all their property which they could carry off upon their cars. After dinner, I again rode to Barquilla, but heard nothing of the enemy.

The firing at and from the place, continued constant but inconsiderable as before. It increased during the night.

Friday, 6 July

General A Campbell[487] called upon the general this forenoon, he was accompanied by Sir [blank]. General Campbell commands a brigade, consisting of [2nd Battalions] 7th and 53rd Foot, 11th Foot, [a] Company 5th B[attalio]n 60th Foot] which is at Castanheira [?] and is at present the nearest part of the army to our division. I rode with the general and Krauchenberg after dinner to Barquilla and from thence to a hill, from which we could see Gallegos [de Argañán], at which place it appears by the account of the natives, that the enemy has only a picquet. A small

---

484 Colonel Edward Michael Pakenham, the Deputy Adjutant General of Wellington's Army.

485 Lieutenant Colonel Henry Hardinge, 57th Foot, was the deputy quartermaster general of the Portuguese Army.

486 Major William Warre, 23rd Light Dragoons, was the aide-de-camp to Marshal Beresford.

487 Brigadier General Alexander Campbell commanded a brigade in the 4th Division.

party of the enemy's cavalry entered Villa[r] de Puerco and Cismeiro [Sexmiro] this morning and plundered them; they had also completely destroyed and plundered everything in [La] Alameda [de Gardón], when they entered it on the 4th. Three squadrons of the 14th [Light] Dragoons are now in Aldea de Bispo [Aldeia do Bispo], with a picquet at Castellejo [Castillejo de Dos Casas]. The rest of our cavalry are in the wood to the right and in front of the infantry camp with their picquets on the Dos Casas. Our patrols go into Villa de Puerco [?] and near to Gallegos. As our force of cavalry amounts to upwards of 800 men mounted, we are now in a state to take more liberties on the flat open country in our front. The weather continues hot and fine. Today we had some thunder and lightning in the afternoon and a shower. Warr[e] and Hardinge returned this evening. The fire continues at the place.

The desertion from the enemy was now pretty considerable; there were 8 yesterday and 12 today.

Saturday, 7 July
Nothing particular occurred today. We rode to the front in the evening.

Sunday, 8 July
I went about ten o'clock this morning to the cavalry camp and arranged a march of the cavalry upon Villa de Puerco [?], to endeavour to cut off some of the enemy's parties which had plundered it this morning. We marched at one o'clock by [La] Alameda [de Gardón] and through the wood upon Villa de Puerco [?], but the enemy had left it and Cismeiro [Sexmiro]. We found their vedettes between Gallegos [de Argañán] and Alameda. I returned by Villa de Yequa [Yegua] and Villa[r] de Ciervo and turned in Gruben's squadron, which had gone to watch the fords there.

Monday, 9 July
Sent No. 5 to H. Unwell during the forenoon and remained in my room. Colonel Talbot[488] and Major Butler,[489] 14th [Light] Dragoons, dined with us today. Rode to the Spanish camp after dinner. The day oppressively hot.

Tuesday, 10 July
The firing has been so heavy from daylight this morning till between nine and ten o'clock am, that there must be some change in the enemy's

---

488   Lieutenant Colonel Neil Talbot commanded the 14th Light Dragoons.
489   Major Charles Butler, 14th Light Dragoons.

batteries; they must either have got up ammunition, which they may have been scarce of, or got up more guns. Since the 1st instant until this morning, the firing has been very slack on both sides. This morning the enemy entered and robbed the villages of Barquilla and Villa[r] de Ciervo.

Nothing particular occurred on the 7th, 8th or 9th, but on the morning of the 10th there was a most material change observed in the enemy's fire. This tremendous fire from the enemies [sic] batteries continued till the evening, when at 5 o'clock the gallant Don Andres Herrasti was obliged to hoist the white flag and surrender at discretion. An immense practicable breach was formed in both the outer' and principal wall of the town; all the guns bearing on the enemy's batteries were dismounted; the town almost totally destroyed and the enemy almost at the bottom by the glacis and on the point of entering the breach by assault, when the gallant governor delivered up his fortress. When the vast advantage is considered, which the enemy had in possessing the height of San Francisco (which commands the town and from which nearly the bottom of the wall is seen, within 500 yards); the disadvantages of the wall of the town in being very perpendicular and scarcely having any flanks; that there was not a single bomb proof in the town, that there was a great deficiency of good artillery men; and above all, when the immense force is considered with which the enemy attacked the place and that he was prepared with a great train of artillery and everything necessary for carrying on the siege with the utmost vigour; it must be allowed to Don Andres Herrasti and his garrison, the honour of having made a most noble and gallant defence. By those who examined the place previous to its investment, it was supposed scarcely possible that it could hold out for more than three or four days after the whole of the enemy's batteries should open upon it. Indeed this opinion was much more correct than is generally known. Whoever reads the above journal of the siege with attention will not fail to observe an extraordinary and unaccounted for falling off in the enemy's fire, from the 1st till the 9th, both days inclusive. On the 10th at daybreak, the enemy's fire was infinitely more furious than it was at any time from the 1st to the 9th and even much more so than during the 25th, 26th, 27th and 28th, for even on the 28th there was a considerable suspension of firing and during the 29th and 30th it did not at all gain upon the fire from the town. If these things are taken into consideration, together with the explosions in the enemy's batteries and the governor's letters of the 29th and 30th June, they will be found very strong proofs that the governor could not have held out for more than six or seven days, against such a fire as the enemy opened from his batteries and kept up until the explosions in his batteries on the 25th.

The following is an abstract statement of the principal operations of the enemy against Ciudad Rodrigo.

Encamped before the place with between 3,000 or 4,000 men which were soon reinforced by about 600 more	April 25
Massena arrived at Salamanca	May 15
His bridge at La Carridad completed over the Agueda	June 2
Ditto at Carboneras [Carbonero][490]	June 7
Place completely invested	June 10
First parallel commenced	June 15
Batteries opened against the place	June 25
And the place surrounded on the evening of	July 10
The enemy were before it	77 days
Completely invested it	30 days
Trenches opened against it	25 days
And battered it	16 days

One circumstance of the siege of the place is omitted in the above account, viz that of its having been summoned to surrender by the General of Division Mermet, on the 12th of May. The governor, the garrison and the inhabitants were offered the most advantageous terms; but they were rejected with disdain.

Ciudad Rodrigo was the last hope of the Spaniards in this part of the country. Their entreaties were most constant and sincere, that the English should relieve their city and they could not conceive what took us there, if we were to remain tame spectators of its fall. The Spaniards in and near to it, who thought that everything depended on its fate, were much enraged at our remaining inactive and although their hatred to the French was most rooted, yet they gave up all idea of resistance upon the fall of the place. The French of course took advantage of the ideas of the Spaniards about our not relieving the town and pretended that Lord Wellington had given the governor false assurance of his support. However people's opinions may differ respecting the policy of His Lordship's having allowed the enemy to carry on their operations against Ciudad Rodrigo without molestation, it is a positive falsehood, that any direct and unconditional promise was made to the governor

---

[490] Molino Carbonero.

of his being relieved by the English army. Upon the approach of Ney's corps to Ciudad Rodrigo, Lord Wellington moved his headquarters to Viseu; also the British and Portuguese Divisions which were at Viseu &c were closed up upon Celerico [Celorico da Beira] and the army was more concentrated than before. It is also certain, that the Quartermaster General made arrangements at that time for the advance of the army upon Ciudad Rodrigo. But the supposition of the commander in chief having made a positive promise that he would relieve the place is quite absurd, as of course however much he might be inclined to do so, his determination on the subject must have depended upon the force &c with which the enemy undertook the operation and the disposition of the enemy's other corps. However, it is pretty clear from the above statement, that His Lordship would have advanced with the army to the relief of Ciudad Rodrigo had he thought the enemy's force warranted his so doing.

The following is an abstract of a letter from Lord Wellington to General Craufurd, dated Almeida 27 June and in answer to a demand made by the governor of Ciudad Rodrigo (on the night of the 26th) of a categorical answer from His Lordship of whether he intended to relieve the place or not.

After referring the governor to His Lordship's former letter (which only promised relief if the circumstances should allow of it) he continues, 'the governor must be aware of the force which the enemy has collected for this enterprise; and how difficult it is for me to provide for his relief as long as the enemy will keep that force collected.'

Wednesday, 11 July

We started at twelve o'clock at night (of the 10th) to carry into effect the following scheme. The enemy have for two or three mornings past made a practice of coming into and plundering the villages of Villa de Puerco [?] and Barquilla. We wished to cut off these parties and for that purpose, six squadrons marched by [La] Alameda [de Gardón] and were placed in the wood near to Villa de Puerco. One squadron was concealed in the house between Villa de Puerco and Barquilla and one squadron and a wing of the 95th Regiment were placed behind the crosses near to Barquilla; also the 3rd battalion of Cacadores was placed behind the bridge of San Pedro and the ford of the Dos Casas, below the bridge on the road from Alameda to Fort de Concepcion. Having waited concealed in this situation till an hour after daylight, we observed parties of the enemy enter Villa de Puerco [?] and Barquilla, according to our expectation. The cavalry then marched off from their right and proceeding on to the Villa de Puerco road, went on at a trot, but were detained considerably by a wall which we had to get over, in endeavouring to get in rear of the village. Having got the leading divisions over, we pushed on at a gallop and now found that the enemy were not in the village; proceeding towards Cismeiro [Sexmiro] we saw upon the hill some of the enemy's cavalry; two or three hussars and Campbell and myself galloped on. Upon my arrival nearly at the summit I came within about seventy yards of a body of infantry, which were formed. Returning immediately to the head of the column, the two leading squadrons formed line and charged the infantry, who by this time were formed in square. The infantry of the enemy's which consisted of only 200 men, remained unbroken and got off without loss. Our loss was in all 32 killed and wounded and 9 horses.

The French officers informed us that Ciudad Rodrigo surrendered at five o'clock yesterday evening and was entered by the French at six. We were pretty well convinced before that the place had surrendered, from our not hearing any firing; this had nearly induced the general to give up his project and to have returned from [La] Alameda [de Gardón]. After the affair at Villa de Puerco [?] we withdrew the cavalry by Barquilla and Castellejo [Castillejo de Dos Casas]. The conduct of the enemy's infantry, which we endeavoured to break, was cool and determined. General Carrera and his division left us today; his instructions from the Marquis de Romana were, to march to Alcantara upon the surrender of the place. I went out with [blank] to Carrera's camp to see him before he went, after which we took a round towards Almeida. The enemy's attention being now of course entirely fixed upon the siege of Almeida, our utmost vigilance becomes extremely necessary, as we have no doubt of his soon forcing us over the Coa.

Thursday, 12 July
Went to the cavalry camp at daybreak in the morning, about eight o'clock am, received a report from the Spanish Colonel Mera (who commanded Carrera's cavalry) saying he had been attacked. The general rode towards Fuentes [de Oñoro] and found it was nothing. I went by Villa Formosa [Vila Formoso] to Fuentes and found Mera gone and all quiet. I dined with Mcleod[491] and rode after dinner to Junca with Johnson. A letter from Lord Wellington to the general this morning expressed His Lordship's wish that the infantry of the division should be placed nearer to Almeida.

---

[491]   Major Charles Mcleod, 43rd Foot.

Friday, 13 July
Nothing occurred worth noticing.

Saturday, 14 & Sunday, 15 July
Were turned out this morning, in consequence of about 7 squadrons of the enemy's cavalry having formed between Fuentes [de Oñoro] and Espeja and having got near to Fuentes, Major Napier[492] and Captain Cotton took a flag of truce into Gallegos [de Argañán] this forenoon. Loison received them. He is quartered there and they think about two regiments. There are some small camps in front of the village. Loison said that there was scarcely a house standing in Ciudad Rodrigo. He desired Cotton to tell Lord Wellington that he would bet His Lordship 500 Louis that he would not relieve Almeida and that the Spaniards were very indignant with us for not relieving Ciudad Rodrigo. The enemy's vedettes were only about a mile on this side [of] Gallegos.

Monday, 16 July
The infantry of the division and guns moved to Junca this morning. The cavalry as before.

Tuesday, 17 & Wednesday, 18 July
Nothing particular. Rode into Almeida. Major Napier dined with Rowan and me.

Thursday, 19 July
Received a report from the officer on picquet at Fuentes [de Oñoro], at 8 o'clock am, saying that columns of the enemy were advancing. The general went off immediately towards Fuentes and I went and turned out the infantry at Junca. This however, proved to be only a strong patrol of the enemy, which drove our picquet back from Fuentes but were driven back in their turn and we took a prisoner. The general now established the headquarters of the division at San Pedro [São Pedro Rio Seco].

Friday, 20 July
I went this morning to Aldea Bispo [Aldeia do Bispo] to receive information from two spies whom I had sent on the 18th, the one to San Felices [de los Gallegos] and the other to Ciudad Rodrigo. By them it appears that the enemy have 4,000 men in San Felices de

---

492   Major Charles Napier, 50th Foot, served as a volunteer aide-de-camp to Craufurd.

Gallegos and 3,000 men in a camp about a league from it; in Castellejo [Castillejo] and Selices Chico [Saelices el Chico], they have 1,500 men; they also occupy Freixenada [Freineda]; but the body of the enemy's army is encamped between Palacios [?], Carpeo [Carpio de Azaba] &c and between that line and Gallegos [de Argañán]. The loss in the town, including both garrison and inhabitants, during the siege, was 500 killed and wounded. The garrison (5,300 men), the governor and the Junta, were all marched off prisoners to Salamanca. They made the members of the Junta walk; all priests and monks of the town are confined, also the writers of the *Diario*.

Saturday, 21 July

About 5 o'clock this morning some firing was heard and soon after a report was received by the general, that the picquet at Castellejo [Castillejo de Dos Casas] was engaged with the enemy. Before we got on horseback we heard an explosion at the fort; the general rode off immediately to Val[e] de Mula and while going there the whole of the mines of the Fort Concepcion went off, I believe nine in all. These explosions appeared to be quite successful. On our arrival at Val[e] de Mula we found the 14th formed behind the villages and the enemy's skirmishers on the right and left of Fort Concepcion. On our left of the fort we saw about a regiment of the enemy's cavalry and a battalion of infantry. On our right of the fort the enemy advanced with two regiments of cavalry and two battalions of infantry. They turned our left and advanced into Val[e] de Mula at the same time. The 14th retired (skirmishing with the enemy) to the stream between Val[e] de Mula and Alameda and about a mile and a half from the former place. The guns were brought up in rear of this stream and the 14th (who were now reinforced by a squadron of the 16th and one of the hussars) formed in front of the guns. Our skirmishers maintained themselves a long time among some rocks in front of the stream till the enemy came on with infantry. The enemy did not pass the stream and about 10 o'clock they retired to Val[e] de Mula. Upon the first alarm, the infantry marched into their position close to Almeida. While the cavalry were skirmishing, the 95th were ordered up, but they only got about half way when the enemy retired and were halted on the road and hutted where they halted; the rest of the infantry hutted in the position, the left of which is within reach of the guns of the place and the right in some enclosures. I went into Almeida to forward a letter to Lord Wellington and wrote to Generals Picton and A Campbell, to mention what had passed. The general went to Junca to dinner and we returned in the evening (after riding round the picquets from Nave de Haver to Malpartida) and took a quarter in the suburbs of Almeida.

Sunday, 22 July
We went out at daybreak to our most advanced picquets on the Val[e] de Mula road &c and saw one or two of the enemy's vedettes, but everything quite quiet. We did not return till 8 o'clock. Our patrols, which went this forenoon to Val de Mula, found none of the enemy there, but saw infantry and cavalry picquets in front of the fort.

Monday, 23 July
Everything remained quiet at the outposts this morning. I went to the camp in the evening and saw Colonel Hull,[493] Captain H [blank][494] and Oglander,[495] who arrived with the regiment this morning.

Tuesday, 24 July
On this day, the Battle of Almeida was fought. What appears in the journal under this date is omitted because as I was wounded in the action, it must partly have been stated on hearsay.

---

[493]   Lieutenant Colonel Edward Hull took command of the 43rd Foot on 23 July and was killed the next day.

[494]   Captain James Watson Hull was severely injured on 24 July 1810. He was the 1st cousin of Lieutenant Colonel Edward Hull.

[495]   Lieutenant Henry Oglander, 43rd Foot.

ADDENDUM

LIEUTENANT COLONEL CHARLES MACLEOD, 43RD FOOT EXTRACTS OF LETTERS[496]

Volume One in this short series contains accounts of the 43rd Foot, including the letters of Lieutenant Charles Macleod, from two sources. A third source of letters was discovered but unfortunately after the book was produced. This source contains extracts of letters not contained in the previous selection and so they are produced here at the end of the final book.

Letter to his father, August 1810

... We made a forward movement again to this place (Freixedas [Freineda]) some days ago, with what object I will not pretend to determine, nothing being half so sickening that I know of (barring Ipecacuanha wine![497]) as the conjectures of people who cannot possibly

---

496   From *The Brave sons of Skye*, by John MacInnes, Edinburgh 1899.
497   Ipecacuanha wine or Ipecac, is an exotic medicinal mixture made since the eighteenth century. It is made by soaking the root of a Brazilian shrub in water or alcohol and added to a syrup or medicinal wine. The active ingredient, Emetine, causes vomiting when given in high doses. This was administered to rid the body of excess bile and thus restore the balance of the humours.

possess the information necessary to form an opinion of what is likely to happen within a hundred chances of being right. Yet everybody can guess and will be more contented with his own guess than anybody else's, so I leave it to you to determine the result according to your fancy, guarding you simply not to be guided by letters you see in the papers from 'officers of high rank in the army' particularly, who always appear to me to be further from the mark than anybody else … I have never written you an account of the affair yet. The truth is I was rather puzzled to give a detailed account. All I can tell you is that it was rather tightish work while it lasted, and indeed until it ended, and who had the worst of it must be settled between the generals … so that if they (the French) say they drove us (and I daresay they will) they 'lie in their teeth' …

Letter to his father regarding the action on the Coa, 4 September 1810

… I find by your letter that you appear to think it not altogether impossible that I shall be superseded again. In my own opinion, which I have only formed upon that of others, it would be an injustice if anybody but myself should be appointed. I very well know how much intriguing and turning and twisting of a subject takes place when people wish to gain a point. Black can almost be made white by plausible talkers. The unfortunate business of the 24th, as some of your papers call it, was as sharp and for those who had any responsibility, as anxious a day as ever was passed and if the troops had not been really good and unalarmed by the commanding superiority of the enemy under circumstances of position &c, which from the beginning to the end were advantageous and encouraging to them and the contrary to us, things might have been bad. As it happened, we put a face upon it, which prevented anything that could be called bad. I am going to write to George[498] who takes notice of the style of a letter of our brigadier. It is a correct account, taking it in general, but no despatch gives universal satisfaction. Lord Wellington's embellishment with respect to myself is what I like least in it. Having commanded the regiment for months before, and it having fallen to me again in the middle of the action, besides having commanded the wing of our own and some riflemen on the other side, and maintained the position until everything had crossed, and then took up the forward line again on this side, makes it appear odd to me that I should not have been mentioned as a commanding officer, particularly as our regiment was

---

[498]   His brother.

most concerned from beginning to end and covered the bridge on both sides directly in front. If General Crawford [Craufurd] had said half what he saaid to me, which I did not want from him, for his opinion is not one I am ambitious of, there could have been no hitch about the matter. I commanded the regiment at least half the action, and five companies during the whole of it. From Lord Wellington I could expect no notice except through the general commanding the division, nor did it ever enter my head until I read the accounts; for recollect that I am writing now my private feelings to you, my father only. Being young and unknown in the army, one cannot help feeling disappointment of this sort, not on my own account as much as on yours, whose good opinion I really covet, and whose happiness or satisfaction I should have felt pleasure in adding to in the smallest degree. Do not imagine that I mean to claim any merit above those, the lowest in the regiment, all of whom did their duty, and if they had not been real good of their sort, particularly the officers, all of whom have raised themselves in my opinion and confidence by their zeal, coolness and gallantry, the trying service we had to perform would have been ticklish work; but it appears to me odd enough where one commanding officer is killed that his successor is not noticed …

Letter to his father dated 3 September 1811

… Both my field officers are sick in the rear and several other officers, I am sorry to say, but this is the most sickly time of year and I am consoled by the men keeping up better than I expected. We have upwards of 900 in the field, which is very fair, and as queer a set of looking fellows for anybody to choose to pick a quarrel with, as you might wish to see …

Letter to his father 20 November 1811

'Orderly – Sir, you can have just ten minutes to write, Sir'. Packet making up for England. We are all rubbing on pretty fairly, nothing to do but course, hunt, and act plays, which Colonel Barnard has set going, and everybody was inclined to assist in. Half my boys are kings, princes, buffoons &c. Tomorrow is to be performed (with variations, no doubt). The most excellent 'Conceited, humorous play of Shakespeare, Henry the Fourth'. It is not true, as the French state, that we are dying of ennui. When they do not amuse us we find some way of killing our other enemy, time, with tolerable success. For my own part, I confess I am a dull actor and my time is spent in the more important, though certainly less profitable or amusing avocation of quarrelling with my general. I course and ride, however as long as the horses can go, but they are I am sorry to say, for want of forage, in a woeful plight. I am glad my friend Bill Napier[499] is improving. If he can get the ball out of his guts, he will do well. If he cannot, he must do well with it in! I hope they will make him a major, but I don't know, I am a little afraid they will put in someone else.

To his father regarding Ciudad Rodrigo, 22 January 1812

I never was more satisfied with the behaviour of my own men and officers than on this occasion. I will say for them, in case nobody else does, that their conduct was excellent. We entered the breach at the same time with the rear of the storming party and amidst the confusion and irregularity that was going on, every man might have gone his own way (as most others did), but we were able to keep them together and as a proof of their steadiness, there was not a single duty furnished in the town that was not taken by our regiment. We got possession of all the gates and both the breaches, and I do not believe a single Frenchman escaped. This is only between you and me, for I do not wish to be the trumpeter of my own forces, except to you. I do not think my own name will appear, although I think it aought, but this I cannot help. There were so many commanding officers of regiments that I daresay they will all be clubbed together as usual; but disappointments in this way are numerous.

Car's[500] idea of muffatees[501] for the men made me laugh for an hour. If she would send them a chew of baccy apiece they would understand what it meant, but the muffatees, you'd puzzle them a good deal.

---

[499]   Later Sir William Napier.
[500]   His sister, Caroline.
[501]   A scarf or muffler.